The Story of the
Institute of Government

The University of North Carolina
at Chapel Hill

ALBERT COATES

The Story of the
Institute of Government
The University of North Carolina
at Chapel Hill

Out of a Classroom in Chapel Hill

I Dedicate this Book

To the men and women

Who in the years from 1933 through 1939 laid the foundations of the Institute of Government and got it going

Who in the years from 1939 through the 1940's held it together and kept it going

Who in the years from the 1940's to 1962 and thereafter have given the prime years of their working lives to building it into a new University of Public Officials within the framework of the old University of North Carolina

and

To the University of North Carolina at Chapel Hill which gave me a classroom and a teaching job—the only job I have ever held and the only one I have needed in order to do what I wanted to do

v

Contents

viii

Introduction

I had known for years that my administrative duties as Director of the Institute of Government would come to an end in 1962 when I reached the age of sixty-five, and I had planned to tell *The Story of the Institute of Government* as the final act of my stewardship.

The first step toward that goal came with the writing of a detailed *Report to the Chancellor* in the middle 1950's. The second came with a pictorial history of Institute activities in the newly opened Joseph Palmer Knapp Building in the latter 1950's. The third step was planned to come with the end of my directorship in 1962—a step prevented by the growing pains of the Institute and the pressure of administrative duties, and visualized as my first order of business for the summer months after returning to teaching duties in the Law School.

At that time I had got the Institute work with public officials going to the point that it would keep on going after I was gone. But there were three programs I had started, stopped, and left unfinished: the program of studies in government with civic clubs and women's clubs; the program with teachers and students of government in senior high schools, the last point of contact between the public schools and the prospective voters, the program with student government officers and their faculty advisors in colleges, universities, and senior high schools.

I had dropped these programs when supporting funds all but dried up in Depression years and I had to concentrate my efforts on holding buckle and tongue together with officials. The coming of World War II and the growth of Institute activities thereafter had prevented me from picking them up. My successor could not pick them up—for the same reasons that I had dropped them. I did not want to see the work that had gone into them go down the drain. I had given them a lick and a promise during the 1940's and 1950's and I wanted to keep that promise in the 1960's. And that is what I did.

I thought I could do it in two or three years. It took me sixteen— to get them going to the point where, like the Institute of Government, they would keep on going after I was gone.

In the latter 1970's I picked up *The Story of the Institute of Government* where I had left it. I decided to tell the story up to the end of my administration in 1962, because each succeeding Director would want to tell the story of his administration. That left a twenty-year gap, from 1962 to 1982, and I didn't want to leave my story dangling in midair. I have bridged this gap—in part by including the report of Director Henry Lewis at the end of his administration on the "State of the Institute in 1978," in part by my own observation on the heartening progress of the Institute since I had left it in 1962, and finally by including working patterns in the Institute written by colleagues most of whom I had brought on the staff in the latter 1940's and were still on the staff in the latter 1970's.

The Story of the
Institute of Government

The University of North Carolina
at Chapel Hill

Chapter I   Background

A Choice of Jobs

In the spring of 1923, during my senior year in the Harvard Law School, I got a letter from Colonel Ed Abell, a lawyer in my home town of Smithfield, North Carolina, offering me a partnership in his law office, and at the same time a letter from President Chase offering me a teaching job in the Law School of the University of North Carolina in Chapel Hill.

I walked up and down the banks of the Charles River in Cambridge trying to decide what I was going to do with my life. I looked at it this way: One lawyer more or less wouldn't make much difference; there would be enough to handle the legal business of the community, and some to spare. One candidate for public office more or less wouldn't make much difference; there would be enough running and being run.

But I had a feeling there was something I could do in Chapel Hill that I could not do in Smithfield, something I could do in a law school that I could not do in a law office, though I couldn't spell out the difference in words. This was a turning point in my life, for better or for worse. In that state of mind, I took the teaching job in Chapel Hill with the expectation that somehow I would find out what the difference was.

1

I finished law study in June, 1923, and started law-teaching in September, without a day of law practice in between. I knew something about law and government in books, but nothing about law and government in action. I discovered a gap between classroom and courtroom, between law school and law office, between law teacher and lawyer, between the law and government as it was taught in my Law School classroom and as it was practiced in the city halls, county courthouses, and the state capitol. Fifty boys and one girl were coming to my classroom every day to learn enough to enable them to go out to make a living, build a home, and start a career; and I was giving them all too little underpinning for those tasks. I could not keep my self-respect as a schoolteacher without trying to bridge that gap—but how was I to do it? Two experiences helped me find the answer to the question.

A Course in North Carolina History

In the fall of 1925, I started sitting in on a course in North Carolina history taught by Professor R.D.W. Connor; there had been no such course while I was an undergraduate. In his classroom I got my first vision of North Carolina as a whole; my first look at the land of North Carolina, stretching from the coastal plain through the piedmont into the mountains and beyond; my first look at the people coming to the land—why they came, where they came from, where they settled, and how they spread across the state, looking for liberty and good bottom land; my first look at the government of North Carolina—the process of dividing the state into counties, sub-dividing the counties into special districts and townships, and overlapping these townships and special districts with cities and towns. I followed the people of the cities, the counties, and the state of North Carolina as they moved "to form a more perfect Union, establish Justice, insure domestic Tranquillity, provide for the common Defence, promote the general Welfare, and secure the Blessings of Liberty to ourselves and our Posterity . . . ."

An Experience in the Mayo Clinic

During the Christmas holidays in 1926, I went to a meeting of the Association of American Law Schools in Chicago. While there, I decided to go on to Rochester, Minnesota, to visit some college friends who were interning at the Mayo Clinic. Their accounts of the working of this famed clinic made me want to know more about it. They told me the best way to learn of its workings was to go through its procedures in a physical examination and that I could do this as a schoolteacher at low cost.

They arranged for me to be examined by the head physician in each department, telling each one that I was using the physical examination to get an understanding of the internal structure and workings of the Mayo Clinic, while the Mayo Clinic was using it to get an understanding of the structure and the workings of Albert Coates.

Each physician started with that part of me that he knew most about: the eye, ear, nose, throat, heart, lungs, blood, bone, tissue, and so on throughout my body. From his own starting point, every physician spelled out the relation of his particular part of me to every other part of me. The process lasted five full days.

On the sixth day, I was ushered into a room with Dr. Charles Mayo and his right-hand man, who had studied the reports sent in by the physicians who had seen me as a man of parts; it was the task of these men to put the parts together. They told me that I was all right; and, what is more, they proved it. Dr. Mayo and his colleague told me that I was all right, and that my body could stand up to the stress and strain of any amount of work, if I would accept and understand one thing: that I was a human being, with all the limitations of a human being, and that the only way a human being could transcend his limitations was to live within them. The process that had begun as an intellectual enterprise had turned into a spiritual experience.

While I was on the way from Rochester to Chapel Hill on New Year's Day, 1927, Professor Connor's course in the history of North Carolina fused in my mind with the Mayo Clinic's revelation of the structure and the workings of the human body, and I knew what I wanted to do for the rest of my life: What Professor Connor had done with the history of North Carolina, I wanted to do with the government of North Carolina; and what the Mayo Clinic had done for the body of Albert Coates, I wanted to do for the body politic of North Carolina.

A Shift in Law School Courses

When I got back to Chapel Hill I looked through the University's catalogues throughout its history, and found that in 1836 the University had started a course in: "A history of national and constitutional law . . . presenting an analytical and historical review, in chronological order, of the Magna Carta . . . the Petition of Right, the Charters of Carolina, the Fundamental Constitutions of Carolina, the Habeas Corpus Act, the Bill of Rights, the Declaration of Independence, the Articles of Confederation, the Treaty of Peace with Great Britain, the Constitution of the United States and North Carolina." It was taught by David Lowry Swain, who had gone out of the University in the early 1800's to become a lawyer, legislator, judge, and governor of North Carolina, and had returned to Chapel Hill as President of the University in 1835.

I found that the substance of this course was expanded in lectures given in the Law School, starting in 1845. These lectures were based first on *Blackstone's Commentaries on the Laws of England,* which had become the "laws of this colony," and later on *Kent's Commentaries on American Law;* and that both of these texts were supplemented by lectures based on North Carolina statutes and decisions. By the 1900's, these general lectures, covering in a summary fashion the whole body of the law, were being grouped and concentrated in separate courses: in constitutional law, criminal law, municipal corporations, administrative law, family law, legislation, and so on throughout the curriculum.

I found that with the exception of constitutional law and criminal law, these courses were taught at irregular times, by different teachers, as odds and ends to fill out schedules for students and

4

teachers, and without any sort of relation to each other. They were considered peripheral to the basic Law School courses such as property, contracts, torts, civil procedure, et cetera. Any teacher would have been horrified with the idea of putting these peripheral courses together as the foundation of a professional career. I picked out four of these courses and staked my academic standing on them—if, as, and when I could get them.

Chapter II   The Starting Point

The Course in Criminal Law

I got hold of the course in criminal law in the academic year of 1927-28 and started teaching it out of a casebook of appellate court decisions. I ran across a recent study by a sociology professor showing that only four-tenths of one percent of the cases tried in the criminal courts of North Carolina during the past thirty years had gone to the Supreme Court on appeal. I asked myself: "Am I trying to teach one hundred percent of a course out of four-tenths of one percent of the knowledge? Is this percentage the measure of the gap between criminal law as it is taught in my classroom and as it is practiced by lawyers on the job?" Of course I knew the gap was not that wide. For these decisions furnished the yardstick for decisions by the lower courts.

If only a percentage of the knowledge of the criminal law is in the books, where is the rest of it? I found the answer to that question in the heads of law-enforcing officers; in the experience they had stored up from years of working on the job; in the methods, practices, and techniques coming out of the originality and resourcefulness of generations of officials; in ways of doing things which had never found their way into printed pages, but which represented no less the habitual processes of the law.

I recalled Chesterton's phrase, "the ignorance of the educated," and realized that I was a good illustration of its meaning.

I Go to School to Law-enforcing Officers

I joined police forces and worked as an apprentice on the job, helping to raid private dwellings where occupants were distilling home brew. The leader of the raiding squad knocked on a door. The man who opened it saw the uniforms which were the "the law" to him and said: "Show me your papers." The officer pulled out of his inside pocket an impressive looking life insurance policy he had taken out that afternoon, embossed in large black letters and stamped with a large gold seal. It was accepted as a search warrant. The officers were admitted, found the distilling works, and arrested the "home brew" makers. I was scared to death. Suppose these people had resisted arrest, and someone had been injured? or killed? and there were indictments for manslaughter? I could see all of us, including me, on the way to jail.

I rode in a light Ford car geared up to go, and going, ninety miles an hour in pursuit of a fleeing Buick loaded down with liquor. When I saw my host pull out a rifle, draw a bead, plug a tire, and bring the car with a screaming zig-zag to a halt, I cried out: "Good God, man, haven't you read the case of *State v. De Herrodora*?", a Supreme Court decision recently handed down prohibiting this sort of conduct.

There were lighter moments. One morning I was passing a police station and an officer called out: "Professor, come over here. We have finally caught that old bootlegger. He is smarter than we are and has outwitted us for the last six months. This morning I caught him in a station wagon full of fruit jars on the floor. 'What is in those jars?' I asked. 'Water', he said. 'Let me taste it', I said, and turned up the jar and started drinking. 'It tastes like wine to me'. 'Lord, Lord,' he said, 'Jesus has done it again!' "

I followed officers into criminal courts, testified as an investigating officer and prosecuting witness, and learned in the agony of firsthand experience how a bulldozing and truculent defense attorney could make the witness stand a mortal terror for testifying officers. I worked with the solicitor in prosecuting cases and saw guilty men escape because cases were not properly prepared and presented by the police, and because officers too often could not match wits with cross-examining lawyers for the defense and would get tangled up in their testimony. I served on juries and watched the workings of the criminal law from the jury box as lawyers and witnesses and defendants went into action before judge, jury, and spectators.

I was appointed by Governor O. Max Gardner to the prison advisory commission which had the responsibility of interviewing all long-term prisoners in state prisons and prison camps who had served half their terms, and recommending paroles on the basis of its findings.

When the commission started its visits to the prisons, I asked for, and got, permission to spend nights in the cells of the prisons we visited. I wanted to get something of "the feel" of the prison, and I got it. To this day I recall the feeling that came over me as I heard the click of the lock and understood why a prison guard was so often called a "turnkey." I would instinctively call out: "Don't forget to come and let me out tomorrow morning." I later spent one unforgettable night in a cell on "death row" in the state prison.

I found the prisoners conducting their own surveys on our criminal law-enforcing machinery, comparing the differing penalties for crimes given by different judges, giving their own ratings of judges, prosecutors, and police. One prisoner had received a five-year sentence for bigamy and told of another who had received three months for a similar offense; the latter had come to prison and gone, and was now free to commit bigamy again. I later read a statistical study showing that one judge was giving suspended sentences in as high as thirty-five percent of the cases coming before him, and another in as low as nine percent; one was giving fines in as high as twenty-five percent, and another in as low as eight percent; one was giving road sentences in as high as thirty-seven percent, and another in as low as seven percent. It was clear that differences in punishment might be due as much to differences in judges as to differences in criminals.

8

Law-enforcing Officers Come to School to Me

I soon found out that law-enforcing officers needed to know what I had learned from studying the books as badly as I needed to know what they had learned from working on the job. I started swapping my research for their experience, my knowledge of criminal law in the books for their knowledge of criminal law in action. One by one they would follow me to Chapel Hill to find "the law" in situations they were facing, and soon the criminal law in books and the criminal law in action were coming together, to their advantage and mine.

I found that police and sheriffs had long been meeting in separate conventions where the program would run like this: a formal meeting; the appointment of committees on nominations and resolutions; a period of fraternization and swapping of experiences by individuals and groups, with lubrication of proper and effective spirits; a banquet with a speech by some political person; a business meeting with the election of officers, adoption of resolutions, and adjournment.

I attended these meetings and got to know the officers well enough to be put on their program for a morning session where I discussed the law of arrest for an hour or more as I taught it in my Law School classroom. This stirred up spirited discussion on questions they faced every day, and changed some of their notions of a "college professor."

A Statewide School of Law-enforcing Officers

In the late 1920's I invited city policemen, county sheriffs, and highway patrolmen, from the newly-created State Highway Patrol, to meet for a three-day school in my Law School classroom in Chapel Hill. I told them in the letters of invitation that we would be in meetings ten hours a day, with no time for convivialities and no need for liquor. I didn't call it a "school"—to which they would not have come. I called it a "convention"—to which they were used to coming.

The older officers freely predicted that no one would come on those terms, that the police and the sheriffs didn't fraternize and wouldn't come together on any terms. I became anxious and took to the road to drum up attendance. My anxiety increased when I went to the sheriff's office in a county courthouse in a fairly large city and talked with the sheriff at some length about the "convention." He walked with me to my car, parked on the street adjoining the courthouse, where I was embarrassed to find a parking ticket. I had come in the interest of law and had stayed to violate the law. "Give it to me," the sheriff said. "You have been talking about cooperation. Here is the way police and sheriffs cooperate in this town," and he tore up the ticket.

I tried to persuade city policemen, county sheriffs, state patrolmen, and federal agents to come together and talk about problems of law enforcement which concerned them all. Policemen told me they would come but sheriffs wouldn't. Sheriffs told me they would come but policemen wouldn't. Some officers in all groups promised me they would take a chance and come whether others came or not. To the astonishment of all, everybody came. A state highway patrolman actually picked up a county sheriff and a city police chief in his territory, and all three rode to the meeting in the same car! And there they were, all dressed up and asking: Where do we go from here?

District Schools

I followed the three-day state-wide school in the summer of 1929 with one-day district schools in the fall of 1929—starting in Wilmington on the coast and going through the state to Asheville in the mountains of the west. In these one-day meetings I tried to get local schools going, with the judges and solicitors of recorders courts doing the instructing at meetings once each week when, with the help of the police chief, they would go over the week's work in court and point out the mistakes made, make suggestions for improvement, and answer questions from the officers. I tried to persuade superior court judges and solicitors to hold one meeting a week with law-enforcing officers in every term of criminal court.

Some judges started the practice of turning the traditional judge's charge to the grand jury into an instruction program for police and sheriffs as well as grand jurors. Their experience in this enterprise led the way toward state-wide schools for prosecuting attorneys, judges, probation and parole officers, and prison officials. The interlocking relationship of these successive links in the chain of law-enforcing machinery required them to understand each other's problems and work together to solve them.

The Going Was Rough

In the beginning the going was rough. There was an old chief of police in my hometown of Smithfield who had known me for most of my life and thought well of me, until he found out that there I was, fresh out of law school and not dry behind the ears, starting schools for law-enforcing officers without ever having walked a beat. He saw me in a crowd in front of Creech's drugstore one day and came up and said: "Look a-here, boy, I knew you when you won't, and you still ain't."

There was the morning when I stood in front of the courthouse in an eastern North Carolina county, greeting officers coming in for a one-day school. A middle-aged police officer was walking up, and one of the officers whispered to me: "This man don't like the idea of these schools and he is bringing trouble." He came up, looked me over, and walked around me, sizing me up. "What are your qualifications for police instructor, young feller?" I knew I could expect no mercy from him, decided the best defense was offense, and replied in kind: "I don't have a pot belly or a flat foot, but give me time." He flashed back: "I had rather be a wart on a [clearly unmentionable but no less clearly discernible part of a dog's anatomy] than to be a college professor talking about something he don't know nothing about." The answer came to me out of the blue, I didn't have time to think it up: "I can understand that," I said, "you are better fitted for that position." There was an explosion of laughter, the officer walked off, and the crowd went into the school. I have often thought: Suppose heaven hadn't taken care of me in that retort and

11

his ridicule had worked on me—would the officers have gone into the courthouse with me or straggled off with him?

I ran into the barrier of "language" among officers who had rarely gone through high school. I soon saw that all of the advantage was not on my side, as I came to know men with little English grammar but more common sense than many a Ph.D. on a college campus. I found they would rarely open a hundred and fifty page-guidebook; but they would read any number of pages if I would send them broken doses of ten to fifteen pages at a time, written in their "language," which I found more and more coming to be my own—their spirit, purpose, and intent had always been my own.

I ran into the barrier of "schools." I found at the start that all too many law-enforcing officers thought "schools" were for children, not for grown men. Going to "school" would be an admission that they didn't know their business, and that might be used against them. It was all right, however, for grown men to go to "conventions." We went from "conventions" to "conferences," and then from "conferences" to "institutes."

Persuading officers to come to these schools was no easy task. I would urge the chief to come; write the mayor, city manager, solicitor, and judge to urge the chief to come; and when I called a joint meeting of them all, I would write each one to come and bring all the others with him. I knew misery loved company. One man came because he was sued along with the county for $150,000 for a killing growing out of an illegal arrest, and he decided that as far as the law of arrest was concerned he had better learn it late than never. Officers began to see they didn't know it all, any more than I did.

I discovered a fear of written examinations. I gave out "certificates of attendance" at first, so that officers could take something home in their hands if not in their heads. Then I saw five of those certificates on the walls of a twelve-man department and wondered what would happen to me if twelve certificates hung there and not much, if any, improvement had been made in the police department.

I started giving written examinations which were difficult for an officer not in the habit of writing. On the eve of the first examination, one of the older officers came up to me and said he "hated the worst in the world" that he couldn't stay over and take the examination because he wanted to carry that certificate back home with him, but his mother-in-law had just died and he had to leave that night for the funeral. Three years later the same mother-in-law died again on the eve of another examination. He could think all right, and talk all right, and was a good officer, but he wasn't used to thinking with a pencil in his hand.

One day I walked through a classroom of law-enforcing officers during a written examination and saw one of the older officers agitated to the point of panic. "What is the matter?" I asked. "Oh, I don't know nothing," he answered. I told him, "I know better than that; you have been the first in your seat at the beginning of a class, and the last to leave it, and you asked some of the best questions." I looked at his weather-beaten face and his hands and said, "Come on out into the hall with me. You remind me of my father. He was five years old when the Civil War ended, and there were no schools to go to. He learned how to read and spell out the words, but it was painful. So was writing. He could sign his name and that was about all the writing he did. His hands were fitted to the plow handle, axe helve, shovel, and grubbing hoe; but a pencil in his hands was out of place. I'll write down your answers, you tell me what to write." He got a better than average grade.

I ran into a fear of "schooling" in itself on the part of some of the old-timers who had come up through the school of hard knocks and were afraid this new-fangled schooling might give the younger up-and-coming officers an unfair advantage. I never will forget the expression which came over the face of an old officer who had been handling fingerprints in the police department when he found that the boy just out of high school whom he had brought along by way of breaking him in as his assistant and who had never seen a fingerprint before, had gotten a higher grade in the fingerprint school than he had.

Shakespeare Helps Out

I heard an officer in a group of officers at one of my schools referring to an absent friend as an s.o.b., in language all his own. "If you are going to call a man an s.o.b.," I said, "why don't you do it in the King's English?" "What is the King's English?" he asked. I got a copy of Shakespeare's plays and read him this passage in *King Lear*, Act II, Scene II, where Kent says to Oswald: "Fellow, I know thee." Oswald asks: "What dost thou know me for?" and Kent replies: "A knave, a rascal, an eater of broken meats; a base, proud, shallow, beggarly, three-suited, hundred-pound, filthy, worsted-stocking knave; a lily-liver'd, action-taking knave, a whoreson, a glass-gazing, superserviceable, finical rogue; one-trunk-inheriting slave; one that wouldst be a bawd, in way of good service, and art nothing but the composition of a knave, beggar, coward, pandar, and the son and heir of a mongrel bitch: one whom I will beat into clamorous whining if thou deniest the least syllable of thy addition."

"He shore knows a son-of-a bitch when he sees him," the officer said. "Who wrote that book?" "William Shakespeare," I answered. He took out his pencil and notepad and wrote down the name of the author and the title. Years later he came to my office with his son who had just finished college and was going into graduate work, and introduced him to me, saying "Son, this is the man who started me to reading Shakespeare. Mr. Coates, me and my son have been reading Shakespeare's plays together as he studied them in college. When a man can put a thing as well as that man Shakespeare put it, I try to learn him."

Noblesse Oblige

I was starting a one-day district school in an eastern North Carolina courthouse full of law-enforcing officers when a six-foot sheriff walked in the door with three strapping deputies. I had held a school in his county the day before and wondered why he had come to this next-day meeting. He walked to the front of the courtroom and asked permission to say a few words, which I granted with fear and trembling. And here is what he said: "This is not my meeting. I was in mine yesterday. And after it was over, me and my men got to talking and said it was the first time in our lives we could remember a man leaving his high place in the colleges and universities and coming down here to work with us fellows in the backwoods. I have come ninety miles to say this to Mr. Coates in this meeting, and that's all I've come for, and now I'm going back home and go to work."

I had not started out with the idea of helping the law-enforcing officers but of getting them to help me—to bridge the gap between the criminal law as it was taught in my Law School classroom and as it was practiced in the criminal courts in city halls, county courthouses, and state judicial and administrative agencies. It was a matter of *noblesse oblige*. They were helping me to double the value of my course to my students.

With the criminal law course, I had laid without knowing it one cornerstone of the Institute of Government, but that was only a beginning. I soon saw that the criminal law and its administration could not be fully understood without being studied in its broader setting of local government law and its administration.

The Course in Local Government Law

The nearest starting point to this field that I could find in the Law School curriculum was the two-hour course in municipal corporations, given as a fill-in when an extra course was needed. No one else wanted to teach it, so I took it on. I found ninety percent of the cases in the casebook dealing with cities and towns, around ten percent dealing with counties, and next to nothing dealing with the bearing of the states and the United States on counties, cities, and towns.

I saw that I could not teach the law of cities and towns without regard to their setting in the counties, county subdivisions, and special districts; nor the law of counties without regard to their setting in the state; nor the law of cities, counties, and the state without regard to their setting in the United States of which they are a part. I knew I had to crawl through the channels of this interlocking structure in order to find out how to close the gap between the law as it was being taught in my Law School classroom, and the law as it was being practiced in city halls, county courthouses, and state departments. I started crawling.

I went to school to city councilmen and county commissioners in their monthly meetings, and to state legislators in their biennial sessions, to see the sort of problems that came up. I went out of these sessions to work as an apprentice on the job with officials in the different departments of local and state government; to sweat with them over their perplexities; to get the swing, the rhythm, and the feel of their work; to find out what they did, and how they did it, and why they did it that way.

Year after year I followed them to the annual meetings of their associations and listened to discussions of their problems in all parts of the state—from counties, cities, and towns in the coastal plain, through the piedmont section, to the mountain region. I read the proceedings of their association meetings from their beginnings to get the background of the problems they were currently facing. I worked with the newly-developing county government advisory commission established in 1929, and followed its work as it started with the counties and went on to the cities and towns, went through the General Assembly, and culminated in the county finance act, county manager act, municipal finance act, and related measures reorganizing local government, and the local government commission.

With this help I expanded the course in municipal corporations into a course in local government law, going far enough into its relationships with state and federal governments to round out the local picture. They helped me double the value of this course to my students. I had laid the second cornerstone.

The Course in Family Law

As I worked my way through the courses in criminal law and municipal corporations, I began to see the family as the underpinning of all governmental units. Out of the home and family came all the citizens that city, county, state, and federal governmental units had to work with. The mother and father were authorized by law to exercise more power over persons in the family unit, during the formative years of their lives, than public officials were authorized by law to exercise over adult citizens in governmental units.

By the 1920's, state and local governments had grasped this fact and had begun holding families together with such programs of governmental assistance as mother's aid and others. In the 1930's, the federal government was coming to the aid of family units with grants-in-aid to dependent children, old-age assistance, and aid tō the blind, followed in later years by aid to the totally and permanently disabled, and by maternal and child health care.

The nearest starting point to this field that I could find in the Law School curriculum was the course in domestic relations, and when it became available to me, I took it.

In an effort to bridge the gap between domestic relations as it was being taught in my Law School classroom and as it was being practiced by officials working on the job, I began working with public welfare officials and juvenile court judges on procedures to be followed in cases involving juvenile delinquency, neglect and custody; with the officials handling matters of abandonment and non-support, bastardy, annulment, divorce, and other legal problems relating to the husband-wife and parent-child relationships; with the clerks of the superior court on adoption procedures, commitment procedures, the appointment of guardians, and the related governmental agencies involved in these problems.

With their help I expanded the course in domestic relations into a course in family law and its administration in local, state and federal government. They helped me double the value of this course to my students. I had laid the third cornerstone.

The Course in Legislation

The problems in these interlocking units of government led me to the General Assembly of North Carolina which was making the laws for the guidance of them all.

I heard a visiting teacher in our summer Law School compare a statute and a politician, saying: "A politician must get elected and a statute must get enacted, and a lot of adjustments and compromises come about between the first draft of a politician's platform, or a legislator's bill, and the last." I started going to the state capitol and following the work of the General Assembly from its organization through its sessions to its adjournment. I talked with the legislators about the problems involved in drafting legislation and found that they would start by drafting a bill to do all that they wanted it to do. Then they found that some legislators would not go along unless one provision was dropped, or another added. Others would not go along unless other changes were made, and this process could go on until the bill was amended to death. At some point in the process the legislator would have to say to himself, "This far will I go and no farther," and draw the line and fight. I saw one legislator get up on the floor of the senate and move to kill his own bill because so little of what he had started with was left in it.

I followed their successive drafts and phrasings until they worked out the bill to be introduced; followed this bill into committee and through committee action in the form of acceptance or rejection or amendment or rewriting; followed it from the committee to the floor of the General Assembly and through discussions and floor fights over amendments to its passage in final form. This process helped me double the value of the legislation course to my students. I had laid the final cornerstone.

Chapter III Building on Cornerstones

Coming events were casting their shadows before and drawing the outlines, form, and dimensions of the superstructure that was to come. While I was teaching these courses in criminal law, local government, family law, and legislation, and working with officials who were involved in the administration of these laws, I became aware of some basic problems which were common to all governmental units and officials.

Gaps in the Governmental Framework

I discovered a gap between outgoing and incoming officials. Every two or four years, literally hundreds of newly elected officials were coming into the administration of public affairs in the cities, the counties and the state of North Carolina, knowing all too little about their powers and duties at the start; learning as they went along; and going out of office at the end of their respective terms to be followed by successors who did not pick up the threads of government at the point where their predecessors had left off, but almost, if not quite, at the point where they had begun.

I discovered a gap between governmental units and officials. On one piece of land the people of North Carolina had built a pyramid of overlapping city, county, state, and federal governmental units. Each unit had its own set of officials working on the same problems for the same people in the same territory, all too often crossing each other's paths, stepping on each other's toes, getting in each other's hair, without coming together in the systematic practice of cooperative effort.

I discovered a gap between the governments of yesterday and the governments of today. Cities, counties, and the state were outgrowing the existing governmental framework as growing boys outgrow suits of clothes. Public officials were being forced to call on outside experts to assist them in reorganizing and adapting old practices to new conditions, to do for us that which we had not yet developed agencies to do for ourselves. The weakness in the practice of relying on them was and is: (1) Through no fault of theirs, they come to us knowing all too little about local conditions. (2) They write their conclusions into a report which goes upon the shelf to be read by all too few. (3) They have no part in or responsibility for the practical operation of the changes they recommend. (4) As soon as their report is written, they leave and carry away with them the most valuable results of all their work—the personal knowledge and experience gained in doing it.

I discovered the gap between people and their government. In the pioneering days of North Carolina, every citizen was a law unto himself. He cut his own paths through the wilderness, found his own water supply in wellsprings or dug his own well, built his own home, fought his own fires, lit his own lamps, collected his own garbage, disposed of his own sewage, looked out for his own health and sanitation, protected his property by serving on the night watch, and provided for his own schooling if he got any at all.

There was no gap between the citizens and the county road gang and the city street department in the early settlements in North Carolina—the citizens were the road gang and street department. There was no gap between citizens and the police department—the citizens were the police department, serving by turns on the night watch. There was no gap between citizens and the water department—the citizens were the water department, digging their own wells and drawing their own water. The gap appeared when people tired of working the roads running by their farms and the streets running by their houses, and paid taxes for road workers to do this for them. When people tired of serving on the night watch, they paid taxes for policemen to watch for them. When people tired of digging their own wells and disposing of their own sewage, they paid taxes for others to do these things for them. When people tired of fighting their own fires, they paid taxes for firemen to do this for them. And that is where the gap between the people and their government began.

How Had These Gaps Come About?

I asked myself how these gaps had come about and answered my question this way at that time:

Here in North Carolina we are committed by two hundred years of political history to the theory and practice of elective offices, short terms of office and rotation of officers. This means that every two or four years hosts of newly elected officers come into the administration of public affairs in the cities, the counties and the state of North Carolina.

These officers are not born with a knowledge of the powers and duties of the offices to which they are elected—the office of sheriff or chief of police, clerk of court or register of deeds, city alderman or county commissioner. Their private occupations and professions do not teach them the powers and duties of public officials. The uncertainties of political life do not offer them incentives to study the responsibilities of a public office before they seek it. The democracy which clothes them with the public trust does not provide them with training to fit them to discharge it.

They go into office to learn by mistakes which might have been avoided, in the school of hard knocks which sometimes knock harder on the public than on the public officer. The learning they acquire in this rough, ready and expensive fashion too often goes out of office with them at the end of their official terms. The mental attitude of a defeated official does not beget a tender solicitude for his victorious opponent. The successor who will gladly learn does not often find a predecessor who will so gladly teach. Retiring officers have been known to walk out of their office doors as the clock struck the end of their official terms without going to the trouble of saying "Good morning" to incoming officers waiting on the threshold. The only tie binding successive governmental administrations together today is the clerical and stenographic help familiar with the office routine. Sometimes this tie too is broken. There are instances where outgoing officers have secured as good or better jobs elsewhere for their clerical and stenographic help in order to guarantee a start *de novo* to their successors.

A generation ago teachers of arithmetic teased their students with this question: A frog in a hole thirty feet deep, jumps up three feet and falls back two; how many jumps will it take to get out? Popular government today is in the hole. Like the frog it starts out with officers fresh from the people, moves forward with them as they acquire knowledge and skill in the administration of the law, then on successive election days drops back to begin again almost at the beginning with new and inexperienced officers, and never breathes a word about its loss. Thus, with every rotation of officers in every general election the continuity of governmental experience is broken. Accumulated governmental knowledge goes over the wheel to waste. Incoming officers start, not where their predecessors left off but almost if not quite where they began. Government is forever in the hands of beginners—who do not always have beginner's luck.

This is costly training for which the people pay—not in the beginning, but in the end. They are paying for it in North Carolina now. They will keep on paying for many years to come and the price they pay is getting higher every year.

How Could I Bridge These Gaps?

How could I bridge the gap in knowledge and experience between outgoing and incoming public officials, and cut down the lost time, lost motion, and lost money involved in a rotating governmental personnel? How could I provide the catalytic agencies to bridge the gap between the government of yesterday and the government of tomorrow, prevent the hardening of governmental arteries and bring about changes in governmental machinery from year to year instead of from generation to generation? How could I coordinate the efforts of city, county, and state officials who were working on the same problems for the same people in the same territory without coming together in the systematic practice of cooperative effort, and cut down needless competition, duplication, friction and waste? How could I bridge the gap between the government and the people, prevent the periodic clashes between taxpayers and tax-spenders, and build an agency which would put the people in touch with their government and keep them in touch with it? While I was working with officials on the job in the 1920's, I could not find a single guidebook bringing together in one place the laws spelling out the powers and duties of a single office and outlining ways of doing them. Those laws were scattered through thousands of pages of statutes, court decisions, and constitutional provisions. Looking for them was like looking for needles in haystacks.

Incoming officials did not have the time or the skill to do this looking. Even if they had the time and skill they did not have the library and research facilities. I did.

A Plan Evolves

(1) *I could go through the thousands of pages of the laws on the books and go to school to officials working on the job* to study the methods, practices, and techniques of government in action.

(2) *I could put these basic studies of government in books and in action into guidebooks* which would bring to every governmental official a clear and concise statement of (a) the powers and duties of his office, (b) the methods and practices developed by his predecessors in the exercise of these powers and the performance of these duties, and (c) the methods and practices developed by other officials in similar offices in this and other states.

(3) *I could teach these guidebooks in training schools* for officials in the period between the day on which officials are elected and the day on which they go into office—bringing to every participating official a

better understanding of the governmental machinery of which he is a part as well as of his part in it, and a better understanding of his responsibility together with information and training which would fit him to discharge it.

(4) *I could demonstrate these guidebooks in a laboratory* which would collect, compare, and demonstrate, for the benefit of every governmental official, (a) the different methods and practices in use in similar offices in this and other states, (b) the different systems of organization, equipment and records in use in similar offices in this and other states, and then (c) in one place provide him with information and guidance he would now have to go to hundreds of places to find and might not even then find available.

(5) *I could distribute this material through a clearinghouse of information,* spearheaded by a monthly journal which would (a) report the results of the governmental studies as they were made, (b) keep the governmental guidebooks up-to-date from year to year, (c) transmit and interpret to officials throughout the state the governmental changes made by each successive legislature, (d) keep every official in every office in touch with improvements in government and its administration as they are made by every other official in the state.

(6) *I could train a group of men with experience and expertness* to do for ourselves what we are now compelled to call on outside governmental experts to do for us. I saw my classroom as a statewide center, with lines of communication to every city hall, county courthouse, state department, and federal agency in North Carolina; with all I was learning about government in books flowing out to the officials in these local centers, and with all they were learning about government in action flowing back to me and coming to a focus in the classroom by letter, telephone, radio, publication, conference, school, and grapevine.

(7) *At this point I added another string to my bow.* It came about while I was talking to my Law School class in the course in local government law. I was saying: "Here in this classroom, we are living as citizens under five overlapping governmental units: the United States, North Carolina, Orange County, Chapel Hill Town-

24

ship, and the Town of Chapel Hill.

In this context, and at that precise point, another unit of government came to mind and I made this observation: Within the limits of the Town of Chapel Hill on the University campus, students are living under another government—student government—with added rules and regulations of its own.

I had served on the student governing council in my junior and senior years, and now in the 1930's most students, faculty, and townspeople recognized the fact that the student council was doing fully as good a job in governing four or five thousand students on the campus as the city council was in governing four or five thousand citizens in the town of Chapel Hill. For this reason the program of the Institute of Government was expanded to include student governing officials along with city, county, and state officials —with studies of student government to be set forth in guidebooks, taught in training schools, and kept up-to-date through a clearinghouse of student government information. This was later extended to include student governing councils in senior high schools and their faculty advisors.

Committee Considers the Plan

William A. Devin, the superior court judge in my judicial district, thought well of what I was doing and agreed to become chairman of a steering committee of fifteen people whom he helped me select, the purpose being to put my plan into effect.

We called this steering committee to meet at Chapel Hill on December 28-29, 1931, to discuss the possibilities of a "Tentative Plan for County, District and State-wide Schools of Governmental Officers, for Continuous Study of the Structure and the Workings of Governmental Institutions and Processes in the Cities, the Counties, and the State of North Carolina." It came together at the Carolina Inn in the trough of the Great Depression. Two of its members left the meeting on receiving news that their home town banks would not open the next morning. The remaining members went over the plan with critical and penetrating care. To illustrate:

The committee members asked the question: Why don't you

confine your effort to the criminal law field before you start in the other fields of government? This was my answer: Because I have four courses to teach, each one in a field that could absorb the efforts of a lifetime, and if I stayed with one I would never get to the others.

They asked a similar question in a different form: Why don't you start with cities, then go on to counties, then to the state? This was my answer: Because the activities of city, county, and state governments are becoming so interlocking, overlapping, and conflicting that the study of any one of them in completeness calls for a study of all together—it is not a matter of choice, it is a matter of necessity.

They asked another question: How are you going to work with all three governments at the same time? This was my answer: City police are arresting people for violating laws within city limits, county sheriffs for violating laws within county limits (chiefly in rural areas), and state highway patrolmen for violating laws within state limits—all under the same law of arrests. There was no need for three guidebooks—one applies to all. There is no need for three schools—all of them can be taught in the same school. This procedure would save time and money. It would also get officers who are working on the same problems for the same people in the same territory in the habit of pulling together instead of pulling apart. The same principle will apply in most if not all activities of city, county and state governments.

The committee put me still another question: You say you want to work with the officials and citizens of today, and the youth of today who will be the officials and citizens of tomorrow—why don't you start out working with one group at a time? I answered this question by showing them a summary of the plan, short enough to go on a four by six card—in these words:

> The Institute of Government is a voluntary organization of public officials and private citizens coming together for the continuous study of the structure and the workings of government, in books and in action, in the cities, the counties, and the state of North Carolina, with the results:
> To be set forth in definitive form in guidebooks, taught in training schools, demonstrated in laboratories, and distributed through a clearinghouse of information.

To be set forth in a more popular form in bulletins and brochures for the use of public affairs committees of civic organizations of men and women.

To be set forth in a more elementary form in textbooks for the use of students and teachers in the twelfth grade in senior high schools— the last point of contact between the public schools and the eighteen-year-old voters.

Persons doing the basic studies and writing the definitive guidebooks for public officials could quickly put this technical knowledge in popular form for civic organizations, and in elementary form for the use of teachers and students in the public schools, thereby costing less than half the price for three separate groups working separately. The committee was satisfied and the plan was approved.

Officials Approve the Plan

We followed up this meeting by calling representatives of city, county and state governments to come to Chapel Hill on May 6, 1932. Two hundred came. For an hour and a half, I outlined the plan and program for their consideration, saying among other things:

The need for training in our governmental personnel is painfully apparent. Within the limits of our governmental experience we have seen the political pendulum swing the balance of power from king to subject; from officers appointed by the crown to officers elected by the people; from the continuity of long-time tenure to the rotation of short-term officers; from the belief that the common man could do nothing to the belief that he can do anything; from the naive notion of birth as entitlement to office to the equally naive notion of birth as a qualification for it; from the aristocratic notion that some men are born to fill an office to the more or less popular notion that all men are born knowing how to fill it.

The letter of the law is in the book. The symbol of the law is in the office. But the life of the law is in the officer. In him the citizen and his government meet, shake hands, and get acquainted. Popular government hangs upon the character of this acquaintance. In every official transaction however minute, in every point of contact between public officer and private citizen, popular governmental institutions are on trial for their life. They are on trial in North Carolina today. One voice says their salvation lies in centralizing governmental power. Another says their salvation lies in localizing it. But the hope of popular government is not so much wrapped up in theories of government, centralized or localized, as in the effective and efficient handling of governmental affairs by effective and efficient governmental officers, responsible and responsive to the people.

More than common honesty is required in public office and likewise more than common sense. A hundred thousand dollars lost through honest inefficiency is as great a burden to the taxpayer as a hundred thousand dollars lost through conscious fraud. Knowledge is no guarantee of character, we are told. Neither is ignorance. The best of governmental systems may be wrecked by men who do not understand it. After two hundred years of practice in the making of governmental machinery here in North Carolina we propose to go into the training of the men who run it.

The two hundred representatives discussed the plan for another hour, and then unanimously approved it. I had my marching orders.

Printing the Plan

But where was the money to print the plan and program and send it out to the rank and file of people it was intended to serve?

I knew that the printshop of the state prison in Raleigh was printing the *University News Letter* because the University had no money to print it, and I asked the editors of the *News Letter* to let me prepare the copy for two successive issues. They did. I wanted more copies than the regular printing, and the prison authorities told me this would be over-time work and that it would be up to me to persuade the prisoners doing the printing to help me on their own time. I went to the prisoners and told them what I was doing and why I was doing it; that I had already put all my money in it and that my pockets were empty; that if they would help me I would get a room in the prison and eat, sleep, and work with them until the job was done. They agreed, and I got hold of the money to pay for the paper for the extra copies. They printed 100,000 copies in over-time work in 1932. I sent them progress reports of the work going on while they were in prison, and after they left. In more ways than one we became brothers in the bonds.

Distributing the Plan

There was no money to distribute copies of the plan after they were printed. I went to the newly-organized State Highway Patrol, whose members were attending the schools for law-enforcing officers, and asked them to help me out. They did. During the next few weeks they personally distributed these 100,000 copies to city halls, county courthouses, state departments, and civic organizations of men and women in every county, city, and town in North Carolina.

I printed the following request at the top of the first page: *It will be a favor to me if you will read this plan, find all the fault with it you can, write down in the margin all of the suggestions you can think of which might make it better, and return it to me.*

I got my fair share of brush-off replies from people saying they had received it and expected to read it with "great pleasure." I knew they never would, for I had written letters like that and knew what they meant. But when I began to get replies running from one to three and four pages, showing the recipients had read the plan and were reacting to it with the criticisms and comments I had asked them for, I knew I had hit pay dirt. It struck a responsive chord with governmental units in the anguished realities of the Great Depression, and scores of responses came.

Working for the Plan

I followed up this printing and distribution by going out to talk to city and county officials, state officials, civic clubs, bar associations, women's clubs, business and professional organizations of men and women, and teachers and students of civics and government in high schools, colleges, and universities. I talked *ad infinitum* to all, and *ad nauseam* to some. I was once asked how small a gathering I was willing to talk to, and I paraphrased the scripture by saying that wherever two or three are gathered together in my name, there will I be also. One observer reported that he had seen me walking along the street talking to myself about the work I was doing, and that was the most interested audience I had ever talked to.

The mayor of Winston-Salem got a few of his friends to listen to me at a luncheon in the Reynolds Grill, and as we went in he gave me a message from one of those present who had heard tell of me, if he had not heard me: "Tell Albert not to try to put every paling in the fence."

Tom Bost, a veteran newspaperman, drew instant and applauding laughter from a group of state officials by saying that "Albert Coates has demonstrated to his complete satisfaction that the way to build an institution is to get hold of an idea and go crazy."

One psychologist on the University faculty found me a perfect illustration of an abnormal type of mind he came across in his studies, and filed a formal report of his conclusions with my superiors.

I found that many public officials in city halls and county courthouses were slow to realize that they needed to know what I had learned from studying the books in my municipal corporations class as much as I needed to know what they had learned from working on the job. They did not know they needed me at all. And when they found out, would they be willing to admit they could learn anything from a school teacher in general, and from a college professor in particular?

I had heard the story of the balky mule that refused to move until an old workman, wise in the ways of mules, held a clod of dirt to his lips. The mule took it in, found he didn't want it, turned his lips wrongside out to get rid of it, and walked off without further prodding. The old workman explained the mystery by saying: "I tried to change the current of his thinking." It was my job to change the current of official thinking; but not too fast, lest it rub my nose in the dirt.

I decided to follow the policy illustrated by Robert Hutchins, the thirty-year-old Dean of the Yale Law School, who was slapped on the back by a United States Supreme Court Justice as he made the jovial comment: "So this is the boy Dean who is teaching his students the Supreme Court of the United States doesn't know any law." "Oh, no, Mr. Justice," answered the boy Dean, "we let the boys find that out for themselves."

But I left as little to chance as I could. I worked to the limit on

30

questions I knew were bothering officials and casually dropped in on meetings when those questions were discussed; then with becoming modesty I volunteered answers, citing chapter and verse by way of authority. Gradually they got into the habit of coming to me with questions.

I had little trouble convincing those officials I needed them. I told them I didn't know anything about the actual workings of government and wanted them to teach me what they knew, so I could do a better job of teaching their sons and daughters. My obvious ignorance had a face value they could not deny. Some of them were a little pleased to find they could tell me things I didn't know. I took what I learned about the practical workings of government from the first official to the second; and what I had learned from the first two to a third; and so on from one official to another in a process that has not ended yet. I had no trouble with officials who didn't know and wanted to learn, even if the learning came from a college professor; and I asked those who knew it all to help me teach the others.

I ran into the fear of some groups that they might lose their separate identities and be swallowed up in the federation of all groups. They lost these fears as they found out schooling activities in co-operating groups increased attendance at their separate conventions. They began to see that the end in view was not absorption, nor merger, but union. They found in union a strength they did not separately possess. Their separate powers ran in rivulets too small to float their independent enterprises; but these same rivulets running together could float a program able to sustain them all.

The Plan Gets Going

I went to my former law school teacher, Dean Roscoe Pound of the Harvard Law School, told him what I had done, was doing, and hoped to do, and asked him if he would come to Chapel Hill and open the first "Statewide School of Governmental Officers for the Study of Governmental Institutions and Processes in the Cities, Counties, and State of North Carolina," on September 9-10, 1932. I told him I had no money to pay him a fee, or even his travel expenses. He came, at his own expense, and announced his enthusiastic support of me and the work that I was doing. In an hour's talk, he showed a complete understanding of it all, put it in words that lettered and unlettered men could understand, pointed out its significance to the cities, the counties, and the state of North Carolina, expressed the hope that other states would follow North Carolina's lead, and said that the Harvard Law School took pride in this work by one of its sons.

Three hundred officials came to the school from counties, cities, and towns throughout the state. O. Max Gardner, the Governor of North Carolina, presided at the opening and said that he knew of no single program initiated by the University of North Carolina in this century that carried greater promise for the people of this state, and that he was throwing the full weight of his office behind it. The programs in each of the sessions of the different groups of officials were carried on by carefully selected officials who had been working with me and knew the problems of the specific groups they were dealing with. They turned these meetings into discussions of their problems in particular and showed how the movement getting under way could help in their jobs.

I had found the answer to the question I had faced in my senior year in Law School in the spring of 1923, the question I had talked over with myself in the night-time walk up and down the Charles River in Cambridge, the question that had then been answered in the feeling that there was something I could do in Chapel Hill that I could not do in Smithfield, something I could do in a law school that I could not do in a law office. I knew now what that something was.

Opposition and a Warning

I had been aware for some time that opposition to my extra-curricular activities had been brewing among some of my Law School colleagues, but I did not know it was brewing so fast or going so far until one morning while I was teaching in my classroom a note marked personal, from a friend high in University councils, was delivered to me, telling me to drop whatever I was doing and meet him at the football stadium—a quiet and unfrequented place at that time of day. I dismissed my class and went to meet him.

He told me that the opposition had come to a head that morning when the Law School Dean had come to the President of the University with a demand from the Law faculty that I give up my work with the officials, or my teaching in the Law School, and that if I refused to give up my work with the officials he was prepared to recommend my dismissal from the Law School faculty. My friend told me that the President had asked the Dean if he had informed me of these complaints and recommendation, and, on his saying no, told him to acquaint me with the complaints against me and discuss them with me, and that both of us would be given a hearing on the merits as soon as the Dean and I were ready.

This friend, who knew me well, thought that my first reaction would be to say that I did not want to stay where I was not wanted, and give up my job. He advised me that, whatever I did, I should hold on to my professorship; that a full professor with his tenure had a secure job in the academic community, and that no one could get rid of him as long as he lived up to the responsibilities of his professorship. He let me know in no uncertain terms that he was not siding with me against my superior; he was simply seeing to it that I was not taken by surprise and catapulted into some instinctive reaction which might have fateful consequences.

A Confrontation

The Dean of the Law School came to my office, told me of his talk with the President, and his request that I quit my work with officials or my teaching in the Law School. I refused to do either. The chips were down and the stage was set for a showdown in the President's office.

The Dean's complaint was direct and aboveboard, with nothing devious about it: that my work with officials was interfering with my Law School duties to the point that my teaching performance was no longer up to acceptable Law School standards. I responded by saying: first, that I was working sixty to seventy-five hours a week on my two jobs while most of my colleagues were working the regular nine to five-hour day and the standard forty-hour week on this one job, and that hour by hour I did not feel that I was much, if any, behind them, and if there was a difference in the hours, that difference was more than made up by the fact that the extra-curricular work I was doing with officials on the job was feeding directly into my classroom teaching in the same way as book work in the Law School library.

At this point President Graham said that he would not require me to give up my work with officials unless it could be shown that this work was undermining the integrity of my teaching. I responded by giving my class rolls to the President, saying: "The Dean has not attended my classes and these students have. You do not need to take my word or the Dean's word—you can take their word. A few of them will put me on the top—where I do not belong. A few will put me on the bottom—where I do not belong. I believe that a majority will put my teaching above the average, and if you find that I have fallen below the average, I will give up my professorship." At that time, students all over the campus were conducting rolls assessing their teachers and it was easy in this atmosphere for President Graham to conduct his own assessment of the Law faculty. He did, and I was rated by the majority as well above average, and my professorship was saved.

President Graham wanted to keep us both. He suggested that I be allowed to take half-time leave from the Law School with full-time pay, as he thought the field work might have value for the University as a whole. The Dean said he was unwilling to allow Law School funds to be used for work which would make the University Law School into the laughing-stock of the American law school world. Things were getting no better fast and the President's efforts at mediation were petering out, when I came up with this way out of the impasse.

34

A Compromise

"Mr. President," I said, "there comes a time in every man's life, when he has to risk all he has on something he believes. The only thing worth dying for is the thing that makes life worthwhile. What I am doing is what makes life worthwhile for me. In order to save it, I propose that the University give me a year or two or more of half-time leave on the same terms that the Pickwick Club gave Mr. Pickwick a trip around the world, at my own expense."

This proposal was finally agreed to with the understanding that my work with public officials was to be a private venture, that the Law School would not be involved, and that I could not use the name of the Law School, or of the University, in promoting the work.

I had made a little better bargain, but not much better, than the farmer whose calf had got loose and trampled and destroyed growing crops in a neighbor's field, and had been shut up and held by the neighbor until the owner paid for the damages. A prolonged hassle followed, and the calf's owner boasted to his friends: "I came out on top in that deal. I agreed that if he would keep and feed the calf for the next six months, he could have the damn thing."

The Morning After the Night Before

The personal consequences of my bargain soon followed. My wife and I gave up the house we were living in, cut expenses to the bleak minimum, and lived in a rented room without the luxury of a private bath for two years. We were getting half-time pay while putting all the summer months and half the academic year on the work that had been called in question. We had left the snug harbor for the open sea.

Up to this time my whole life and interests had been focused on and concentrated in the Law School, with the unswerving belief that everything I wanted to do in this world could and should be done through the Law School. There I had lived and moved and had my being for seven years, and there I expected to grow and develop, with my classroom and extra-curricular work re-enforcing each other from day to day.

To this moment I recall my feelings on the first morning of the new adventure. I was lying in bed thinking about the move I had made, and heard the college bell ringing for 8:30 classes—I had always taught 8:30 classes, but this morning that bell was not ringing for me—and I kept on lying there until I recalled a chapel talk about discipline by President Edward Kidder Graham in my college days:

> It is easier for some men to charge through barbed wire on the cold steel of German bayonets than to crawl out of a warm bed on a February morning to attend a first-hour math class. Yet the whole problem of democratic civilization is symbolized in this test of whether when the obviously right thing to do presents itself, the intelligent free man will choose it, and be strong enough to do it. We are fighting Germany for the privilege of staying in bed if we want to; but the victory of democracy will not be won unless when we win the right to stay in bed we choose to get up.

That memory rang a bell for me. I got up and got going. I was thirty-six years old.

Appraisals of the Plan: 1927-1933

From a newspaper editor:

The first of many heartening responses to the plan came from Ben Sronce, editor of *The Wilkes Patriot:*

> This morning I received your general letter and . . . the initial number of "Popular Government." Tonight, after chores were done, I began thumbing through the issue to determine whether I wanted to read it. I decided that I did want to, and began. I was tired, and . . . rather dreaded the highbrow presentation that I expected to find. It is 12:30 now, yet I feel refreshed. "Popular Government" should refresh any soul that takes life seriously.
>
> "Popular Government" is as fine a thing as I ever read and with as splendid purpose. I shall read it again and again and I hope that I may miss no future issue, no matter what the cost.
>
> Mine is a mind handicapped educationally, but I would like to strike hands with you across the distance, and pledge you every

feeble cooperation that I can give, because hereafter the name Albert Coates will mean something more to me than simply a University professor.

From a city official:

"I believe that the program of the Institute of Government offers an investment which in terms of dollars and cents, in terms of improved and simplified governmental methods, in terms of public knowledge, understanding and confidence in our governmental institutions, will pay higher and surer returns to the citizens and taxpayers of this and future generations, than any other ever offered to the people of North Carolina."

From a county official:

"The preliminary plan for the schooling of governmental officers and for the study of governmental institutions and processes is splendidly conceived and expressed, and if put into operation will meet one of the most crying needs of our people and their government. Private business would soon go bankrupt if conducted with the overlapping waste, the embarrassing ignorance, and the perpetual change of personnel that characterize the conduct of public business."

From a stenographic report of the speech by O. Max Gardner, Governor of North Carolina, to the statewide school of law-enforcing officers in Chapel Hill in September, 1931:

"It is my considered judgment that this movement here inaugurated today has in it more potentialities for the welfare of North Carolina, her government and her people, than any movement heretofore inaugurated in the history of this University. And when I say that, I am not unmindful of its long historic past."

From J. Edgar Hoover, Director of the Federal Bureau of Investigation:

I have been so happy in watching the great work which you and your associates in the Institute of Government are accomplishing in North Carolina.

I have always felt that what we have tried to do in a National way in regard to Federal agencies could be accomplished in a local way with local agencies. You have actually done this. I know that you must get a great deal of satisfaction out of having brought this about, for one can not help feeling a certain degree of pride in being a builder, particularly in such a great cause as that in which you and I are enlisted.

As I go about the country I have a great sense of satisfaction in being able to point to North Carolina and the fine work that you are doing in that state . . . .Your name will certainly be at the top of that list of names, which, in years to come will be viewed as the pioneers in the advanced field of scientific crime detection and law enforcement training.

From the President of the United States:

My dear Governor:

The Institute of Government, its purposes and its organization, as conceived and established in North Carolina, has and will render fine service to the State and the Nation.

It is my hope that other States will recognize the leadership of North Carolina in what it is doing through this Institute and that States having no comparable agency will accept and follow your leadership. Some of the most progressive and original developments in the whole field of education have been in North Carolina and I take this occasion to congratulate you on that as well as on the Institute itself.

Very sincerely yours,

Franklin D. Roosevelt

To J.C.B. Ehringhaus
Governor of North Carolina

PRELIMINARY DRAFT OF A PLAN FOR

COUNTY, DISTRICT AND STATEWIDE SCHOOLS OF
LAW ENFORCING OFFICERS

For the Continuous Study of the Problems of Crime and Criminal Law
Administration in the Cities, the Counties and the State of
North Carolina

Submitted by Albert Coates
Teacher of the Criminal Law and its Administration,
in the University of North Carolina

With the request that you find all the fault with it you can, write down in
the margin all the constructive suggestions and criticisms you
can think of, and return it within the next few days
in the enclosed envelope.

Contents

I. Independence

    A. Agencies for the investigation of crime and the apprehension of criminals
    B. Agencies for the trial of persons accused of crime
    C. Agencies for punishment, pardon and parole

II. Co-ordination

    A. Common problems for the judges to discuss
    B. Common problems for the prosecuting attorneys to discuss
    C. Common problems for police officials to discuss
    D. Common problems for judicial, prosecuting and police officials to discuss
    E. Common problems for judicial, prosecuting and police officials to discuss
        with city managers and attorneys and the state commissioner of pardons
    F. Common problems for judicial, prosecuting and police officials to discuss
        with clerks--the record keeping officers--of the city, county and superior
        courts

III. Training

    A. Knowledge is no guarantee of character--neither is ignorance. "I want
        to qualify," said a newly appointed justice of the peace to a clerk of
        court. "I can swear you in," said the clerk, "but all hell can't
        qualify you." This is the all too common attitude of the public to the
        public agencies for the investigation of crime and the apprehension of
        criminals

IV. Schools taught by judges, prosecuting attorneys, and practitioners in city,
     county, state, and federal courts for law enforcing officers

    A. Statewide schools
    B. District schools
    C. County schools
    D. Local schools

PRELIMINARY DRAFT OF A PLAN FOR
COUNTY, DISTRICT AND STATEWIDE SCHOOLS OF
LAW ENFORCING OFFICERS

*For the Continuous Study of the Problems of Crime and Criminal Law
Administration in the Cities, the Counties and the State of
North Carolina*

Submitted by ALBERT COATES
*Teacher of the Criminal Law and its Administration,
in the University of North Carolina*

*With the request that you find all the fault with it you can, write down in
the margin all the constructive suggestions and criticisms you
can think of, and return it within the next few days
in the enclosed envelope.*

———————

Popular Government

VOL. I.   JANUARY, 1931   No. 1

Permit to enter as second class matter applied for.
Published Quarterly.

THE UNIVERSITY OF NORTH CAROLINA

ALBERT COATES, *Editor*

Contents

THE CONVICT'S QUESTION

THE STATEWIDE
SCHOOL OF GOVERNMENTAL OFFICERS
FOR THE
STUDY OF GOVERNMENTAL INSTITUTIONS AND PROCESSES
IN THE
CITIES, COUNTIES AND STATE OF NORTH CAROLINA

CHAPEL HILL, SEPTEMBER 8-11, 1932

CONDUCTED BY
THE INSTITUTE OF GOVERNMENT

PROGRAM

The discussions will center around seven major themes:

I. Problems Connected with Taxation: (A) Allocation of Sources of Revenue Between City, County, State and Federal Governmental Units. (B) Assessment of Property for Taxation. Levy, Collection and Distribution of Taxes. Safeguards Around Public Funds in the Cities, Counties and State. (C) Cost of Collecting Taxes. Percentage of Taxes Collected.

II. Problems Connected with the Public Debt—City, County, State: (A) Present Status of the Debt by Governmental Units. (B) Financing and Refinancing. (C) State Control Over Local Expenditures. (D) Constitutional Limitations on Indebtedness. (E) Methods of Enforcing Public Obligations.

III. Problems Connected with Simplification of Governmental Machinery: (A) Overlapping Agencies in City, County, State and Federal Governmental Units. (B) Coördination of Efforts in Overlapping Governmental Units. (C) Trends Toward Simplification.

IV. Problems Connected with the Administration of the Criminal Law: (A) Penal and Correctional Policies in North Carolina: Punishment, Probation, Parole, Pardon. (B) Juvenile Delinquency. (C) Criminal Procedure: Codification and Revision. (D) Limits Within Which the Law Allows Law Enforcing Officers to Enforce the Law: Constitutional and Legal Rights of the State and the Citizen.

[38]

V. Constitutional Changes Under Consideration by the Constitutional Commission.

VI. Governmental Problems Growing Out of Unemployment.

VII. A Program of Governmental Education in North Carolina: (A) In High Schools, Colleges and Professional Schools. (B) In County, District and Statewide Schools of Governmental Officers. (C) In Different Groups of Private Citizens.

The following group programs are suggestive and tentative. They are submitted to the members of the different groups as starting points for discussions. They will be revised in the light of these discussions to fit the needs of individual members.

SESSIONS

The *morning sessions* will be devoted to separate meetings of the different groups for the discussion of problems of primary interest to themselves; the *afternoon sessions*, to joint meetings of two or more groups for the discussion of problems in which they are jointly interested; the *evening sessions* to a joint meeting of all groups to consider the broader relations of city, county and state governmental units to each other and to the country of which they are a part. To illustrate: police officers will want to discuss some problems among themselves; other problems with township constables, county sheriffs, state patrolmen, federal agents, who are working on similar problems in the same territory; other problems with the prosecuting officers of city, county, state and federal courts, who follow up the work of the police; other problems with the judges of city, county, state and federal courts, who follow up the work of the prosecuting officers; other problems with prison officials and the commissioner of pardons and paroles who follow up the work of the judges; other problems with city, county, state and federal legislators who enact the laws to be enforced and prescribe the procedure to enforce them; other problems with the people who take offenders back into their ranks when the courts and penal institutions turn them loose.

THE WHITE HOUSE
WASHINGTON

May 29, 1933.

My dear Governor:

To you and my many friends in North Carolina who have been good enough to invite me to attend the first meeting of The Institute of Government, I can but express my very real regret that conditions over which I have no control literally make me a prisoner in the White House and make impossible even a twenty-four hour escape.

I have been looking forward with genuine anticipation to the pleasure of participating with you in the meeting of The Institute and my inability to do so is consequently a deep disappointment. The Institute of Government, its purposes and its organization, as conceived and established in North Carolina, has and will render fine service to the State and the Nation.

It is my hope that other States will recognize the leadership of North Carolina in what it is doing through this Institute and that States having no comparable agency will accept and follow your leadership. Some of the most progressive and original developments in the whole field of education have been in North Carolina and I take this occasion to congratulate you on that as well as on The Institute itself.

Will you, in my behalf, extend greetings and best wishes to those who have the good fortune of attending these sessions of The Institute.

Very sincerely yours,

Franklin D Roosevelt

Hon. John C. B. Ehringhaus,
Governor of North Carolina,
Raleigh, North Carolina.

300 representatives of officials, civic organizations and schools attend the first statewide school

42

Chapter IV The Institute of Government is Born

What's in a Name?

I said to myself: You have got to start from where you are, with what you've got, how you got it, how it works, and answer the question, where do you go from here? You can no longer fly the Law School flag. You can no longer fly the flag of the University of North Carolina. What flag are you going to fly? You have got to have a name. What shall it be?

The word "institute" occurred to me, because the organization was to be a new thing in the University, and "government", because that label was not in current departmental use, and so on the spur of the moment I called it the Institute of Government.

A battle of "academic imperialisms" was immediately joined. The very name "Institute of Government" had, it seemed, very ominous implications. Did I mean to trespass on the territory of "Public Administration"? of "Political Science"? of "University Extension"? These properties had been listed in the catalogue for years, and the boundaries posted. Why did I use the word "government" in my title? Why didn't I call it the "institute" of something else?

I agreed with the objectors that any one of several departments might register a valid claim to the sort of work that I was doing under the particular label I had chosen, that all of them ought to have been doing it for a hundred years. But I thought that in the eyes of the law constructive possession yields to actual possession, and the statute of limitations eventually runs in favor of persons holding under color of title; that I ought to be accorded at least the dignity of "squatter's rights" in territory I had already occupied; and that I was perfectly willing to take another name if they could help me find one equally suited to my purposes without an academic patent on it.

From the viewpoint of all parties in this controversy, any wedding of my work with any other department at that time would have been a shotgun wedding. My opponents claimed that my work was the "illegitimate" offspring of the Law School; the child conceived of academic hope was fast becoming the bastard child of academic rape. My answer, far from turning away wrath, was that I had never been bothered by bastards born out of wedlock, it was the bastards born in wedlock that had always bothered me. When the battle subsided, I had won "squatter's rights" for the Institute of Government, but no academic standing.

That is *how* and *why* the Institute of Government was born. Whenever I am asked *when* it was born, I give the inquirer three choices: (1) In that moment on New Year's Day 1927 when my experience in Professor Connor's course in North Carolina history and my experience in the Mayo Clinic fused in the vision of doing for the government of North Carolina what Professor Connor's course had done for the history of North Carolina and of doing for the body politic of North Carolina what the Mayo Clinic had done for the body of Albert Coates. (2) In the moment when the plan to fulfill this vision was fully formulated and approved by two hundred city, county, and state officials, and the first statewide school of public officials was held in September 1932. (3) At the moment when the first full-time member of the Institute of Government staff, outside of myself and my wife, came to Chapel Hill and started to work—that was in April 1933.

Acquiring a Staff

I had come face to face with the fact that I had bitten off more than I could chew. My Law School courses had outgrown my Law School classroom—and the work was far beyond the capacity of one teacher.

Up to now I had paid all expenses of my extra-curricular efforts out of my Law School salary, and had carried on the extra-curricular activities with the full-time, and unpaid, assistance of my wife. But the combination of our efforts was not enough.

To solve this dilemma, I needed to acquire a staff of four men to supplement myself and my wife. I would continue to teach the course in criminal law and carry on the work growing out of it. I would break in three men to teach each of my other three courses, and add a fourth to teach a new course on overall interlocking relationships between city, county, state and federal governments. If I couldn't do this, my plan would die a'borning. Money was scarce at this very bottom of the depression, with hardship everywhere and the spending of a dime a matter for serious thought. Where was I to get money?

It was Ben Cone, a former college mate and the chief executive of the Cone Corporation in Greensboro, who pulled me out of the quicksand and started the Institute of Government on its way. Over and over again he took time from busy office hours to listen to my plans and needs. He gave me the first money I received outside of my own pocketbook to keep my efforts going, a gift of $500 in the spring of 1932, and told me to keep him in touch with what I was doing and wanted to do. He gave me a second gift, $1,000, in the fall of 1932. Early in the next year, he called me to his office and told me he was satisfied with the possibilities of the movement and that he was going to give me $5,000 a year for three years to get some full-time help. I will never forget that morning in his office. Feelings deep down inside me welled up and overflowed, and for awhile I could not speak. A few months later Ben Cone persuaded his brother, Caesar, also of the Cone Corporation, to follow his lead with a gift of $5,000 a year for three years.

45

The following year, James G. Hanes, a long-time mayor of Winston-Salem and chairman of the Board of Commissioners of Forsyth County, came in to help and brought his fellow townsmen: Robert Hanes, Huber Hanes, Clay Williams, James A. Gray, and A.H. Bahnson, all business men in Winston-Salem who added gifts. A year later, George Watts Hill and Ashby Penn, who were former students in my Law School classes, came in with gifts, as did Ed Millis, a businessman in High Point. These gifts ranged from $300 to $2,000. With these funds I could start building a staff to assist me in the work I had begun, which was rooted in my Law School classroom.

I wanted lawyers because I expected them to share with me the teaching of my Law School courses. I wanted young lawyers, because I did not have the money to attract older and more experienced men. I wanted men who would come as partners with a vested interest in a going concern—men who would help to get it going and keep it going because I knew from my own experience that I could get more and better work out of myself than anybody else could get out of me, and I was sure they could get more and better work out of themselves than I could get out of them. I wanted men with first-rate abilities and a native mother-wit who could work with people as well as with books. I knew the old story of the tortoise and the hare but, I thought to myself, God pity the tortoise that runs against a hare that doesn't go to sleep. I wanted men with the qualities of both. I wanted men on the staff who had the actual or potential capacity to push me for first place, and I found them.

The first man who came on the staff was *Henry Brandis, Jr.,* a graduate of the University of North Carolina and a former student in my Law School classes, who had finished at the Columbia Law School and was then practicing law in New York City. The second was *Dillard Gardner,* a graduate of the University of North Carolina and of the University of North Carolina Law School, who was then practicing law in Marion, North Carolina. The third was *Nelson (Buck) Grice,* who had graduated from the University of North Carolina School of Commerce and was then with the Price Waterhouse Company in New York City.

These were the pioneering three. A year or two later they were followed by *Marion Alexander* and *Harry McGalliard,* both of whom had graduated from the University of North Carolina and the University of North Carolina Law School.

Other colleagues came and went in these hectic beginning years, staying for shorter times ranging from a few weeks to a few months: Moore Bryson, George Bradham, Jack Thompson, Malcolm Seawell, Elmer Oettinger.

Six of these men had been my students in the UNC Law School and the other two were UNC graduates.

The Staff Goes to Work

Henry Brandis. Ben Cone's gift of $5,000 a year for three years brought Henry Brandis on the staff, and for a year he was the one and only full-time staff member. He put to the test the working pattern which had evolved out of my own experience. He started studying the property tax which was, at that time, the source of around two-thirds of the supporting revenues of counties, cities, and towns.

First, he went to the books. There he studied the tax provisions of the Constitution and the statutes passed by the General Assembly to lay down the guidelines for the administration of the property tax. He went through the court reports to find all of the decisions handed down by the Supreme Court of North Carolina, interpreting the Constitution and the statutes and settling the questions that had been raised.

Against this background of the law in books, he started studying the law in action, to find out what officials had learned from working on the job first in Guilford County and in its cities of Greensboro, High Point, and Gibsonville, and thereafter in a dozen or more counties, cities, and towns, in the eastern, piedmont, and western sections of the state. He worked with the tax supervisors, tax listers, tax assessors, tax leviers, tax collectors, tax attorneys, boards of equalization and review, and city and county governing boards as he went through every step in the process from the discovery of property and putting it on the books to the collection of taxes, and through all the problems involved in these procedures.

He then set forth the results of these studies in a series of guidebooks on: *The Listing and Assessing of Property for County and City Taxes, The Collection and Foreclosure of County and City Property Taxes, The Levy and Collection of Ad Valorem Taxes.* He then conducted schools for tax officials in eight districts of the state. He followed up these district schools with a statewide school of tax supervisors, lasting for two days and held in the House of Representatives of the General Assembly in Raleigh. In those guidebooks and district and statewide schools, the fate and fortune of the Institute of Government was riding on the shoulders of a twenty-four-year-old boy. I knew it. He knew it. The attending officials knew it.

As a backstop for the proceedings and an insurance policy for the success of the school, the first in the state's history, we invited the Attorney General, a fine lawyer of great experience who had for years as a county attorney been the loyal advisor of the tax supervisors in his home county.

As Director of the Institute of Government I opened the meeting, told what had been done by way of preparation, and Henry began outlining the topics which would be discussed. As the meeting got under way, the tax supervisors began putting the tough questions to the Attorney General, but they soon found that he had not made the detailed studies Henry had made, and gave them general answers such as: "Use sound judgment," when what they wanted was specific answers to technical questions. Before the morning session was over the questions were all going to Henry, who was answering them with chapter and verse from the Constitution, statutes, and court decisions. The Attorney General did not come back for the afternoon or the next day's sessions. Henry Brandis had become the answer to their prayers, and remained so as long he was on the staff. Henry had won his spurs, and the Institute of Government was on its way.

Dillard Gardner. Caesar Cone's gift brought Dillard Gardner on the staff to work on the administration of justice in the courts. He used similar methods of studying the constitutional provisions, legislative enactments, and court decisions, and he followed his studies of the law in the books with studies of the law in action. Starting with justices of the peace at one end of our trial court system, he surveyed the field from the intermediate city and county courts to the superior court at the top of the trial court system, working with judges, prosecuting attorneys, clerks of court, registers of deeds, and local bar officials along the way.

Buck Grice. The gift of Jim Hanes brought Nelson (Buck) Grice on the staff. He used the same methods, practices, and techniques in his studies of accounting and financing policies and procedures, culminating in the budget-making process. He worked with city and county accountants, clerks, managers, and other officials having to do with budget making. He worked out a calendar setting forth the duties of city and county officials in chronological fashion for every working day in the year which was distributed to all of these officials.

Later gifts brought *Marion Alexander* and *Harry McGalliard* to the staff.

Marion Alexander started the Institute's clearinghouse of information by making a detailed study of the multiplicity of services that North Carolina state government was offering to counties, cities, and towns, and the services the United States government was offering to North Carolina and its counties, cities, and towns.

Harry McGalliard started his studies of public welfare and health activities by observing and consulting with the superintendents of public welfare in Orange County and the State Department of Public Welfare in Raleigh, and by taking formal courses in family law, juvenile delinquency, and public welfare organization in the University's Department of Sociology in Chapel Hill. With the family as his starting point, he began tracing the legal status and relationships of the family unit and its members through constitutional provisions, legislative enactments, and court decisions from colonial beginnings to the 1930's.

Edward Scheidt. I continued teaching my criminal law course in the Law School, adapting my teachings to the needs and uses of sheriffs and police, prosecuting attorneys and judges, together with officials involved in the supervision of convicted persons on suspended sentences, on parole, and in the state prison and city and county jails. My efforts were supplemented by Ed Scheidt, who had gone to work with the Federal Bureau of Investigation on graduating from the UNC Law School, and had been in law-enforcement work for several years. The Director of the FBI gave him a twelve-month leave of absence, at Institute of Government expense, to continue and expand the police-training program.

With the coming of Ed Scheidt from the FBI we held another series of one-day district schools in the fall of 1935 in order to lay the foundations of a ten-day school in the spring of 1936. Sixty-six officers attended the latter school, with ten hours of instruction and discussion each day, followed by a comprehensive written examination, and the giving of certificates to those who had made the grade. It is not too much to say that this school was a significant event in the life of the state—important enough to move the Governor of North Carolina to leave his office at the busiest time of the bicentennial session of the General Assembly and come to Chapel Hill to make the graduating address and present certificates to members of the graduating class. Eighteen of the graduates were promoted to the rank of chief of police in their departments within the next seven years.

I taught the courses of instruction in the elements of crimes and in the laws of arrest, search and seizure. Judges and solicitors of the Recorders Courts, the Superior Courts, and the Supreme Court of North Carolina taught the courses in evidence, procedure, and the preparation of cases for trial. Special agents of the FBI taught the courses in criminal investigation, scientific aids in crime detection, fingerprinting, and police organization. Ed Scheidt was the organizing genius of this school and in complete charge of its day-to-day operations.

We made plans to follow up this ten-day school with ten one-day schools at thirty-day intervals, with the hope of attracting sixty-six officers or more for each school, adding up to ten days of systematic instruction for six hundred or more officers. And so on until this instruction was brought within reach of every law-enforcing officer in North Carolina.

Institute Services

A Clearinghouse of Information. The men on the Institute staff were growing into the lives and the work of officials in counties, cities, and towns where they were making their studies, writing their guidebooks, and conducting their schools. Inquiries began coming in by letter, telephone, telegraph, and from personal visits of officials to Chapel Hill—first one by one and later in groups, including a full board of city councilmen or county commissioners, or a state commission. The clearinghouse of information had started before we knew it.

Questions and Answers. A mayor of one town wanted to know the steps to be taken in holding municipal elections, explaining that for the past several years the citizens had "neglected" to hold an election. A newly-appointed county attorney wanted an outline of the steps to be taken in foreclosure for delinquent taxes, together with the forms of notice, pleadings, judgments, and orders. A police chief wanted to know if it was lawful to sell confiscated tax-paid liquor to the county commissioners. A county accountant wanted to know if there was any way to get around the constitutional limitation on the rate of the tax levy for general county purposes, explaining that it had become impossible to carry on the expanded county activities within the statutory limitation. A clerk of a recorders court sent in a copy of a schedule of court costs that had been in use in his court for a number of years, and asked that it be corrected and brought up-to-date. A county commissioner inquired to what extent it was lawful for the county to give financial aid to the local boards of a variety of federal agencies operating within the county. A city attorney sent in a long list of proposed appropriations and wanted to know if they were permitted under the constitutional limitations on expenditures for special purposes, necessary expenses, and public purpose. A clerk of the superior court wanted to know whether he could compel the production of a letter referred to in a will as containing instructions for the disposition of trust funds. And a town clerk wanted to know what his duties were in regard to the approaching town elections, in view of the fact that none of the incumbents would file for reelection and no other candidate for any office had come forward.

Answers to one inquirer became answers to all. When we found questions in the mind of one official were likely to be in the minds of many officials, we began bringing these questions and answers together in a systematic way in mimeographed bulletins sent to officials all over the state.

Attorney General's Rulings. We went further and asked the secretaries and clerks to city councils and boards of county commissioners to send in copies of the minutes of their meetings so we could analyze and classify them and send digests of their doings to officials in every other city hall and county courthouse. We added to the value of these bare-bone minutes by clipping daily and weekly newspapers in the state for news stories and editorials describing and commenting on official activities everywhere—all of which served as windows through which we could look in on meetings of city councilmen and county commissioners, and provided starting points for the researches, writings, and teachings of the staff. We extended this practice from our own inquiries and answers to include our own digests of Attorney General's rulings and Supreme Court decisions. In the early 1930's we started digesting the sporadic rulings given by the Attorney General's office to local officials as a matter of courtesy, and sending them out in mimeographed bulletins to officials in city halls, county courthouses, and state departments. This practice stimulated questions from local officials to the point that answering them became an accepted part of the work of the Attorney General's office. The Attorney General's biennial report in the 1930's carried the following comment on this practice:

> This service, while having no legal sanction, has come to be one of the very important functions of this office and, in my opinion, the necessary method of deciding questions of administrative law, for

the decision of which no tribunal is provided . . . . The Institute of Government publishes a magazine "Popular Government" which has for several years carried a digest of opinions of the office given to local units of government. This service has tended to unify practice and procedure with local governments and has made available to them the digest of the opinions of the office on subjects in which they are interested.

Calendar of Duties. Buck Grice combed thousands of pages and administrative regulations to find the duties of local officials required by law to be performed on or before specific days. He listed these on the calendar of duties for county, city, and town officials with specific references to the pertinent statutes, and sent the calendars at the beginning of every year to all appropriate officials to be put on the walls of their offices. We also prepared for our own use, and published for the use of others, a directory of city, county, state, and federal officials in North Carolina. And thus came our calendar of duties and directory of officials.

Popular Government. We launched *Popular Government* as a quarterly publication in January, 1931; but because of lack of time and money, the second issue, which contained an extended discussion of the program of the Institute of Government, did not appear until the autumn of 1932. In 1934, we turned *Popular Government* into a monthly magazine, with twenty-four pages, nine by twelve inches in size, carrying most of the clearinghouse features already developed and described, together with other features of its own; and going to eighty-five hundred government officials operating in the territorial limits of North Carolina. Every month, this magazine gave each Institute staff member a direct avenue to officials with whom he was working throughout the state. It provided a way for carrying experiments and experience from one governmental unit to another, and became a liaison between local units and state agencies in Raleigh as well as with federal agencies in Washington.

The Library. The beginnings of the Institute of Government library may be found in the materials sent in reply to letters I wrote in the early 1930's to government agencies asking for all the free publications, studies, and reports they could send us in exchange for *Popular Government*. Still more significant materials came in exchanges for guidebooks, special studies, and periodic bulletins growing out of the work of Institute staff members. Most of our books on government came in exchange for reviews in *Popular Government*. Each man on the staff was his own librarian, looking for what, if anything, he could find in a miscellaneous collection of materials, full of wheat and chaff, and classified by amateurs into a system which was rougher than it was ready. At last the library was beginning to serve the staff, in hit-or-miss fashion, as source material bearing on governmental developments throughout the nation came in. It was also becoming a significant addition to the library resources of the University in the fields of public law and government.

The Legislative Service. We found that the General Assembly had little or no systematic machinery for keeping its members in touch with the content of bills introduced during the sessions; their progress in the committees to which they were referred—the amendments, rewritings, and killings; or the days on which the bills approved would be reported back to the floor of the General Assembly for discussion and vote. Henry Brandis outlined the Institute's plan for a legislative service meeting these needs.

The first step in the development of the Institute of Government's legislative service began in 1933 when Brandis attended sessions of the General Assembly, analyzed and classified the public laws enacted, and summarized them in a two hundred-page book published and distributed by the Institute to five thousand local and state officials in North Carolina.

Early in January, 1935, Henry Brandis and Buck Grice, with the staff secretary, went to Raleigh for the beginning of the 1935 General Assembly. They attended every session of the House and Senate, analyzed and digested all bills as they were introduced, and followed them through committees, noting amendments and recording calendar actions, until the bills failed or passed the final reading.

At the end of each day's sessions they wrote summaries of the proceedings, mimeographed them, and put them in the mails so that the following morning these mimeographed reports appeared on the desk of the Governor, Lieutenant Governor and Speaker, all legislators and state department heads in the state capital, and officials in every city hall and county courthouse in North Carolina. In addition to meeting the needs of the General Assembly, this service met the needs of heads of state departments and city and county governing boards to keep in touch with all legislation affecting their interests, and cut down on the time and expense involved in sending representatives to Raleigh to keep in touch with what was going on. Special weekly bulletins in the progress of legislation were prepared and sent to all daily and weekly newspapers in North Carolina to help them keep the general public informed.

As soon as the General Assembly adjourned, these members of the Institute wrote final summaries of all public, public-local, private laws and special acts, for distribution to officials in city halls, county courthouses and state departments. These reports came out several months before the session laws came off the press and were an ever-present help to officials and to lawyers and business men as well.

In the summer of 1935, the Institute called a two-day meeting of city and county officials and state department heads in Chapel Hill for the interpretation of the laws of the 1935 session of the General Assembly, and hundreds came. In succeeding years this statewide meeting in Chapel Hill was broken down to five one-day district meetings to reach more officials. Both Governor Clyde Hoey and Governor Gregg Cherry thought these meetings were important enough to take five days of their time to establish the practice of participating in them after the close of each session of the General Assembly.

In the latter 1930's and 40's, the Institute service during the sessions of the General Assembly, and after it adjourned, was extended to aid the General Assembly before its sessions began. Three or four months before it met, we would send out requests to city, county, and state officials asking them to point out old laws that in their opinion ought to be amended or discarded and new laws that ought to be enacted, and to spell out the reasons why, for the guidance of members of the General Assembly in drafting bills. We would sort out these suggestions, edit, and print them in a report which was sent out to all concerned.

When Henry Brandis and Buck Grice began attending the meetings of the General Assembly in Raleigh in 1935, they faced the difficulties typical of pioneering efforts. There was no place for them at reporters' desks under the stands of the reading clerks in either House or Senate, nor in the open spaces around the dais of the presiding officers—only in the galleries, where in single and solitary isolation they wrote down on notepads on their knees what they picked up by ear from the intonations and the chants of the reading clerks and the comments of legislators, supplemented by a tortuous and precarious accessibility to copies of bills because of the uncertain whereabouts of introducers, the uncertain leftovers of the press, and the uncertain grace of office helpers too busily engaged in tending to their own business to help us tend to ours.

Without precedents to go by, they blazed their own paths, during the lengthiest session of the General Assembly this generation of North Carolinians has experienced, under more mentally wracking, physically exhausting, and long-continuing strains than any single set of staff members of the Institute of Government has ever faced.

They commuted the twenty-eight miles to and from Chapel Hill each night and morning, got four or five hours of sleep at night during the week and caught up on Saturdays and Sundays, so as to be ready to go again on Monday mornings. On two memorable occasions in the rush of work in the closing days of the long drawn-out five-and-a-half-month session, they worked forty-eight hours in a stretch, with no sleep or rest, and grabbed bites to eat whenever they could find the time.

Special Projects

Sometimes the questions of officials would call for answers running to ten or fifteen pages or more of single-spaced typing, and out of these complicated problems came our special studies. These are illustrated by: *Standards of the Bar,* by Albert Coates, in answer to a question from the North Carolina Bar Association in its efforts to raise requirements for admission to the bar; *Everybody Wants the Highway Fund,* by Henry Brandis, in answer to requests for information on tax sharing; *The Great Bond Age,* and *Refinancing of Bonded Debt by Counties, Cities, and Towns,* by Buck Grice, in answer to inquiries about the state debt and plans for its management; *The Proposed Changes in the State Constitution,* by Dillard Gardner, in answer to demands for an analysis of changes planned in the fundamental law of the state; *Local Government Debt Problems in North Carolina,* by Buck Grice, in answer to pleas from local officials for information on city, town, and county borrowing and its significance; *The School Debt Fight,* by Henry Brandis, in answer to queries about a proceeding which posed the problem of whether the counties should assume the school debts of the cities and what would be the effect on tax bills and city schools; *Women and the Law in North Carolina,* by Harry McGalliard, in answer to a growing need to be informed about the changing legal rights of women. Similar special studies by other members of the staff included *Centralized Purchasing, Permanent Listing of Property in Mecklenburg County, Traffic Bureaus to Handle Minor Violations, Problems in Governmental Accounting, Liquor and the Law in North Carolina, Zoning Ordinances and the Police Power,* and *The Police Officers Pension Fund.*

All in the Day's Work

I told my colleagues that we would never turn down any job that came to us, no matter how controversial it was, and no matter how much it cut across party lines or special interest groups and opposing points of view; that we would not lobby for or against anything or anybody, no matter how good or how bad, either in the General Assembly or out of it; that we would take on any problem, analyze it in all its detail, set out the advantages of opposing points of view, and leave it to the people involved to decide what they wanted to do about it; that I wanted us to build a reputation for intelligence and integrity to the point that if the General Assembly of North

Carolina, or any other institution or agency, should be split in a bitter controversy which would turn on the finding of a particular fact, it would trust us to find that fact.

The fact that we did not take sides did not mean that we did not go to the root of controversies, no matter how explosive. The only thing we would fight over would be the fair and impartial integrity of our work. We tried to phrase all of our studies and guidebooks and other writings in terms so plain and simple that anyone with common sense who could read could understand them; and to make them so accurate that any official relying on them could go in court or any other forum, public or private, and defend them.

The Highway Fund. A tug of war developed in the General Assembly over the highway fund. The cities wanted part of it for city streets. The counties wanted part of it for upkeep of county roads (this was before the state took all county roads into the state highway system). The state wanted all of it and more for the state highway system. Henry Brandis took on this problem, traced its background in history, analyzed the issues involved, went to the contending parties and got every argument each could make for itself and against the others, and spelled it all out in a report with the title, "Everybody Wants the Highway Fund," which became the basis on which the General Assembly began making appropriations to cities for the building and maintaining of city streets.

The Police Pension Fund. Here is an illustration of a hotly contested issue in which all parties involved turned to the Institute of Government to find the facts: A fight over the police pension fund developed in a statewide meeting of police executives. The fund had been oversold by its sponsors. Officers had been led to believe they could get enough to live on when reaching retirement age, but the pension fell far short of this goal. The actuaries said that to pay what had been promised would jeopardize and undermine the fund and leave nothing for others to come. The officials of state and local governments were siding with the actuaries on the smaller payments and the soundness of their figures, while the officers were shouting them down and calling for the larger payments at any cost.

Both sides agreed to submit the issue to the Institute of Government. I made our position clear:

"The issue is as simple as it is profound: Do two times two equal four, or five, or three? In the present fighting atmosphere, we can please some by saying five, others by saying three, and run the gauntlet between you by saying four. I want you to know at the start that we are going to take the soundness of the fund as our only guideline—to the exclusion of all others. We are going to stand on the proposition that two times two equal four, regardless of the enemies we make by saying so. We are going to keep our own self-respect at the risk of losing your goodwill, on the ground that when the excitement over this fighting issue dies down, as it surely will, your respect for us would be forever gone when you found that we had told you that two times two equal three or five."

By this time, most of them were getting the point, and we got a majority to agree that the only question at issue was the soundness of the pension fund, and whether it would in fact be sacrificed by payments larger than the actuary recommended.

Drafting Laws. There were many other controversies. Henry Brandis drew a bill for a legislator in a partisan local squabble. The legislator said, "I thought the Institute was non-partisan." "It is", Henry replied. "I put in this bill exactly what you told me to put in it. It is your bill, not mine. If your adversary comes in and asks me to draw a bill to kill it, I will draw that bill too. And it will be his bill, not mine." This statment dramatized the position of the Institute of Government: that no controversial question was too hot for us to handle in a non-partisan way.

A Policeman's Question. There was the time when Frank Little-john, chief of police in Charlotte, telephoned and said: "Professor, didn't you tell us at the police school in Chapel Hill last week that the word of a fellow police chief that a specific person had committed a murder was sufficient evidence to justify me in arresting him without a warrant?" "Yes," I answered. "Well," he said, "I did just that this morning in court and the judge and the defense lawyer jumped all over me for doing it."

I was in a quandary. If I was wrong, the news would go all over the state by the grapevine and police officers wouldn't come to any more schools. I replied that the law as I understood it was that an officer could arrest without a warrant whenever he had reasonable ground to believe a felony had been committed, and reasonable ground to believe the man he arrested had committed the felony; that the word of a fellow law-enforcing officer and competent investigator constituted "reasonable ground" for such belief; and that he could tell the judge that if it was arranged for the question to go to the Supreme Court on appeal, I would represent him without charge. Then I thought a moment, and said: "Don't tell the judge and defense lawyer anything. I will go to Charlotte and tell them myself." I went armed with Supreme Court decisions, and found there had been a misunderstanding about the facts and that the judge sustained my opinion. He was good enough to clear up the matter in open court, paying tribute to the Institute of Government, and word of this spread to officers all over the state.

Listing Property. There were cases in which tax supervisors, coming to Institute schools and finding out about new methods of discovering unlisted property to go on the tax books, learned more about the meaning of assessing property at its "fair value in money" as required by the Constitution. When they put their l·arning to work back home, many big landowners complained that the tax supervisors were learning "too damn much" for their own good, and threatened to cut our revenues in the General Assembly to stop us from teaching subversive doctrine. In one memorable case, Henry Brandis had called the attention of a county tax supervisor to a Supreme Court decision authorizing the listing for tax purposes of a certain class of intangible property which had not been listed in North Carolina up to that time. On the strength of this Court decision, the Attorney General had told the supervisor that the listing was proper. At this point a citizen of the county, owning millions of dollars in securities he had considered not taxable, came to me and said that Brandis was getting the Institute of Government into trouble and ought to confine himself to academic matters. At that point it seemed to me that academic freedom had ceased to be an

60

academic question, and I asked him how he would feel if his personal attorney had failed to call his attention to a court decision which might involve a gain or loss of tens of thousands of dollars. He got the point and backed off from his attack.

Backfire. There was the time when a prominent lawyer sued his home town to prevent the use of local tax revenues from paying the expenses of local police officers to attend the Institute of Government training schools for law-enforcing officers. The local police chief had brought about a first-degree murder conviction by the use of investigation techniques he had learned at an Institute of Government School, and that lawyer had lost the case for the defense. The city attorney was a former law student of mine, and called me in to write the brief and argue the case for the city. I won a decision from the Supreme Court of North Carolina saying that such expenditures were authorized by the city council as a "necessary expense." If the Court had gone the other way, the training schools for law-enforcing officers would have been crippled to the wrecking point.

Under Fire. And here was another intriguing case. In the middle 1930's, the Institute was called on by the state's constitutional commission to make a study of the new constitution proposed for North Carolina. Dillard Gardner, who had taken the lead in the studies tracing the origin and evolution of every provision in the constitution from 1776 to the 1930's, analyzed the rewriting proposals, outlined the arguments being made for and against each one, and left the decision to the commission and then to the people.

The commission members were impressed with the work and asked the Institute of Government to lead the fight for ratification. We refused. "Don't you believe in it?" they asked me. "Yes," I replied. "Then why are you unwilling to fight for it?" Again I stated our position:

Because this sponsorship would destroy the very foundations of our existence. The Institute of Government will never lobby for or against anything or anybody, in the legislature or out, no matter how good or how bad. That proposition and the integrity of our

work are the only things we are willing to fight about. They mean more to government in North Carolina than the success or failure of any particular venture we study and report on.

I had a chance to illustrate my meaning while the campaign for ratification was under way. It came about in this way. A high state official, bitter over the failure of the then Governor to endorse his candidacy for the office, undertook to turn the statewide referendum into a political issue which would take the political power in the state out of the hands of those in control. He advised the Institute of Government not to hold the non-partisan schools it had planned for civic organizations of men and women in different parts of the state to study the proposed constitution. To him it was a partisan political fight, and non-partisan education discussions had no place in the picture.

When we refused to acquiesce, he began to attack the integrity of our work—taking one crucial sentence out of context. Dillard Gardner had written that the old Constitution adopted in 1868 was a constitution largely written by "carpetbaggers". In speech after speech, this high state official began by saying: "The Institute of Government tells us this old Constitution is a carpetbag Constitution. But let me tell you that this 'carpetbag' Constitution is the best Constitution North Carolina has ever had." And he was citing provision after provision in order to prove it.

I went to his next scheduled speech, and sat on the front row, with the Institute's study open before me. He made no mention of the Institute of Government or the "carpetbag" Constitution in his speech that night, nor the next, nor the next, as I followed him, sitting on the front row in open view. Why? Because on the very next page of our study Dillard Gardner had gone on to say that the 1868 Constitution was the best constitution in the state's history, and cited to prove it the very same provisions this official was using in rebuttal against us! He knew I was there to point out this fact and demonstrate his duplicity. He could not afford this demonstration of his double-talk. It broke the back of the argument he was hypocritically using against us. He never used it again, and we went on with our schools and studies and guidebooks.

62

Finale. On the back porch of my house one day, I was chiding my colleagues for allowing a competing organization to copy Institute digests of legislative bills in the General Assembly and send them out under its own name, without stopping it or informing me. In an effort to temper the wind to the shorn lambs, I said: "You are too much the gentlemen. You ought to be more of a sonofabitch like me." Whereupon Harry McGalliard, the youngest man on the staff, remarked to the hilarity of all: "Maybe under your expert tutelage we will get there before our allotted time!"

Moving Toward Our Goals

By the latter 1930's, we were moving toward our goals.

We were beginning to bridge the gap between outgoing and incoming officials throughout the state. We were bringing officials together in statewide, district, and local training schools, and conducting systematic studies and discussions of the ways and means of pulling together instead of pulling apart. We were bringing together the different methods and practices of governmental units and officials in a governmental laboratory, laying the foundation for working toward a uniformity of governmental standards by lifting the poorest practices to the level of the best.

Here is a summary of Institute activities from 1933 through 1938, as recorded in the March 1938 issue of *Popular Government:*

Criminal Law Administration

Seven statewide institutes from two to ten days in length for city, county, state and federal law-enforcing officers have been held in successive years, beginning in 1930. The attendance has steadily increased from around forty to nearly two hundred. Two series of district institutes have been held: the first in September, 1935, with the state divided into eight districts; the second in September, 1936, with the state divided into five districts; with an average attendance of six hundred officers to the series. A ten-day statewide training school for police instructors was held January 5-15, 1937, followed by two series of one-day schools in 1937 and 1938. Many local institutes have been conducted with the cooperation of judges and solicitors in counties, cities and towns throughout the state.

Courses arranged for the following official groups [in 1939-40]: city police, county sheriffs, state patrol and other state agencies; prosecuting attorneys and judges; probation, prison, parole and pardon officials; city and county attorneys, managers and commissioners.—Planned by Albert Coates with the cooperation of representatives of the foregoing city, county, state and federal law-enforcing agencies.

Finance Administration

Two statewide institutes for finance officers of counties, cities and towns have been held in connection with the statewide institutes for all officials heretofore described. One series of district institutes has been held for city accountants, clerks, treasurers, purchasing agents and other finance officers, with the state divided into five districts. The first statewide institute for city, county and state purchasing agents and the first statewide institute for municipal finance officers have been held.

Courses arranged for the following official groups [in 1939-40]: city and county accountants, managers, treasurers, purchasing agents, clerks, and other finance officers.—Planned by T.N. Grice with the cooperation of representatives of city, county and state finance officers.

Administration of Justice in the Courts

Two statewide institutes for court officials have been held in connection with the statewide institutes for all officials heretofore described. One series of district institutes has been held for sheriffs, one for clerks of court, and one for registers of deeds, with the state divided into five districts and a total attendance of two hundred twenty-five sheriffs, deputy sheriffs, and newly elected sheriffs, ninety-seven clerks and deputy clerks of court, and eighty-six registers and deputy registers of deeds.

64

Courses arranged for the following official groups [in 1930-40]: clerks of city, county and state courts; sheriffs; registers of deeds; justices of the peace and other judicial officers; state and local bar officials.—Planned by Dillard S. Gardner with the cooperation of representatives of city, county, state and federal court and bar officials.

Legal and Governmental Aspects of Public Health, Welfare and Relief Administration

Two statewide institutes for welfare, health and public works officials have been held in connection with the statewide institutes for all officials heretofore described. One series of district institutes has been held for welfare officers in their capacity as juvenile court and probation officers.

Courses arranged for the following official groups [in 1939-40]: city, county and state health officials; city, county, state and federal welfare officials; juvenile court officials; probation, parole and prison officials.—Planned by Harry W. McGalliard with the cooperation of representatives of city, county, state and federal health and welfare officials.

Federal, State, Local Relationships

Three statewide institutes have been held by the legislators' division including city councilmen, county commissioners, state legislators and congressional representatives; the first in September, 1932; the second in June, 1933; the third in June, 1935; with an average attendance of six hundred. One series of district institutes was held in 1937. Prior to the meeting of the General Assembly in 1935 the legislators' division of the Institute of Government invited representatives of the counties, cities and towns to appear before the newly elected legislators to discuss their respective legislative programs. Subsequent to the sessions of the General Assembly in 1933 and 1935 and 1937 institutes were held for the interpretation of state and federal legislation to officials and units affected by it.

Courses arranged for city councilmen, county commissioners,

state legislators, . . . and other city, county, and state administrative . . . officials.—Planned by Marion R. Alexander with the cooperation of representatives of the foregoing groups.

Laws Affecting Married Women's Rights

Course arranged primarily for public affairs committees and other members of women's organizations.—Planned by Harry W. McGalliard with the cooperation of representatives of women's clubs.

As a basis for instruction in the foregoing course [in 1939-40], a guidebook has been prepared by Harry McGalliard, setting forth the history of the laws governing the Legal Rights of Married Women from Colonial Times to the Present.

Students and Teachers of Civics and Government in the Schools

Institutes for students and teachers of civics and government in the schools will equip them to interpret the current developments in government and its administration in the classroom at the classroom hour. Four statewide institutes have been held for superintendents, principals and teachers of civics and government: the first in September, 1932; the second in June, 1933; the third in November, 1934; the fourth in June, 1936. One series of district institutes has been held in November, 1935, with the state divided into eight districts, and a total attendance in excess of one thousand. [Planned by Albert Coates.]

Public Affairs Committees of Citizens' Organizations

Four statewide institutes for representatives of citizens' organizations of men and women have been held in connection with the institutes for officials: the first in September, 1932; the second in June, 1933; the third in November, 1934; the fourth in June, 1935.

Courses arranged for public affairs committees of civic organizations and other interested citizens. [Planned by Albert Coates.]

Here is a chart summarizing Institute of Government services planned and announced in the middle 1930's:

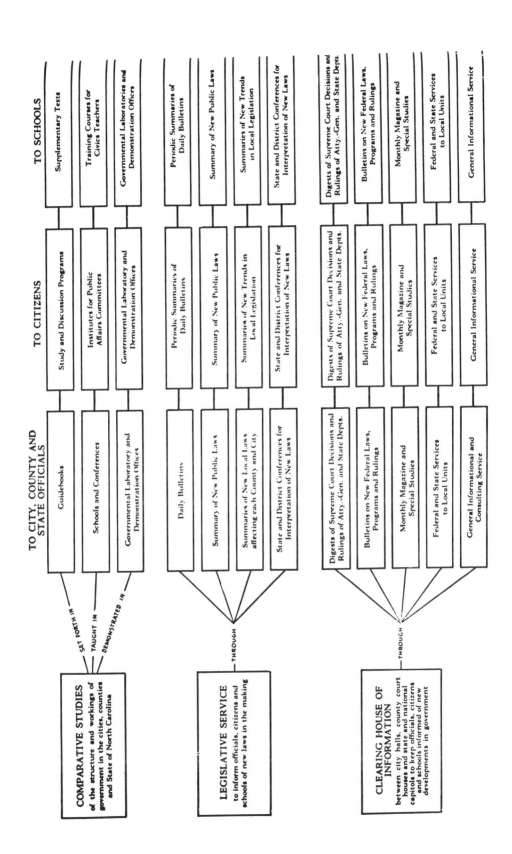

Financing Institute Activities

While my academic life was being questioned, the life of the Institute of Government was hanging in the balance for the lack of money. Chancellor House, in one of his off-hand classics, supported me in an open meeting, saying that "every North Carolinian worth his salt was born in a panic, brought up in a depression, and buried on a debit balance." That sounded good to me until I got to thinking about it while talking to myself: The Institute of Government had been born in a panic all right—two men had been called out of one of our early meetings by the news of breaking banks. It had been brought up in a depression—which we were not yet out of. But the flaw in the third item of his trilogy, as far as it concerned me, was that I was still alive and did not want to be "buried on a debit balance." Not money, but the lack of it, became the root of all evil for me.

Private gifts from private citizens had started the Institute of Government on its way and continued to finance its activities. We lived in the expectation that public support would gradually pick up the financing as private support left off. In the middle 1930's some of the mayors, chairmen of boards of county commissioners, and city and county managers who had sampled Institute services asked us to fix a flat rate which would bring all of the Institute services to all of their officials. This rate was fixed at one-half of one cent per inhabitant, and city and county membership dues came in as the beginning of public support.

While Brandis and Grice were working with the General Assembly, Dillard Gardner went on the road soliciting city and county memberships in the Institute of Government. Here is an extract from one of his reports:

> I had to go twelve miles out of my way to find the chairman, over a muddy detour, but his signature is on the dotted line. Expect no miracles but I'm still fighting in mud and sleet against the damnedest inertia and indifference I've found in the state. Wish me luck .... This is a lousy hotel, and worse bed. Thank your lucky stars for your own home, bed and family .... To drive in these mountains

now is pure torture and deadly dangerous. Please don't mention this to Janie because she knows these roads in winter and it would only cause her needless worry.

It's a long story but slowly—one by one—they came over. Originally, the board stood solidly against it. It had three times previously turned it down unanimously . . . . By the stove in his country store a county commissioner discussed everything from ABC liquor control to the packing of the Supreme Court—but I kept edging in comments on our work. Finally, he limbered up, wanted to know about how the Institute was started, what its goal is, etc. From then on only a cyclone could have prevented him from signing . . . .

The chairman was the "key" official. All the county officers recommended that he sign up. So, I had to strike out after him. He wasn't at home, so I went into the swamp after him. Left the car and walked a mile, then rode the dinky engine down to the "skeeter" where they were loading. Once the chairman considered the matter, he was with us completely. This "selling game" is funny business. You win where there isn't a chance, and the door is slammed where it (the membership) is practically "in the bag."

I went by the courthouse to thank the officials for their work in getting the county to join. They received me with open arms. The clerk had a dozen questions ready for me and kept me over an hour answering questions. In the register's office there were even more questions, and it took even more time. Even the sheriff had questions. Their interest and cooperation is ideal. I wish there were 99 other counties just like this one.

The mayor is glum and totally uninterested, and left the impression that he regarded the Institute as the romantic dream of a long-winded teller of jokes. The mayor said their rate was 25 cents on the $100 and as it was the lowest in the state, they didn't have a thing to learn from anybody. He assured me that they could tell the rest of the state a lot about running towns . . . . For God's sake, see that a deposit is placed in the bank for me. Checks from every member county in the East will be turned down on me . . . . As it is now I have had practically no expense money for the past month on the road—and it costs like Hell!

These travels took Dillard Gardner into most if not all counties, cities and towns in North Carolina. They marked the beginning of the transition from private contributions to public support. But city and county membership dues were not coming in fast enough to pick up at the point where private revenues were running out. At that point the only way I saw out of our dilemma was a move to tie in Institute operating expenses with an Institute housing plan. It came about in this way.

Operating Expenses and Housing Plans

Throughout the latter 1920's and 1930's our activities migrated from one working place to another: from my home, to my Law School office, to the Law School basement, to the Law School attic, to Peabody Hall basement, to an abandoned fraternity house, to an abandoned church building. In the mid-1930's the Public Works Administration was giving 45% of public building costs. The North Carolina Senators and Congressmen in Washington got us a grant of $45,000 towards a $100,000 building.

At this point a friend offered to give $25,000 toward a $100,000 fund; $55,000 of this fund was to be used to match the Public Works Administration grant of $45,000, with the remaining $45,000 of the fund to go for operating expenses until public support took over where private gifts left off. Another $25,000 gift followed this initial lead, but those two gifts left me with a $50,000 distance to go before I could use the $45,000 earmarked for operating expenses. I was missing payrolls. My colleagues were living on credit. And Christmas was coming on.

I went to see a friend in Morganton who *could* help me if he *would*, but he was out of town for the winter months. On the way back to Chapel Hill I stopped in Greensboro at a little restaurant where the proprietor was giving a free meal to a hungry man and telling him he could eat all he wanted, but not to eat too fast. I saw Ben Cone sitting alone in a booth. He had told me to come to him for help if I ran into a stone wall. He told me now that he had just sent out twenty-five hundred hams as Christmas gifts to Cone Mill employees and he was in a mellow mood. I told him about the plight of my colleagues. He took out his checkbook, wrote out a check for almost as much as he had given to start the Institute of Government on its way in 1932, and told me to count it toward the $100,000 fund and use it for operating expenses now—Christmas money, he called it. When I got back to Chapel Hill, I found a $2,000 check in the mail from Gordon Gray, a fellow alumnus of the University, practicing law in Winston-Salem. This money paid back-salaries to my colleagues on Christmas Eve. A little later, Caesar Cone came in to supplement his former gifts. Watts Hill, who had been a student in my Law School classes, went beyond his previous gifts, and endorsed my note to his bank for a personal loan to help meet operating expenses. He later renewed the note with new endorsements until there was no more room for further endorsements and a new note had to be signed and endorsed.

These added gifts kept the Institute going but they did not add up to the $100,000 mark. The PWA grant lapsed again. The PWA director quite understandably refused a further extension. Senator J.W. Bailey took the issue to the President of the United States in person, with the result recorded in the following letter:

> Dear Albert: I sent you a wire just now containing good news which I now confirm with the original letter from the President, which you may keep if you wish as a souvenir. I think it would be fine for you to write him a letter and thank him.

Here is the personal letter from Warm Springs, Georgia, to Senator Bailey:

> Dear Senator: I have your letter of November 14. Generally speaking, I am reluctant to grant any extension of time within which a PWA project must be under contract because if I vary the rule for one I will be asked to do it for others. However, considering the circumstances set forth in your letter with respect to the laboratory building at the University of North Carolina, Docket 1089, I will extend the deadline to January 15, with the understanding, however, that the contract must be signed and work ready to begin not later than that date. Sincerely, Franklin D. Roosevelt.

Time Runs Out

I hit the road running day and night. Stresses and urgencies crept into my voice and showed in my face as I talked to men I knew and didn't know. Some of them thought they smelled a rat, others thought they saw one. One night, coming back to Chapel Hill with Harry McGalliard near midnight—hurried, worried, and tired—I must have dozed, for the car slowed down almost to a stopping point before it went off the road on a curve and turned upside down. Both of us were knocked senseless at first. When we came to ourselves and managed to scramble up to the road, a passing motorist picked us up and took us to the University infirmary where we were treated. Harry suffered a painfully sprained arm while I had a concussion and a scalp wound as a result of my head hitting the rear-view mirror. Harry later reported that on the way to the infirmary I made the most moving plea for the Institute he had ever heard. Though I do not remember making this plea, by the next morning my head was clear enough to call some of my colleagues and say, "Boys, for God's sake go out with the garage man to bring in the car. There are five thousand highway safety pamphlets on the back seat and I hate to think of the story some inquiring reporter could write if he found them." When they carried out my request they also found copies of the Bible and Shakespeare which my wife kept in the car—she was often the driver—to read while I went in to talk for half an hour with prospective donors and stayed for an hour and a half, or more. She has had time to read and digest them both.

During the following days, the bed I was lying in seemed to me to turn over every few hours. The doctor said I was simply reliving the experience of turning over in the car. While I was out of the running, the PWA grant lapsed beyond the hope of resurrection, leaving a longer and deeper cut in my mind than the rear-view mirror had made in my head.

I was out of a building. Out of money. With a staff of five men—four of them married, and two with children. With salaries behind schedule, and no bread and butter in sight. My University salary was already mortgaged for two months in advance and divided among my colleagues. From going all out to hold the staff together, I went all out to get them off one payroll and on to another.

At this point, the value and effectiveness of the work of the men of the Institute staff to the cities, the counties and the state of North Carolina came to my aid. I got a job as research director with the State Tax Commission for Henry Brandis, who had been working with tax officials in the counties, cities, and towns. I got a job with the Supreme Court of North Carolina for Dillard Gardner, who had been working with local and state court officials. I got a job with the State Auditor for Buck Grice, who had been working with city and county auditors and finance officials. I got a job with the North Carolina Bar Association for Marion Alexander, who had been working with local and state officials on the clearinghouse of governmental information. I got a job with the state Attorney General for Harry McGalliard, who had been working with local and state officials in health, welfare and family law. Ed Scheidt returned to the FBI.

Their bread and butter was provided for, and more than that— they were working in the same fields in which they had been working with the Institute of Government and building on the knowledge and skills they had acquired in the work with which they had earned statewide reputations on their own. They were getting more money than I had paid them and were no longer living from hand to mouth. They had in their new work a future more dependable, at least, than the Institute could give them.

What Had Gone Wrong?

But this rescue operation did not gloss over the fact that the Institute of Government had lost the men who had made it.

It had lost the knowledge and experience that had come from the staff's five years of study of the Constitution, statutes, court decisions, and administrative rulings defining the powers and duties of officials, and from their five years of going to school to local, state, and federal units and officials working on the job. It had lost the momentum of a going concern.

What had gone wrong?

Not the idea or the plan of the Institute of Government. They were still sound in wind and limb, and were steadily attracting support—but not enough, or fast enough.

Not lack of support from the President and Chancellor of the University. They had never loaded the dice—for me or against me. They did something more important than that. They held the scales in balance; kept the avenues of effort open, free, and clear; gave me a fair chance to fight for the life of something I believed in with a consuming passion. They stood up to be counted for me in academic battles involving high stakes and hair triggers—and at times when they had much to lose and nothing to gain. They zeroed in at many a critical moment with the admonition to my adversaries: "Thou Shalt Not Kill." I had heard about "due process of law" in Law School, I had studied it in Constitution, statute, and decision, but in Frank Porter Graham and Robert Burton House I saw those words become flesh and dwell on this campus.

Not my colleagues on the Institute staff. In the late 1930's when the Depression was closing in, money was giving out, Christmas was coming on, and salaries were a month or more overdue. I had put in all I had, borrowed two months ahead on my salary, as far as the University allowed, and I was out on the road day and night trying to get help. My colleagues knew I was doing all I could. Without my knowing it they came together, put their savings into a common fund to meet the needs of those nearest to the breadline and told me nothing about it. Years later I found it out by accident. Their action struck deeper into my being than ever plummet sounded.

I recalled the examination I had given in the course in property in my early Law School teaching days. Two-thirds of the students had flunked it and in the face of a riot of protest I had stood by my grades. And then it had occurred to me that the examination had been not so much a test of how much they knew as it was a proof of how little I had taught!

That recollection brought to mind an observation of Mr. Justice Holmes in the case of *Abrams v. United States:* "When men have realized that time has upset many fighting faiths, they may come to believe even more than they believe the very foundations of their own conduct . . . that the best test of truth is the power of the thought to get itself accepted in the competition of the market place." I had not met that test. It was just that simple, and just that profound.

Appraisals of Institute Work: 1933–1939

From Clyde R. Hoey, Governor of North Carolina:

I have watched with interest the progress and development of the Institute of Government. I have been acquainted with its activities from its first organization and have watched with increasing admiration its growth and expansion. While city and county attorney at Shelby, N.C., I was familiar with the service it rendered the officials of the cities and counties and had occasion to profit by this instructional service.

After I became Governor I met with the Institute frequently and attended the many classes conducted at Chapel Hill, and I have had occasion to observe at first hand its efficiency. It is gratifying to me to note the cooperation of city police officers, sheriffs of counties, commanding officers of the State Highway Patrol, and officials of the State Bureau of Investigation and the various Federal law-enforcing officers. The cost is small, the service is excellent, the training important, and the results achieved justify the efforts put forth in this field of service.

Training schools conducted by the Institute of Government during the past several years have demonstrated their value and have laid a solid basis for their extension to all groups in the systematic program now getting under way. I am glad to see this education and instruction in government extended to all groups of officials in city halls, county courthouses, and State departments, and to the public affairs committees of civic organizations and to those who teach civics and government in our school system.

From the General Assembly of North Carolina:

WHEREAS, the services rendered by the Legislative Staff of the Institute of Government, a division of the University of North Carolina in analysis of bills, preparation of pending calendars, daily report of calendar action and other assistance to legislators have been of great value to members of the General Assembly and to interested citizens throughout the state: NOW, THEREFORE,

Be it resolved by the House of Representatives, the Senate concurring:

Section 1. That the General Assembly of North Carolina express its sincere appreciation to the Trustees and Faculty of the University of North Carolina, to the Division of the Institute of Government, and to members of its Legislative Staff, for the valuable assistance rendered by them to members of the General Assembly in the conduct of its business . . . .

From Roscoe Pound, Dean of the Harvard Law School:

I doubt whether anything which has taken place in connection with American Government in the present century is as significant as the movement for planned, intelligent official and administrative cooperation which began some years ago in North Carolina, and has now taken on enduring form in the Institute of Government . . . .

In the typical American state polity, police, sheriff's office, coroner's office, public prosecutor's office, were independent. Each might, each frequently did, conduct its own separate investigation of the same crime. They might cooperate, they might cross each other's tracks, or they might get in each other's way as they liked. Each was not at all unlikely to be willing to score at the expense of the other, and it happened not infrequently that one or another was not unwilling to aid the other as a rival candidate for publicity . . . .

One might justly compare our policy in respect of cooperation to Artemus Ward's military company in which every member was an officer and the superior of every other.

Of late, consciousness has been growing that in the unified, economic order and urban industrial civilization of today such things will not do. We have been seeing that the several agencies of government must be brought to work together intelligently toward common purposes . . . .

North Carolina has taken the lead in organizing this spirit of cooperation, in making through organized effort for consciousness on the

76

part of officials from top to bottom of the administrative scale that they are co-workers towards the ends of government, and as such need to understand what each is doing and why and how in order that through that understanding the task of each may be better achieved.

What seems to me particularly significant in the North Carolina movement is that it is a voluntary movement. In this respect it is in line with a general movement of the time. On every side, trade, professional and civic associations are organizing men's efforts toward a better and more effective general social control. Recently the Federal government has been able to use this spirit of voluntary association with conspicuous effect. To rely on the enlightened free action of officials rather than a system of command from above in a centralized administrative system is in accord with the characteristic polity of English-speaking people. It is in accord with the spirit in which our political institutions were conceived. It is evolutionary, not revolutionary, and does not involve the institutional waste which too often accompanies significant changes in government.

From Robert B. House, Chancellor of the University of North Carolina:

Chancellor Robert House called me into his office and said: "Albert, you are over the hump. For a long time a lot of people around here thought you were full of wind. Then they thought you might be pregnant. Then they predicted that there was going to be a miscarriage. Now everybody knows a baby has been born. Everybody is swearing it's a bastard. And everybody is secretly hoping the paternity will be ascribed to him."

The fourteen officials shown below represent their respective divisions on the State Board of Advisers, The Institute of Government: (1) A. H. Graham, Hillsboro, President of the Legislators Division; (2) R. L. Harris, Roxboro, Vice President of the Legislators Division; (3) Andrew Joyner, Jr., Greensboro, Vice President of the City Attorneys Division and President of the North Carolina League of Municipalities; (4) John L. Skinner, Littleton, Secretary of the County Commissioners Division; (5) R. L. Stowe, Belmont, President of the County Commissioners Division; (6) Clarence E. Blackstock, Asheville, President of the City Attorneys Division; (7) J. Wallace Winborne, Marion, President of the County Attorneys Division; (8) D. W. Newsom, Durham, President of the County Managers Division; (9) A. C. Hudson, Greensboro, President of the Tax Supervisors Division; (10) J. A. Orrell, Wilmington, President of the Accountants Division; (11) R. H. Wharton, Greensboro, President of the Registers of Deeds Division; (12) George C. Eichhorn, Greensboro, Vice President of the Street and Safety Division; (13) C. W. Smedburg, Greensboro, President of the Engineers Division; (14) A. S. Brower, Raleigh, President of the Purchasing Agents Division.

The above officials represent their respective organizations on the State Board of Advisers, The Institute of Government: (1) Judge W. A. Devin, Oxford, President of the Judicial Officers Division; (2) Judge M. V. Barnhill, Rocky Mount, Vice President of the Judicial Officers Division; (3) E. B. Jeffress, Greensboro, President of the Street and Highway Safety Division; (4) Charles M. Johnson, Raleigh, President of the Public Treasurers Division; (5) Major L. P. McLendon, Greensboro, President of the Election Officers Division; (6) Clawson L. Williams, Sanford, President of the Prosecuting Attorneys Division; (7) N. E. Aydlett, Elizabeth City, President of the Clerks of Court Division; (8) J. G. Wooten, Winston-Salem, President of the Police Officers Division; (9) Oscar F. Adkins, Marion, President of the Sheriffs Division; (10) Dr. C. R. Wharton, Ruffin, President of the Coroners Division; (11) George Lawrence, Chapel Hill, President of the Welfare Officers Division; (12) J. B. Roach, Raleigh, President of the Prison Officers Division; (13) Samuel E. Leonard, Rocky Mount, President of the Correctional Officers Division; (14) Captain Charles D. Farmer, Raleigh, Head of the State Highway Patrol.

Above are shown eight of the educational leaders of the colleges and public schools of North Carolina who are coöperating with the officers and citizens in building The Institute of Government: (1) Dr. Frank P. Graham, President of the Greater University of North Carolina; (2) Dr. Thurman D. Kitchin, President of Wake Forest College; (3) Dr. Walter W. Lingle, President of Davidson College; (4) Dr. W. P. Few, President of Duke University; (5) A. T. Allen, State Superintendent of Public Instruction; (6) G. B. Phillips, of Greensboro, President of the North Carolina Education Association; (7) Paul S. Daniel, of Raleigh, President of the City and County Superintendents organization; (8) Needham Y. Gulley, Dean of the Wake Forest Law School and Chairman of the City and County Boards of Education Division of The Institute.

Above are shown representatives of various citizens groups who are serving on the State Board of Advisers, The Institute of Government: (1) Mrs. W. B. Aycock, Raleigh, President of the North Carolina Parent-Teachers Association; (2) Mrs. J. Frank Sprulll, Lexington, Citizenship Chairman, Parent-Teachers Association; (3) Mrs. R. H. Latham, Asheville, President of the North Carolina Federation of Womens Clubs; (4) Mrs. Clyde A. Milner, Guilford College, President of the North Carolina Division of the American Association of University Women; (5) Miss Mae Reynolds, Raleigh, President, Business and Professional Womens Clubs; (6) Mrs. M. H. Shumway, Lexington, President of the American Legion Auxiliary, Department of North Carolina; (7) Millard F. Jones, Rocky Mount, President of the State Bankers Association; (8) R. R. Lawrence, Winston-Salem, President of the State Federation of Labor; (9) Earl S. Vanatta, University Station, Master of the North Carolina State Grange; (10) W. C. Meekins, Hendersonville; (11) Dr. L. M. Edwards, Durham; (12) Eugene F. Rimmer, Charlotte.

Pictures of the following were not received in time to be included in this edition: Mrs. Charles W. Tillett, Jr., Charlotte, President of the League of Women Voters; Frederick L. Willis, Asheville, District Governor of the Civitan Club; Mrs. W. R. Absher, North Wilkesboro, retiring President of the American Legion Auxiliary; Neal S. Zeigler; Charlotte, representing the Certified Public Accountants of North Carolina.

Above are shown accredited leaders of various citizens groups who are serving on the State Board of Advisers, The Institute of Government: (1) Harold D. Cooley, Nashville, President of the Local Bar Officials Division; (2) C. W. Tillett, Jr., Charlotte, President of the State Bar Association; (3) I. M. Bailey, Raleigh, President of the North Carolina Incorporated Bar; (4) Rev. T. A. Sykes, High Point, District Governor, 57th District of Rotary International; (5) Ralph C. Barker, Durham, Governor, Carolinas Kiwanis District; (6) Guy O. Bagwell, Charlotte, District Governor, Lions Clubs; (7) O. Arthur Kirkman, High Point, Lieutenant-Governor, American Business Clubs; (8) D. Hiden Ramsey, Asheville, President of the State Press Association; (9) H. E. Olive, Statesville, Department Commander, the American Legion; (10) Arnold Schiffman, Greensboro, Past President, North Carolina Merchants Association; (11) W. C. Denmark, Goldsboro, President of the North Carolina Commercial Secretaries Association; (12) Dr. Paul P. McCain, Sanatorium, President of the State Medical Society.

Harry Woodburn Chase,
President, UNC

Roscoe Pound, Dean, Harvard
Law School

R.D.W. Connor,
Professor of History,
UNC

80

W.A. Devin, Judge, Superior
Court, Chairman, Organizing
Committee

Judge Junius G. Adams,
Organizing Committee

Lucius Polk McLendon
Lawyer, Legislator,
Political Leader

81

Financing the Institute

Ben Cone

Caesar Cone

James G. Hanes

George Watts Hill

M.E. Hogan

Original Staff

Henry P. Brandis, Jr.   Dillard S. Gardner   T.N. (Buck) Grice

Harry McGalliard

Marion Alexander

83

Elizabeth Coates

Illustrative District Schools

Law-enforcing Officers, Winston-Salem

Law-enforcing Officers, Asheville

Tax Officials, Kinston

84

Illustrative Statewide Schools

1936 graduates of first ten-day Police School, Governor Clyde R. Hoey, front and center

Police Conference

Tax Supervisors

1937 Conference of State Government Officials endorse Institute of Government, Governor Clyde R. Hoey, front and center

Registers of Deeds

Tax Supervisors

Ed Scheidt teaching Law-enforcing School

Police Officers on firing range, left to right: Ed Coffey, FBI; Albert Coates; Ed Scheidt, FBI

Superior Court Judge Hunt Parker swearing in Wake County Officials

Dillard Gardner reading legislative bulletin

88

Schools of Officials

Chapter V   Between Bases: 1939-1949

For a week or ten days after the automobile accident I lay in bed recovering from physical exhaustion, loss of blood, shock from the concussion, and the inevitable loss of the men who were the quick and core of the Institute itself. On the campus, not-so-friendly critics were thinking, feeling, and saying to themselves and their friends: "The Institute of Government is dead."

Taking Stock

Temptations like these ran through my mind:

I could put all my time on Law School teaching, which would gratify both my students and my colleagues on the law faculty.

I could call my salary my own, which for a long time I had not been able to do.

I could call evenings, weekends, holidays and summer vacations my own.

I could renew my fellowship with family and friends and enjoy more of what is commonly known as life.

Men who had put up the money for my pioneering venture did not blame me for this situation. They knew that I was taking calculated risks and that they had been parties to my calculations. They had backed me with their eyes open. I had done all I could, and they knew it and sympathized with me.

My former students who had come to the Institute staff did not blame me. They knew the limited resources I had when they came on the scene; they knew that I had doubled those resources while they were there, and they knew that all along the way my salary and credit had been shared with them. Law School authorities would welcome me back to put full-time on my Law School job as a sadder and a wiser man.

But I knew that as long as I lived I would look into the faces of businessmen who had written me off as a risk and venture that had failed. I would look into the faces of colleagues who had followed me down a blind alley to a dead end. I would look into the faces of University authorities who had prophesied that dead end. And beyond all, I knew that as long as I lived I would have to live with myself.

My colleagues had come for something more than bread and butter. They had left places of security and prestige in the practice of their professions and had come with me for little pay, on a pioneering venture, in the trough of a great Depression. They had followed the glimmer of a dream into an uncertain economic future.

Henry Brandis had left a law firm in New York City where he had made a record so good that the lawyer he had worked with was planning to start a firm of his own with Brandis as his partner. Dillard Gardner had left a secure and lucrative partnership and a bright law-practicing future with one of the best lawyers in western North Carolina. Buck Grice had left a responsible position as a certified public accountant with a bright future in one of the great accounting firms of the nation. Marion Alexander and Harry McGalliard had turned away offers from solid law firms to come with me. These were men who had

> ... toil'd, and wrought,
>   and thought with me—
> That ever with a frolic welcome took
> The thunder and the sunshine, and
>   opposed
> Free hearts, free foreheads—
> [to all the lurking hazards of the way.]

I recalled the Old Testament story of King David exclaiming in his weariness after a great battle, "Oh that one would give me drink of the water of the well of Bethlehem, which is by the gate!" I went to the King James version of the Old Testament and read over again the story of how, in answer to David's longing, "three mighty men brake through the host of the Philistines and drew water out of the well of Bethlehem, that was by the gate, and took it and brought it to David: nevertheless he would not drink thereof, but poured it out unto the Lord.

"And he said, . . . is not this the blood of the men that went in jeopardy of their lives?"

The way King David felt about his "mighty men" is the way I felt about Henry Brandis, Dillard Gardner, Buck Grice, Marion Alexander, and Harry McGalliard.

Back to Work

Memories came flooding in with a lifting power.
I remembered a generous letter from Dillard Gardner saying:

> Of course, there were times of frustration and of irritation, but as I look back, I realize that had you been a methodical, systematic, traditional personality—there would never have been an Institute. To me the grip of the Institute idea upon you had always been understandable. The miracle is that the rest of us took your dream, made it our own, and equally became slaves to it. Driven by the throbbing dynamics of a great idea the impossible is done as a matter of course and miracles become a commonplace. In a sense our faith was greater even than your own, for we had to believe not only in the "idea" but also in you. However, in a more realistic sense, it was the greatness of your own faith which fed our own and renewed it. Institutions, indeed, are the lengthened shadows of men, but it is ideas which lift men's heads to the sun and thus make shadows.

I remembered an evening in the early 1930's when I was riding on a late bus from Raleigh to Durham with Justice Brogden of the Supreme Court of North Carolina. He told me this story: He had been attorney and director in a bank which had failed in the depression. The officers and directors had assembled in a room on the

92

third floor to face the fact that the bank could not open its doors next morning. The double-liability provision in the law had swept away the life-time savings of nearly every man in the room. Some men were unashamedly crying. One was being forcibly restrained from jumping out of the window. The meeting was turning into bedlam. Judge Brogden called on them to stop the panic and listen to him. And here is what he said:

The trouble with us is that we have lost our sense of values. We have gone crazy over things. We have accumulated things until we have become slaves to the things we have accumulated. And now that we have lost all these things, we think we have lost everything. Over in India, Ghandi has kept his freedom. He wears a loin cloth and eats a few grains of rice and drinks a cup of goat milk every day and he is happy. He does not carry excess baggage. He is not a slave to things.

Look at me. All my property is gone. All the things I have accumulated in twenty years are gone. But I have not lost everything. I have all the strength and health I had when I started to accumulate the things I have lost. I have all the brains and mother wit I had to start with, and they have been seasoned with experience along the way until I am more of a man than I was when I started out. I have a wife and children acquired along the way and they are inspirations I did not have to start with. All of these values will help me build back to where I was, if that is what I want to do. I have lost nothing that is really worth keeping when the chips are down.

With these words Judge Brogden had brought his colleagues back to their senses, and they sat down to pick up the pieces and go on.

I, too, could start again, with all the abilities I had in 1923; schooled in the trials, errors, fumbles, and mistakes I would not make again; seasoned with experience that money could not buy; aware of most, if not all, of the pitfalls in my path. These things would give me a harder-hitting power than I had begun with.

My wife once read to me the words of Miss Madeira, head of a school for girls: "I try to teach my girls two things: to function in disaster and to finish with style." I knew that the time had come for me "to function in disaster and to finish with style." To the critics who were saying "The Institute of Government is dead," I could give this answer, "Not while I'm alive."

My sense of humor returned as I recalled a story told me by Senator Josiah Bailey from the days around the turn of the century when he was sent by two distinguished North Carolinians to see if an equally distinguished bishop and educator was willing to call off the dogs in a long and bitter feud. The bishop had scented victory in the wind as he looked at Senator Bailey with the olive branch in hand, and in a mournful voice he said: "Bailey, I don't want to quit; but maybe I ought to quit." He then got down on his knees and took the question to the Lord in prayer. As he prayed, his voice grew audibly stronger as the significance of the visit grew clearer. He jumped to his feet without saying amen, and with tears streaming down his cheeks cried out: "Bailey, God don't want me to quit!"

I understood exactly how the Bishop felt—God didn't want me to quit either. But how was I to keep on going? I understood how Marshall Foch felt at the Battle of the Marne in World War I when he wrote the famous message: "My center is giving way, my right retreats, situation excellent, I am attacking." There was no doubt about the fact that this was my Battle of the Marne.

Holding Buckle and Tongue Together: 1939-1942

In the early 1930's, I had started out working with three groups: officials of today, citizens of today, and the youth of today who would be the officials and citizens of tomorrow. The officials were the taproot of this trio. Obviously, to stay in business at all the Institute of Government had to hold buckle and tongue together with officials. The program with them was basic—if we lost them we lost all. The programs with the citizens and the schools were derivative. If the Institute survived with officials, there was hope for picking up the other programs in later and better days. The civic and school groups agreed, and I dropped the programs with them for the time being, with the mutual understanding that we would continue to give them a lick and a promise, and pick them up again if, as, and when we could.

94

This step lightened our operating load, but how was I to carry forward the program of services with officials?

My first step. One thing I could do on my own, as a teacher of the course in local government law, without calling for outside help. I could and did persuade Billy Mitchell, a third-year student and *Law Review* editor who was taking my course in local government law, to use the time he was going to spend on writing for the *Law Review* in helping me with the research for two studies which could go from the Institute of Government to city and county officials: one on the "necessary expense" doctrine in North Carolina and the other on the doctrine of "special purpose." These studies were of direct interest and basic importance to city and county managers, attorneys, budget-makers, and governing boards, and were put into guidebook form and sent to them as Institute of Government services to officials in every city hall and county courthouse.

My next step. There was another thing I could do on my own as the one remaining member of the staff of the Institute of Government still teaching the course in criminal law and its administration in the cities, the counties, and the state of North Carolina. I could continue to adapt my teachings to students in my Law School classroom to the needs and uses of police agencies, prosecuting attorneys, judges and governing boards in city halls, county courthouses, and state agencies. That would be holding buckle and tongue together on a second front.

I no longer had the money to pay the salary of Ed Scheidt, and when he returned to the FBI I went to J. Edgar Hoover with the request that Ed Scheidt's work be looked on as the beginning rather than the end of the relationship between the Institute of Government and the FBI. That the FBI build on the beginning that had been made, and instead of sending Ed Scheidt back to Chapel Hill at Institute expense (obviously the FBI could not pay the salary of an Institute staff member), send a variety of FBI instructors to Chapel Hill for two or three days to a week at the time to assist the Institute of Government in a comprehensive program. The FBI Director complied with my request. *Popular Government* for September 1940 carried this outline of the plan agreed on:

The Institute of Government Announces---

A Series of Seven-Day Police Schools
One Each Month --- Starting October, 1940

Criminal Law, Procedure and Evidence

Instruction will include analysis of the law in North Carolina pertaining to the principal criminal offenses as established by ordinances, regulations, statutes, and decisions of the courts, including:

Crimes Against Public Morals, such as violations of liquor laws, narcotic laws, prostitution laws, gambling laws, and related crimes.

Crimes Against Property, such as arson, burglary, housebreaking, larceny, embezzlement, obtaining property by false pretenses, receiving stolen goods, trespass, and related crimes.

Crimes Against the Person, such as assaults and batteries (including simple assault, assault with deadly weapon, assault with intent to kill, secret assault, false arrest and false imprisonment), homicides (including murder, manslaughter, and self defense), rape (common law, statutory assault on females, and other sex crimes), kidnapping and abduction, and related crimes.

Instruction will include (1) analysis of the structure and jurisdiction of the various criminal courts, (2) analysis of the laws governing the conduct of officers in making arrests, searches and seizures, and questioning defendants and witnesses and procuring of confessions and admissions, etc., (3) analysis of procedure in preliminary hearings and on trials, (4) preparation of cases for trial, (5) testifying in court, (6) rules governing the admissibility of evidence, (7) analysis of laws governing extradition of fugitives (including federal statutes against unlawful flight to avoid prosecution and to avoid testifying in criminal cases).

Outline of Courses of Instruction

Investigation of Crimes

Great emphasis will be laid throughout in making this instruction extremely practical, and the presentation of these topics will center around actual cases, illustrations, demonstrations, and practice work. Special attention will be paid to effective methods of investigating the more serious crimes and crimes occurring most frequently with the methods and techniques applicable to each offense.

Investigation of crimes against public morals and related crimes as listed above,

Investigation of crimes against property and related crimes as listed above.

Investigation of crimes against the person and related crimes as listed above.

Scientific Aids in Crime Detection

Criminal Identification: document identification; firearms identification; blood stains; making casts of footprints, tiretracks, toolmarks, and other physical evidence of crimes; techniques for the study of glass fractures, soils, fibres, metals, woods, and other laboratory aids in the solution of crime.

These subjects will be approached entirely from the viewpoint of the investigator in the field and not from the laboratory technician's viewpoint. Emphasis will be placed upon making clear what the criminal laboratory can and cannot do, and the discovery, preservation, and handling of physical evidence.

Police Techniques and Skills

Practical work and instruction on tactics employed in making arrests, searches, and seizures. Intensive training and practice to improve skill in the use of firearms as a defensive weapon. Effective methods of conducting interviews and questioning persons to obtain desired information. Mechanics of preparing confessions which will stand up in court. Detective methods and other special techniques and skills required of police officers.

Apprehension of Fugitives

Effective techniques and methods in bringing about the apprehension of wanted persons. Valuable sources of information in tracing the movements and determining the whereabouts of fugitives. Practice work in solving fugitive cases.

Police Administration

Personnel, equipment, records and statistics. Rules and regulations. Report writing. Police patrol work. Achieving efficiency and economy in the administration of police departments.

Cooperative Measures

Between city and town police, township constables, county sheriffs, state patrolmen, State Bureau of Investigation, Federal Bureau of Investigation, and other federal agencies. Between the foregoing police and investigative agencies and prosecuting attorneys, in city, county, state, and federal units, probation officers, prison officials, pardon and parole officials.

Public Relations

Problems which arise in dealings of law enforcement agencies with the public. Methods of winning the cooperation and support of the public. Crime prevention work. Instruction and practice in public speaking.

My next step. The General Assembly was to meet within a few weeks, and I had to keep the legislative service alive, as evidence that the Institute of Government was still active. This gave me the opportunity to cover up my predicament further by expanding the legislative service which had been going to one or two designated officials in each county, city, and town. I began sending it to most if not all officials—impressing them with a greater volume of services than they had received before. I could pay for this service with receipts coming in from commercial subscribers while the legislature was in session.

Elmer Oettinger came in to take charge of this service, with the assistance of others, including George Riddle, Newbern Piland, Tom Alderman, and Bill Parker.

Elmer and his assistants attended the daily legislative sessions, digested the bills, mimeographed the digests, and put them in the mails each night, so that these would be on the desks of local officials the next day. Each week some 7,000 officials received a daily summary of the work of the legislature, and about 7,000 bulletins went out weekly to local and state officials to keep them abreast of all legislation affecting their particular county, city, or town.

I took pride in the fact that these men of the Institute earned the official recognition of the General Assembly, expressed in another joint legislative resolution at the end of the 1939 session.

My next step. I started picking up the frazzled ends of work left by departing colleagues. The wires they left behind them were live wires, and I used them as ignition points to keep the Institute's fires burning. Some revenues continued to come in from city and county membership dues—enough to bring on a few men for limited periods of time and for part-time services, coming mostly from my former and present students. Bill Speight, Phil Lucas, Leon Roebuck, Tom Long, and Bill Parker came in under this temporary arrangement.

These men could not carry on the in-depth programs of the former full-time staff members, but they could, and did, carry on the clearinghouse of information serving all city and county officials on a day-to-day basis. Whenever an inquiry would come in from one official we would mimeograph the answer and send it out to all officials whenever it was of general interest—giving the assurance that the Institute of Government was alive and kicking.

My next step. For the first time, I put the names of all these men on Institute stationery as Assistant Directors, and listed the former staff members as Consultants, as indeed they were, giving the impression to all officials that the Institute of Government was a going concern with more men than ever on its staff, when in fact its very life was hanging in the balance. It did the officials no harm and it did me great good, for I was in so bad a fix that I could not afford to tell anybody the fix I was in. I gave out the impression that the Institute was expanding its activities from city and county government into state government—as indeed it was; that the former staff members were serving as apprentices in their new jobs and would return to expand the Institute's programs to state levels—as I devoutly hoped they would.

My next step. In 1941 I turned to Terry Sanford and Bill Cochrane, third-year students in my Law School classes, who were working their way through school by managing dormitory stores, working one hundred hours a month for fifty cents an hour. I could offer them that much money out of my own salary. This proposal had some advantages for them, since they would be putting their efforts in the field of law and government, thus furthering their legal education and preparing a future for themselves in the Institute of Government when they finished Law School, if we could keep going. They accepted the offer and started working twenty-five hours a week at fifty cents an hour.

98

My next step. My wife, Gladys Hall Coates, picked up and carried on the studies in student government as it developed under the Di and Phi Societies up to the early 1900's, and under the Student Council up to 1941. We collaborated in a series of lectures to student government officers in 1939, 1940, and 1941. During those years we began to work with student governing officers and their faculty advisors in senior high schools and held a statewide Institute for them in Chapel Hill.

My next step. During these same years the Institute of Government began pouring its studies in city, county, and state government into a series of seven-day programs for rising high school seniors sponsored by the American Legion under the heading of Boys State. This program tied in with and reinforced Institute programs with students and teachers of government in senior high schools for the training of youth of today who would be the citizens and officials of tomorrow.

High Stakes and Hair Triggers

While my colleagues were keeping Institute life lines open, I was carrying a full-time teaching job in the Law School and wrestling with financing problems in a rhythm of hope and despair. I had one holdover promise of $25,000 from my former fund-raising efforts toward a smaller building and a modest operating fund. I got the promise of another $25,000 on similar terms. With more nerve than sense, I got an architect to draw preliminary sketches of the exterior of the building; got an artist's drawing of the building sketches; persuaded the Orange Printshop in Chapel Hill to print, on credit, five thousand pictures of this drawing; and sent them to officials in every city hall, county courthouse, and state department in North Carolina, to hang on their walls.

I got my friend Sandy (A.H.) Graham, Lieutenant Governor, who trusted me, to go to Robert Hanes and Richard Stockton, businessmen in Winston-Salem who trusted him, to persuade them to go to Will Reynolds, another business man in Winston-Salem who trusted them, for the difference between the money I thought I had and the money I knew I needed. Mr. Reynolds promised part of the difference—enough to buy a valuable piece of land which was a strategic building site.

I wrote out a statement of the charitable and educational features of the Institute of Government which made the University of North Carolina look like a commercial enterprise by comparison, and sent it to William B. Umstead, a former college-mate and the congressman from my district, with the request that he take it to Internal Revenue Commissioner Helvering in person, stay with him while he read it, argue for it if necessary, and not leave his office until he got an approval which would be worth exactly $10,000 to me. He did, and we bought the building site.

Time passed, and no building started on the land. People got suspicious and began to talk. To allay suspicion and stop the talk, I borrowed money to hire a contractor to dig a hole on the land—the exact size and depth for the foundation and basement of the building. I told him to dig it slowly; to fit it in to his other work and give priority to all the jobs on hand and any coming in later; to use this basement as a last resort to work on when he had no other work to do. The digging started and seemed to satisfy the most cynical; for who could be fool enough to dig such a hole if he did not have the wherewithal to fill it up? I was, in fact, so big a fool that they could not conceive how big a fool I was.

Then the rains descended and the floods came and filled the hole with water. This gave me more time, but not enough, because the water stood still, then got stagnant, then bred mosquitoes, then bred talk, and then became a public nuisance, which I was called on to abate. I hired a man to pump the water out, and told him to pump it slowly; in short, to put this job last on his list and keep it there, so as to give me time to raise the rest of the money for the building before the water was out.

While the land-buying, the hole-digging, and the water-pumping were going on in the slowest possible succession, I was getting nowhere fast in raising money.

To make bad matters worse, one $25,000 promise was withdrawn upon the acknowledgement from some of my friends that I had not raised the matching money and their belief that I never would.

Institute operations were again suffering from malnutrition. Some of my more observant critics even noticed signs of scurvy. I understood the Confederate soldier who said that he was eating green persimmons "so as to draw up my stomach to fit my rations." I had the taste of green persimmons in my mouth.

When salaries were cut, my wife and I moved out of a house and lived for two years in a rented room. As revenues ran low, we sold the lot we had bought as a site for the house we hoped to build. As Institute revenues ran low, I pieced them out with my salary. As my salary frazzled out, I resorted to credit.

When credit ran low, Bruce Strowd, owner of a garage in Chapel Hill, allowed me to run up a bill of several hundred dollars for gasoline, oil and repairs at his garage.

When traveling money ran low, I resorted to the long-distance telephone as a substitute for travel, and local officials allowed me to use vacant beds in fire stations when I did travel.

When I had gone beyond my own telephone credit limits on long distance calls, my friend and classmate in the University, Burt Linker, loaned me the use of his telephone on his own credit.

When light bills reached the limit and the lights were cut off, we resorted to candles.

When grocery bills ran up to shaky heights, George Livas, a native of Greece who had established a successful restaurant in Chapel Hill, invited us to eat for months at his Carolina Coffee Shop on a credit which went as high as a thousand dollars but never ran out; and when I had to travel by train and had no money, he would tell me to write out a check for what I needed and let him know when I had money in the bank to meet it.

I had reached the point of no return. Any further falling had to be uphill.

Saved by Grace

In that moment the Institute of Government had a single life line; if that broke, its life was gone. Gordon Gray had given $2,000 for operating expenses in 1936. A year or two later his brother, Bowman, a business man in Winston-Salem had joined him in a $25,000 gift toward the $100,000 building and operating funds. I could not meet their condition now, and I could not afford to lose the gift. I went to them with my problem. They had a more than perfect out, if they wanted it; and if they had taken it, they would have taken the bottom out from under me.

I would have been left with a piece of land, with a big hole in it, filling up with water in every rain, breeding mosquitoes in every drought, with no money to haul back the dirt that had been hauled away, no money to pump out the water, no money even to spray for mosquitoes, and with pasteboard pictures on city hall and county courthouse walls to advertise a building which still existed only in my imagination.

They withdrew the condition, and told me I could use their gift in a smaller building without PWA funds. I was saved, and the Institute of Government was saved, by the grace of Gordon and Bowman Gray.

The First Institute Building

I needed $25,000 more and, with the backing of John Umstead, a life insurance man in Chapel Hill and long-time friend, went to Julian Price, president of the Jefferson Standard Life Insurance Company, with this extract from the University auditor's report:

> The records indicate that Albert Coates has been meticulous in recording funds received by the Institute but prodigal to the same degree in the use of his own personal funds for the Institute. In the early years of its life, the Institute was financed entirely out of his pocket; later with the help of private sponsors. It seems reasonable to estimate that, over a 15-year period, from $25,000 to $30,000 of his own funds have gone into this undertaking. In addition he has for many years given his time to it without pay for the three summer months when he could have turned that time into money for himself. This would add up to $50,000 or more as years went by.

Using the auditor's statement of what I had done in the past as evidence of what I would do in the future, I asked Mr. Price to lend me the money I needed to erect the building, secured by salary assignments over a period of years. He looked at me a long time, and then said: "Albert, I'll do it." He put his arm around my shoulders as we walked out of the room. In later years I learned that it was Julian Price's personal endorsement of my note which had guaranteed the loan and got it.

The contract for the building was let. Brick and concrete took the place of mud and water in the basement. But, no matter how fast the building went up, it could not go up fast enough for me. We set the day for dedication in the Thanksgiving holidays (the year was 1939), six weeks beyond the builder's completion date, and even that saving margin was barely enough to complete the building for the opening. My wife has described these hectic hours:

Albert thought he had given plenty of time for the completion of the building before the dedication but it turned out that it was far from finished when the day arrived that had been set. The painters were still painting, the floormen were still finishing floors, and the night-shift men worked far into the night to lay the brick walk up to the building. Debris was in piles in the building and I had to oversee and sometimes take a hand myself to get it swept up. I recall chasing painters out of rooms so that visitors would not ruin their clothes when they came—all in friendly fashion, of course, as I realized they didn't want to lose a day's work.

Still we had to get the building in some shape to receive. Many complications beset us at the last. Albert had ordered murals, blown-up photographs, for the assembly room and upstairs hall, but the frames for these did not fit and all had to be straightened out in the few hours before the great day. The furniture arrived for the building and had to be moved in on barely dried floors. I was so busy seeing about all of these things that it was not until I was showing some visitors over on the day after the dedication that I realized I had not gotten toilet paper for the new lavatories. This occurred to me only when someone asked to use one! Horrible omission but the building was so brand-new that we hadn't even had a chance to look after the primary things. We were still sweeping up when the first delegate arrived, and I met him at the door with a broom in my hand and registered him.

After that I decided it was time to cease operations. I went home to get a bath and dress before trying to become hostess at the buffet supper scheduled for the notables that night at an old house on Columbia Street which was used as a faculty club at that time.

The supper passed off all right, though the food left much to be desired. The University had no facilities then such as the Morehead Building, and since the Institute was still outside of the University there was no cooperation that I recall to help us put over the occasion. I do remember that Fred Weaver helped me work out some problems about the supper at the faculty club, but evidently the facilities were primitive, for the supper was anything but elegant. However, the guests were fed and seemed to be enjoying themselves. I suppose they did not expect too much at that time from an institution as struggling as the Institute of Government.

This event was preceded by such excruciating labor and concern about the completion of the building, as well as for the occasion of the dedication itself, that the wonder is that either of us came through it in our right minds! After it was over, the tension and anxiety of these days continued and I was not able to sleep for three nights. Finally, Albert got a heavy sleeping tablet from our doctor, Bill Morgan, and I slept for about twenty-four hours from sheer exhaustion. As soon as I had gotten the needed relaxation I was all right and I do not recall any bad after-effects.

The front door of the building opened into a hall which lead into a large reception room with a handsome mantel and an open fireplace in the north wall. Large conference tables on each side were surrounded by comfortable chairs and a leather sofa faced the fireplace in which a fire was kept burning during the winter months. On the wall over the fireplace was a mural of the colonial plantation mansion, Orton, in New Hanover County, symbol of hospitality and welcome. Covering the upper half of the east wall was a great mural of the sand dunes fronting the ocean on the eastern shore of North Carolina, and covering the upper half of the west wall was a similar one of the western mountain ranges including Mount Mitchell and Pisgah Forest. Above the central door of this room was a mural depicting water-power sources, the first cotton-mill site in North Carolina. Flanking the door and covering the upper half of the walls facing the fireplace were two other great murals—one, a field of cotton, and the other of tobacco, the principal crops of the state. Under the murals on three sides of the room were racks built into the wall for the display of most if not all of the daily and weekly newspapers coming from all parts of North Carolina and the monthly magazines portraying governmental activities throughout the country—local, state, and national. This reception room doubled as a browsing room, and trebled as an assembly room comfortably seating fifty to seventy-five people, and seventy-five to a hundred could be crowded in.

Above this room, on the second floor, was the library, with the North Carolina statutes and court reports, texts on government and related fields, and reference works accessible to all the working staff as a workshop center. On each side of the first floor reception and assembly room and the second floor library were rooms of equal size for Institute staff working in their different fields. These rooms doubled as classrooms for officials coming from all parts of the state, trebled as consulting rooms for individual and small official groups, and quadrupled as subsidiary library and reference rooms for specialized text and reference materials supplementing the central library.

On one side of the full basement—half above ground—were ample restrooms for men and women, and on the other side was room for the mimeograph machine and related equipment, with additional room for staff work in assembling, addressing, and mailing bulletins, guidebooks, and the monthly magazine of *Popular Government*—all of them carrying the researches and teachings of the Institute staff to public officials throughout the state.

At first there were bedrooms in the basement and on the third floor of the building to house officials attending Institute schools, but they were too few to take care of all who came, and after two or three years they were converted into offices for staff members as the Institute grew.

The Building Dedication

The dedication, on Thanksgiving Eve, 1939, was a community affair. University students who were going home for the Thanksgiving holidays invited officials from their home counties, cities, and towns to occupy their dormitory rooms without charge, while a token number of students from each county remained to greet arriving officials, show them to their rooms, and look after their needs. Terry Sanford, Bill Cochrane and Clifford Pace were among these.

Two former Governors attended, O. Max Gardner and Clyde R. Hoey. All of the North Carolina Congressmen came and held separate meetings with city, county, and state officials from their respective districts. Ninety-nine of the state's one hundred counties were represented at the dedication ceremonies in Hill Hall. Someone asked me why I didn't make it a hundred for the sake of completeness. By way of answer, I told him the story of the man who got liquored up on another Thanksgiving Day, went hunting, and came back with the tale of finding one hundred squirrels lined up on a limb, sighting them at the right angle, and killing ninety-nine of them at one shot. "Why don't you make it a hundred and be done with it?" queried an indulgent friend. "Sir," came the reply with the imperturbable sobriety of a truly drunken man, "do you think I would tell a damn lie for the sake of one squirrel?"

My former colleagues at the Institute were in places of honor on the stage—Henry Brandis, Dillard Gardner, Buck Grice, Marion Alexander, and Harry McGalliard—and heard me say: "No teacher ever had a finer set of students, and no teacher ever paid his former students a more ungrudging tribute than I pay these men tonight."

William B. Bankhead, Speaker of the National House of Representatives, said in his dedication speech:

> This Institution has pioneered in recent years in many fields of special and economic research, which make it outstanding in progressive thought and action. It is a fortunate thing that it has been thought wise to select such an environment for the location of the North Carolina Institute of Government, which we are now assembled to dedicate. This is in my opinion a civic agency which in the long reach of coming years will not only prove of incalculable value to every citizen of North Carolina, but it will also prove to be not only the pattern but likewise the inspiration for the establishment of many other similar activities in many states of our Union.
>
> I have fortunately been furnished with the *prospectus* of the ac-

tivities that are contemplated by this Institute and I have been frankly amazed at the details, compass and thoroughness of the program which it proposed to follow. Its formulation has doubtless taken years of intensive practical study and research into the intricate channels of all branches of federal, state, county and municipal governments, as well as of the judicial, taxation and educational system of the state. If the program is pursued, as I am sure it will be, a startling recompense will come to your people in economy and efficiency in every branch of your state government and practically an awakening of the consciousness of the individual citizen of his responsibilities to this community. I give wholehearted praise and congratulations to all those who have shared in this monumental and historic work.

I felt that it was your will to make this a great occasion. It is indeed a milestone on the highway of your progress. It is typical of the mind and heart of the people of a great state.

You once lost a romantic and pioneering colony at Roanoke; but you have found those methods of thought and action that lead always onward to a better and happier life for your people.

"This building is your monument," said my friends; but, knowing more than they did, I responded, "It remains to be seen whether it will be my tombstone." I thought of the Biblical observation: "The last state of that man was worse than the first." For now that the festivities of dedication were over, in the cold gray dawn I faced the sobering facts:

There was a $25,000 mortgage on the building covering the loan of money to complete it, and I had the personal responsibility of meeting the yearly payments by the methods of rake, scrape, and borrow.

I found that I could rake, scrape, and borrow no longer. I was at the end of my rope. I had come face to face with the question that had been put by some humorous nineteenth century skeptic: "If God is all powerful, can He make a rock so big He can't tote it?" Maybe He couldn't. But I knew I could, for I had already done it. "A man's reach should exceed his grasp," the poet had said, "or what's a heaven for?" I began to see the truth in the old song: "Everybody talking 'bout heaven ain't goin' there." A gallon of water poured into a pitcher pump would not bring up water from the bottom of a dry well, and the Institute well was slowly running dry. The theory

107

of "priming the pump" would not work much longer. I needed to find a stream of flowing water which would come welling up strongly enough to sustain the operations before they faltered. I found it. It was a life-saving find, and came about in this way.

Coming Home

On a memorable evening in the fall of 1940, I was working in my office in the new building on Franklin Street when Billy Carmichael, the newly appointed Comptroller of the University, saw the lights on in the building and came in. He said he had been going through the University budget operations and could find no provision for the support of the Institute staff, no reference to operating revenues or to building maintenance, and he wanted to know why. "Because," I said, "the Institute of Government is a private venture growing out of my Law School classroom and is supported by private individuals supplemented by city and county membership dues." "Why hasn't the University been in on it?" he asked. "Because," I answered, "University appropriations have been cut to the bone in Depression years since 1931, and it has all it can do to hold on to what it has got and restore these cuts to former levels before it can taken on new enterprises." "Well," he said, "I am going to do everything I can to bring it into the University where it belongs."

In a meeting with Billy Carmichael and Frank Graham, I said: "The University of North Carolina is your lookout and responsibility. The Institute of Government is mine. It is a going concern but I need help to keep it going. I understand why the University has not come to the aid of the Institute in the past, and why it cannot help it now. But I know that I have given fifteen years of my life to building something that ought not to die. I do not believe that public officials in the cities, the counties and the state of North Carolina are willing to see it die. I believe there are enough of them who will reach out to help it live if they are told the facts about its condition.

"There is Charles M. Johnson, chairman of the local government commission, who will be glad of the chance to take over and run it as an avenue of service to local governments. There is Thad Eure,

Secretary of State, who will be glad to take over and run its legislative service. These two state agencies, and most if not all others who have profited by the Institute's services will, I believe, be willing to scrape the bottom of their budget and channel into the Institute of Government funds now reverting to the state's budget at the end of the year, and that will be enough to keep the Institute going until the next meeting of the General Assembly when they can ask for a state appropriation which the Institute of Government has never had.

"If the University cannot find it possible to come to my aid, I am going to call a meeting of these state agencies in Raleigh, put the life or death of the Institute of Government in their hands, offer to work for them without pay—full-time during the summer months and part-time through the rest of the year and as long as necessary thereafter—as for fifteen years I have been working without pay to keep it going in Chapel Hill. I shall do this without rancor or resentment at the University but for the sole purpose of keeping so much of my life from going down the drain. You have the chance to keep its flag flying in Chapel Hill if you think that the Institute of Government is worth the University's having."

From this point on, Billy Carmichael took the lead in efforts to bring the Institute of Government into the University. With the approval and support of President Graham, Carmichael worked out refinancing plans to extend outstanding obligations over a longer period of years—with the help of Julian Price, who was the biggest creditor by far. James H. Clark, chairman of the state budget commission, on his own motion called for a list of the personal obligations I had incurred in keeping the Institute going, and the budget commission unanimously agreed to retire them at once. Governor Broughton brought the state into the financing picture for the first time by agreeing to recommend that the General Assembly appropriate $15,000 a year for five staff members at $3,000 a year—a living wage in those days. He did this in recognition of the fact that the Institute was serving the state no less than cities and counties, and that the $15,000 from the state would match the membership dues of counties, cities, and towns.

All of this planning and work by Frank Graham and Billy Carmichael brought us within $20,000 of the amount needed to guarantee operations of the Institute until the General Assembly could come in with state appropriations to supplement city and county revenues. Where could it be found?

At this point Miss Cornelia Love, whose father and grandfather had been professors at the University, came in to point the way. She invited me to meet her brother, Spencer Love, of the Burlington Mills, at her home on a Saturday afternoon when he was in Chapel Hill for a football game, and later told me that she thought he might help us. Frank Graham and Billy Carmichael went to see him in his office in Greensboro. He asked them what they thought was the most pressing need of the University at that moment. "Bringing in the Institute of Government," was their reply. He gave the $20,000 needed for that purpose.

Billy Carmichael and Frank Graham brought me the news of Spencer Love's gift just before Christmas in the winter of 1941. The financing plans were approved by the Executive Committee of the Board of Trustees in December, 1941, and the Institute of Government became part of the University of North Carolina on January 26, 1942.

Spencer Love's interest in the Institute of Government did not stop with his gift of $20,000. Later, I received a telephone call from my former student, Ed Hudgins, in Greensboro, saying that he had a client, whose name he was not authorized to disclose, who was thinking of including in his will a gift of $50,000 to the Institute of Government and wanted to know how to phrase the terms of the gift so as to achieve the purpose I had in mind. I told him to make it to the University of North Carolina for the unrestricted use and benefit of the Institute of Government at Chapel Hill. I also told him that my instant and instinctive response to the unknown giver, and the way I felt toward any man who thought enough of the Institute of Government to contemplate such a gift, was that I hoped he would live forever so that we would never get it.

Ed Hudgins called me back a few days later and said that if there had ever been any doubt in his client's mind it disappeared when he relayed my message. His client's name was Spencer Love, and he converted the provision of his will into a direct gift. The Institute of Government received the $50,000 in a few weeks.

"There is many a slip 'twixt the cup and the lip," and that sort of slip almost occurred in the 1943 budget while it was on its way to the General Assembly. The $15,000 appropriation was put in the budget, as recommended, under the heading of "Appropriations." A friend in the General Assembly and on the budget commission told me about it and said I had nothing further to worry about. He had called me from his hotel room in Raleigh and read out the glad tidings. "Do you have the copy of the budget in your hands?" I asked, and he said he did. "Turn to the heading of 'Receipts'," I suggested. He ruffled audibly through the pages and exploded: "Well, I'll be damned!" "What is the matter?" I asked. "Fifteen thousand is written under the heading of 'Receipts!'" he replied. A slip, perhaps, of the budget officer's pen had nullified the $15,000 appropriation by putting in $15,000 under "Receipts"! That meant that I was expected to raise the $15,000 Institute appropriation. It was my friend John Kerr, Jr., a collegemate, a Warrenton lawyer and Speaker of the General Assembly, who saw that the entry was corrected and secured the first state appropriation the Institute of Government ever had. As Wellington had said about the battle of Waterloo: "It was a damned near thing!"

The history of the Institute of Government for 1939 to 1942 is the history of the improvised staff—all of them had been, and some still were, my students. They had worked for these years on a shoe-string—a shoestring which had been broken, knotted, and tied and broken, knotted and tied again. They had kept its services going and its life lines open during the heartbreaking days, after the Institute of former days had gone with the men who built it, and were part and parcel of its strivings to be born again. They have the satisfaction of knowing that their achievement still stands as one of the brightest chapters in its history.

Holding Buckle and Tongue Together: 1942-1949

The 7th day of December, 1941, brought the news of the Japanese attack on Pearl Harbor, the United States entered the Second World

War, and students and faculty left the campus for the armed services. In the early months of 1942 men on the Institute staff left
more quickly than they had come: Sanford for the Army combat
paratroopers; Cochrane, Oettinger, and Long for the Navy; Samray Smith for the Marines; and others for war activities in one form
or another. For a long time I had had a staff without a building.
Now I had a building without a staff.

It was as difficult to find men for the staff in the early 1940's as it
was to find money in the early 1930's. Ordinary men would not
do—they had to be first-rate men. I found them in the 1940's as I had
found them in the 1930's, men who were not eligible for military
service, wanted to be in some form of public service activity, and so
joined the Institute staff for the war years: Peyton Abbott, Joel Denton, George McGehee and Clifford Pace, who had been my students; Maurice Hill, a University official; William Barfield, a city
official; Joseph Reid, a graduate student in political science; Louis
Cherry, a librarian; and John Fries Blair, a young lawyer from
Winston-Salem.

Civilian War Services Save the Day

Gas rationing came in and began cutting down to near the
vanishing point all travel that was not "defense-related," and it
looked as if district and statewide schools were out for the duration
of the war, and that most if not all traveling contacts between the
Institute staff and its clientele in city halls, county courthouses, and
state agencies would cut our Institute life lines. At this point we
were rescued from catastrophe by the work the Institute had carried
on with civic organizations of men and women throughout the
1930's; because of these connections, the Office of Civilian Defense
in North Carolina called on the Institute of Government to take
over the training of people engaged in the civilian war services
throughout the state. I was sent to a War Department School for
those in charge of similar training in the southern states; and I did
spadework studies in civilian war-service activities for local governments and the state.

These activities called for the training of citizens to serve as auxiliaries to supplement police, waterworks operators, and other public services in cases of manpower shortages or in other emergencies. At the Institute, we put our studies and teachings into a 200-page guidebook; and in the next two or three years held seventeen statewide training schools running for five days each, and six one-day district training schools, attended by two thousand or more people coming from just about every local government center in North Carolina.

Since this was "defense-related" work, all participants were permitted extra gasoline rations so that Institute staff members could travel to these training schools held in strategic centers throughout the state, and state officials, citizens, and teachers could come to the Institute of Government in Chapel Hill. This flow of effort strengthened the vital relationship between the Institute and the governmental agencies, school systems, and civic organizations throughout North Carolina.

National Recognitions Help at Home

The Director of the Institute of Government was invited to tell about its work in South Carolina, Georgia, Florida, Alabama, California, Washington, Michigan, Illinois, New Hampshire, New Jersey, New York, Pennsylvania, and Virginia.

Articles about the Institute of Government were published in various periodicals, including: *Reader's Digest, National Municipal Review, National University Extension Division Studies, Newsweek, Pathfinder, Collier's, County Officer, American City, Saturday Evening Post, Criminal Justice, Journal of Chicago Crime Commission, Melbourne Graduate, Time,* and *American Bar Association Journal.*

This national recognition brought the Institute of Government to the attention of thousands of people in North Carolina outside of official circles, people who had barely heard of it before, and strengthened its standing with city and county governing-boards and with the General Assembly of North Carolina when we needed help. It caused a fresh look and some re-thinking among local critics—"Maybe there is something to it after all." One of them met me on the street and said: "I see you've made the *Reader's Digest*." "Oh, no," I replied: "The *Reader's Digest* has made me." There was truth in that reply.

In 1944 DeWitt Wallace, owner and editor of the *Reader's Digest,* invited me to New York City at his expense—I couldn't have gone on my own—took me to the Ritz for lunch, the first and last time I ever got there, questioned me at length about my work, and offered to finance me for a year or more to go to every state in the union to get a similar program going in them all, with a dazzling salary and expense account. I had never made half that much money in my life, nor had so lavish an expense account. I had no choice but to refuse the offer, for if I had gone away for a year at that particular time and tried to get an Institute of Government started in every state, I knew that there would not have been an Institute of Government in North Carolina when I got back home.

Transition Years

The years from the coming of the Institute into the University framework as its "public service department" in January 1942 to the end of World War II in 1945 and its aftermath in the latter 1940's were transition years and some of the most productive in the history of the Institute.

It was during these years that Peyton Abbott picked up and carried on the work in the tax field that Henry Brandis had begun, and in a series of local, district, and statewide schools widened and deepened the Institute's working relationships with city, county, and state tax listing, tax assessing, tax collecting and foreclosure officials.

It was during these years that John Fries Blair did the painstaking and thoroughgoing research work into the history of the motor vehicle laws and their enforcement and administration from the horse and buggy days in the early 1900's to the 1950's. His work covered the evolution of legislative enactments, court decisions, and administrative rules and regulations and resulted in a series of

114

articles in *Popular Government* and a guidebook on motor vehicle laws in North Carolina which became the standard text for the State Highway Patrol and local officers, prosecuting attorneys, and judges at all levels throughout the state.

It was during these years that Clifford Pace organized and developed the massive and far-reaching programs for the Motor Vehicles Department for driver license examiners, hearing officers, and other administrative personnel; supplemented by the invaluable work of David Monroe on all fronts in the safety field.

It was during these years that Maurice Hill and George McGehee initiated the Institute's work with city, county and state purchasing agents, and that Samray Smith and Lewis Cherry developed the Institute's library into an invaluable service agency for the Institute staff, public officials, and related departments in the University of North Carolina at Chapel Hill.

It was during these years that the Institute of Government with the help of the FBI and lawyers from the bench and bar expanded the programs for prosecuting attorneys, judges and other court officials, police, sheriffs, and the State Highway Patrol.

It was during these years that the Institute took on the task of organizing and conducting refresher courses for lawyers returning from the armed services, and laid the foundation for continuing legal institutes conducted by the North Carolina Bar Association to keep lawyers up-to-date in all fields of the law.

It was during these years that Bill Cochrane, returning from the Navy, began the work which later grew into Institute training programs for planning officers, local jailers, state prison officers, and public health officials.

It was during these years that Terry Sanford, returning from the Army, located and transferred barracks used by soldiers in army camps to be used by recruits in training for the State Highway Patrol and police and sheriffs in the Institute's expanding program for law-enforcing officers—a program carried forward into the far-reaching law-enforcement training programs of later years.

Throughout the years while the Institute of Government was between bases the short term staff members, working from 1939 to

Pearl Harbor in 1941 and from Pearl Harbor into the aftermath of World War II, turned their hands to anything and everything that had to be done to keep the Institute of Government a going concern. They remained with us into the 1950's while we were recruiting and breaking in a new staff for future years. They have the satisfaction of knowing that they had held buckle and tongue together and saved the life of the Institute of Government.

It is not more than simple justice to say that Peyton Abbott's work in the legislative service, his researches and writings in *Popular Government*, his guidebooks, his teachings in local, district, and statewide schools, his first-rate abilities working for the Institute of Government on many fronts, prove him one of the ablest and most productive men who have ever served the Institute of Government.

Appraisals of Institute Work: 1939 to the Latter 1940's

From the Attorney General of North Carolina:

> I think it is pretty generally understood throughout the State that the Institute of Government has, during its existence, rendered a service of incalculable value to our counties, cities, and towns in carrying on the functions and duties which, under the law, they are required to perform. To mention only one service with which I have been thoroughly acquainted, the listing, assessing, and collection of taxes, I will say that the aid given by the Institute of Government to the taxing authorities in our local units of government has been of tremendous value. Issuance and use of the handbooks on these subjects has given the local authorities ready reference to the law and practices and procedures, which otherwise it would have been impracticable for them to get.

From the President of the State Association of County Commissioners:

> The Institute of Government's record during the last Legislature is something to be proud of. The bills introduced were presented to counties over the state with utmost speed and accuracy. This saved the counties a lot of money and kept the legislature from passing, some crazy bill. I recall one bill that if passed would have cost the counties of the state $100,000 at least and this bill could have easily been passed but for your bulletin service.

A member of the 1943 House of Representatives, referring to his personal file of the daily legislative bulletin placed on his desk each morning of the session, said, "This is my bible."

Another wrote: "Placing the Institute of Government's legislative bulletin in notebooks, readily available, on the desk of every member each morning is the biggest improvement in the General Assembly since I have been a member."

Another wrote: "In the course of a hurried legislative session, there are many opportunities for errors of many kinds to be enacted into law, unless detected and corrected during the process of legislation. Errors are particularly apt to occur in bills amendatory of existing laws, and because of the usual method employed in effecting amendments—by striking a certain line in a certain chapter of the laws of a certain session, and adding some other phraseology—errors have a good chance to go undetected unless the bill receives close scrutiny and comparison with the existing law."

The following are samples of some errors that were detected and corrected during the last session: One bill would have placed the sheriff in complete care and custody of the prisoners. Another bill, intended to place one county under the provisions of a statewide bill that authorized the appointment of certain subordinate officials, was so drawn that it would have literally made the county responsible for the salaries of those subordinate officials all over the state. Another bill, intended to repeal a part of a local act of minor importance, would have cut the heart out of a major statewide bill because of an erroneous citation in the repealing clause. And one bill would have repealed an act that was not to be found in the books: the chapter number was in error, with the result that the act intended to be repealed would have remained in force.

From the Supreme Court Librarian:

I have your letter of the 27th asking for comments and suggestions concerning the Bulletin Service. It has been quite helpful and of very genuine service—as always. It was a pleasure to note that the General Assembly itself publicly acknowledged its value, finally giving some credit where credit has long been due. I followed the Bulletin closely and noted, with pleasure, the very high character of reporting. Aside from the many other values, often noted, which the Service has revealed, it has, apparently, accomplished at least one major legislative reform: The "sneak" bill is now obsolete. As far as I was able to learn, not a single instance of attempting to bury in an other wise innocuous bill some vicious or unpopular change was attempted during the last session. If there ever was a major triumph for popular government in this State, this is it. What was once a popular legislative pastime has, it would seem, now followed the brontosaurus and the saber-toothed tiger down the twilight path to extinction.

From the Commanding Officer: Headquarters District Number Two Fourth Service Command Fort Bragg, N.C.

During the critical days of World War II, the Institute of Government rendered outstanding service in aid of the defense of the soil of North Carolina against enemy invasion. The concept of amalgamating all local, municipal, county, and State forces with the Federal forces in defense of the life and property of the citizens of your State was your idea and was matured and made effective by you in the Institute of Government of the University of North Carolina. The plans fashioned on the campus at Chapel Hill for the utilization of all State and Federal forces in the days of crisis when submarines were lying off the North Carolina Coast line and enemy agents were threatening landings were of inestimable value to the Army in its plans for the defense of the Atlantic Coastal Area.

From the Regional Director of the Office of Civilian Defense:

To say that I highly commend the Institute of Government on the excellence of the material contained in your guide to civilian defense, would be putting it all too mildly. As much literature as I have had to read on the subject of civilian defense would cause most people in my position to hope that they would never have to read another article on this subject. However, I can honestly say that the intelligent and readable manner in which you have arranged and composed the various subjects covered caused me to enjoy reading every work of your defense issue. I think you have made it possible for anyone who reads this issue to have as comprehensive a view of civilian defense as they could possibly have from reading any other one given publication. Even the technical matter covered in this issue is written in a readable manner. All in all, it constitutes an excellent civilian defense handbook.

From Howard W. Odum, Director
The Institute for Research in Social Science:

The Institute of Government, evolving through experiment and exploration as a private voluntaristic organization in the 1930's, became officially an integral part of the University of North Carolina in January 1942. Like the Institute for Research in Social Science, it grew out of the day's work. And like many another American effort it followed the rough road of frontier work and blazed its trail as private effort before joining the family of publicly supported institutions.

Inaugurated and developed by Albert Coates, professor of law, it represented the attempt to perform services and meet needs not ordinarily met by a university's regular departments and to experiment through procedures not available in the academic field.... [Coates] was restless under the limitations of formal instruction and explored the possibilities of several avenues of approach.

None of these avenues proved satisfactory for various reasons. One was that Professor Coates' programs offered too sweeping, too individualistic, and too much outside the standard set-up and practice of the several university departments. Another was that some of his plans were in conflict with a previously conceived effort to set up an ambitious academic school of public administration. Other reasons included the usual and inevitable diversity of opinions, limitation of staffs, conflict of personalities, and the usual logical difficulties involved in pioneer work. It seems quite likely that no American university was ready for so distinctive and revolutionary departure as Professor Coates wanted. Certainly this was true of the University of North Carolina....

The logical next step, therefore, was for Professor Coates to undertake a voluntary private arrangement through which experimentation could be carried on. Such an arrangement, therefore, eventuated in the founding of the Institute of Government which began in the early 1930's, continued under private auspices in its constantly changing and expanding program for a decade when the Institute became a part of the University officially at the January 1942 meeting of the University Board of Trustees. Just as it was clear that in its earlier stages the University was not prepared to inaugurate the Institute under the premises proposed, so it became clear that such an Institute could not function as adequately as a private institution as it could as an integral part of the University. And in the meantime, there was an amazing amount of experience to study, a vast experiment in practical contact with governmental officials, scores of private individuals who had become interested and involved on many levels, the idea and plan had caught the imagination of the nation, and the time was ripe for the next step.

Institute of Government Building, Franklin Street, 1939

Speaker Bankhead, left, and Comptroller Lindsay Warren look at picture of Institute Building

Gladys and Albert Coates

121

North Carolina Congressional Delegation invites Speaker Bankhead to speak at dedication of Institute Building in Chapel Hill

At the dedication, left to right, seated: Governor Clyde Hoey; Speaker William Bankhead; former Governor O. Max Gardner. Standing: UNC Chancellor Robert House; Albert Coates; Gregg Cherry, State Chairman Democratic Party; Congressman Robert Doughton; Comptroller Lindsay Warren; Jake Newell, State Chairman Republican Party; Ed Coffey, FBI

122

At the dedication, left to right: Lindsay Warren, Clyde Hoey, Speaker Bankhead, O. Max Gardner, Graham Barden, Albert Coates, Frank Graham

A.H. (Sandy) Graham

Robert Hanes

Richard Stockton

Will Reynolds

124

Gordon Gray

Bowman Gray

Julian Price

Bruce Stroud

George Livas

Institute Staff–Between Bases

Terry Sanford

William Cochrane

Peyton Abbott

John Fries Blair

Clifford Pace

William Mitchell

Elmer Oettinger

Edna Clark

Maurice Hill

Malcolm Seawell

Samray Smith

Lewis Cherry

George McGhee

*Pictures not available for: Tom Long, W.C.
Barfield, Joel Denton, Joseph Reid, Claude
Edwards, Betta McCarthy, William B. Parker,
George Bradham, Moore Bryson, Bill Speight,
Phil Lucas, Leon Roebuck, George Riddle.*

128

Illustrative Schools of the Early 1940's

Tax Supervisors

Scientific Aids in Crime Detection School. Kneeling, left to right, Institute staff members: Abbott, Blair, Cherry, and extreme right, Pace

Registers of Deeds

Tax Officials. Top row, second from left, Institute staff member Brandis

Sheriffs

Superior Court Clerks

Law-enforcing Officers

Law-enforcing Officers. Front row on left, Abbott and Cherry; on right, Blair, Coates and Pace

John Fries Blair with Police Officers

Civilian Defense School

Tax Official Officers with
Peyton Abbott

Moot Court Trial

Coates with Police School

Postwar Planning School

134

Police Executives Training Committee

Peyton Abbott congratulating Police School graduates

Supreme Court Justices at graduating exercises of Police School. Left to right: Devin, Clarkson, Schenck, Seawell, Thompson

Illustrative Schools of the Latter 1940's

Tax Supervisors

Fingerprint School

Institute staff members with Mecklenburg County Commissioners. Standing, Sanford, Cochrane, Allen. Seated, extreme left, Coates; center, Lewis

Local Service Officers School

Refresher Course—State Highway Patrol. Front row, Institute staff members, extreme left: Machen, Hayman. Extreme right: Pace, Edwards

Scientific Aids in Crime Detection School

Police Records School

State Highway Patrol Schools and Related Groups

State Highway Patrol Training School Staff

Terry Sanford, at right, with Training Officers

Traffic Law
Enforcement School

Barracks, School conducted October 13—December 7, 1946

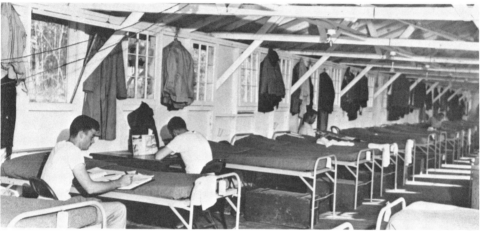

State Highway Patrol Training School for recruits

Law Refresher Courses for Veterans returning to the Bar in North Carolina

Brandis, Lowndes, Adams, Rice, Thigpen, Vaughn

North Carolina Bar Association Committee on Law Refresher Courses. Present for the opening of the first law refresher course for lawyer veterans, conducted by the Institute of Government for the North Carolina Bar Association on February 8, 9 and 10, were the members of the Committee appointed by Louis J. Poisson, President of the Bar Association. First row, left to right: Luther Hartsell of the Concord Bar; Louis Poisson of the Wilmington Bar, President of the North Carolina Bar Association; Charles R. Jonas of the Lincolnton Bar, Chairman of the Committee; E.L. Cannon, Raleigh, Secretary of the North Carolina Bar Association; and Charles W. Tillett of the Charlotte Bar. Second row: Alan Marshall of the Wilmington Bar; Albert Coates, Director of the Institute of Government; and Isaac T. Avery, Jr. of the Statesville Bar.

Schools

141

1945 Legislative Service

After discussion of final plans, Albert Coates wishes Peyton Abbott good luck as he leaves the Institute Building in Chapel Hill to set up the Legislative Office in Raleigh prior to the 1945 session.

One or more representatives of the Institute attends every session of both the House and Senate. Leaving the Capitol after gathering all necessary information for the daily bulletin are, left to right: Peyton Abbott, Clifford Pace, Nancy Fewell, Louis Cherry and John Fries Blair.

Now the grind begins. Bills must be digested, statutes consulted, amendments checked and inserted, and the daily report prepared. Engaged in the process are Blair, Pace and Abbott.

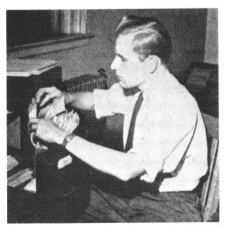

Copies of all bills in both original and final form must be obtained and files kept. Cherry is shown checking the bill files.

Nancy Fewell posts the day's entries in the journal which shows a record of all bills introduced and all legislative action taken.

143

The process of getting out bulletins begins in Chapel Hill. Edna Mae Clark pre-addresses envelopes for the daily and weekly mailings.

Rosanne Guess sorts the envelopes according to counties and towns to facilitate handling in Raleigh.

Jack Atwater takes a direct part. Here he boxes up a batch of envelopes to be put on the Raleigh bus.

144

Proofreading goes on for hours at a sitting. Here Abbott and Cherry proof local weekly stencils which are cut from the card index kept for each county and municipality.

Quire upon quire of stencils must be cut. Engaged in this task are Margaret Wilson and Corinna Sherron.

The mimeographing and assembly room is a little crowded, and so is the time. Shown above is one of the alternate crews of part-time assistants hard at work in getting out the bulletin.

145

His own work completed and bedtime long since passed, Blair lends a hand in "tying up" in order to expedite the process.

It's three o'clock in the morning . . . .

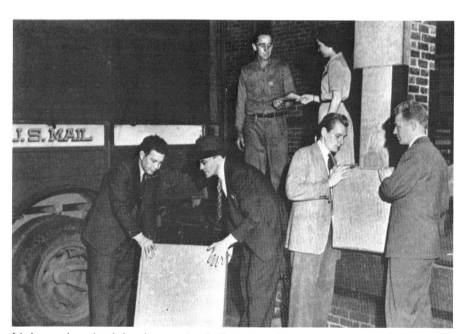

It's been a long hard day, but another bulletin is on its way.

Governor R. Gregg Cherry

John Harden, Secretary to the Governor

State Treasurer Charles M. Johnson

Secretary of State Thad Eure

State Auditor George Ross Pou

Principal state officials, as well as local officials throughout the state, receive each morning a copy of the daily legislative bulletin. In addition the Institute of Government prepares for the Governor, members of the Legislature, the Council of State and State Department heads in Raleigh a special notebook which keeps in chronological order digests of all bills. Shown on this page are the Governor and other officials in the Capitol Building examining their notebooks and bulletins.

147

Chapter VI   The Institute Of
Government Is
Born Again

I was twenty-seven years old when I started teaching in the UNC Law School in 1923. I was thirty-six years old when the first full-time person was added to the staff of the Institute of Government in 1933, apart from my wife and myself. I had by then spent nine years experimenting with the plan and purpose which brought the Institute of Government into being—and thereafter spent nine more years in fighting for its life. I was forty-six years old in 1942 when the Institute of Government came into the framework of the University of North Carolina. I was forty-nine years old when the war was over in 1945 and I began recruiting another staff. I had seventeen years to go before 1962, when trustee regulations would require my withdrawal as Institute Director at the age of sixty-five. I wanted to make the most of those seventeen years.

Fitting into the University Framework

My first problem was to find the Institute's footing within the University framework. The path into the University had been full of hurdles. Many skeptics had pointed with justifiable alarm to my record of expanding the horizons of my Law School classroom, taking over one activity after another simply because I thought it ought to be done, acting on my own initiative without asking permission from the accredited authorities—all vagrant performances without any visible means of financial support. "Albert cannot be trusted to operate within the limitations of a budget," they said.

To which I had answered: "How can you know I cannot operate within a budget when I've never had one? I have always started out with things to be done, and started doing them in the expectation of raising the money to finance them as I went along, and paying out of my own pocket the difference between what I had spent and what I had raised at the end of the year. Reversing this process, and having the money in the bank at the beginning of the budget year, instead of scraping it up on the go, will be a new experience for me, and I will revel in that."

It was also objected that if Albert gets into the University he will claim the same backing of the University authorities that the present insiders claim for going to the General Assembly and the foundations for support, whereas now the University President has enough insiders to take care of without adding any more. To this I answered: "Why not?"

There was the problem of dealing with University budget officers. I ran into four types of budget officers: one who would put pitfalls in my path; one who would not tell me where the pitfalls were, when he knew and I didn't; one who would go out of his way to point out the pitfalls and help me stay out of them, or help me get out after I got in; one who took the view that I was the youngest calf in the pasture and had to "suck hind tit."

Being enveloped in the mind of the usual budget officer reminded me of a fellow student nominating a man for president of the Phi Society in my college days, saying: "Mr. President, I have in mind a man," and a critic rising to a point of personal privilege, saying: "Mr. President, I would like to observe that that man is in a mighty cramped position." My only escape from that cramped position was to take the budget allocation as a starting point rather than a stopping point, as a hunting license rather than a dead-end. And that is what I did.

149

There was the problem of status. It came about in this way. Teachers of semester courses to freshmen, sophomores, juniors, and seniors in the University curriculum were considered members of the faculty. Teachers of short courses running for a few days or a few weeks in the University Extension Division were considered employees of the University with fewer academic rights and privileges than the faculty, even though their native ability and academic training might be fully the equivalent. Which category did the newly organized Institute of Government and its staff come into? It was a question of status.

After a prolonged argument the Institute of Government won recognition with the status of a School with its Director the equivalent of a Dean or a Department head in the academic hierarchy, and its staff members became faculty members with all their rights and privileges.

There was the problem of the work year. The victory of status brought on another argument which was also prolonged. Faculty members taught for nine months in the year, with their salaries spread over twelve months, and had the privilege of supplementing their pay for the other three months by teaching in the University summer school, or finding other supplemental jobs on a catch-as-catch-can basis. University Extension employees worked on a twelve-month basis and were paid accordingly. It was seriously argued that since Institute staff members had become University faculty members, they should be paid by the University for nine months, with the privilege of scrambling on their own for supplemental jobs during the remaining three months—as all other faculty members had to do. Having pointed out the similarity of Institute staff and University faculty, I was now called on to point out the difference which was this: the Institute faculty was working for officials whose jobs ran twelve months in the year, who had to be on the job twelve months in the year, whereas the University faculty was serving a different clientele of students coming for nine months in the year. At long last this argument prevailed, and the faculty of the new University of Public Officials in the framework of the old University of North Carolina were paid, and worked, on a twelve-month basis.

With these administrative problems settled, I faced the question: Shall I give up my Law School teaching job and put full-time on the job of directing the affairs of the Institute of Government? Certainly this was a full-time administrative job, testing the vision, the stamina, the skills, and the endurance of any man at the height of his powers.

I decided to do both for this reason among others: My work had become a bridge between the teaching of government in the classroom and the teaching of officials working on the job, with each reenforcing the other, and giving up one would be undermining both.

I was learning from officials working on the job, giving an added dimension to what I was learning from reading constitutions, statutes, and decisions in the Law School library. In supervising the work of my Institute colleagues, I was adding to my knowledge and insight what they, too, were learning from the study of law in books and in action. I believed it to be literally true that this work was doubling the value of my courses to my students.

Recruiting a New Staff

The problem that transcended all others was the work of recruiting new staff members, for the Institute of Government would never rise above the level of their quality, character, competence, and their continuity.

The work of new men and women coming to the Institute of Government would be made easier by the fact that those who had gone before them from 1933 to 1945 had laid a solid foundation of achievement to build on in the future. It would be made still easier by the fact that the Institute was now an integral part of the University of North Carolina at Chapel Hill and thereby had acquired a stability that a purely private organization could not provide. It would be made easier still by the fact that they could start in the paths charted by their predecessors until they could begin making

151

tracks of their own. I wanted the same sort of people for the new staff that I had found for the old.

I believed in individualism to the point of anarchy and spent thirty years of my life in demonstrating that belief. I carried this notion to the point of saying in later years, even boasting and proclaiming, that there were twenty-four directors on the staff, with every man directing himself in his own field, and one assistant director, myself, who was assisting all twenty-four directors without supervising them.

I not only gave them independence—I insisted that they use it. I would tell a staff member all I knew about an assignment indicating that he would learn more about it as he went along, would revise my guidelines, and finish with something far different from what I had originally envisioned. It was important that he be free to change course and direction as he saw fit. I would then turn him loose with the assurance that he was free to come back to me, if, as, and when he wanted to.

Now and then someone missed the point I was trying to make. One man worked zealously on a project for three or four weeks and brought back the results of his work. I looked at it and exclaimed: "This will never do!" "But I've done exactly what you told me to do," he replied. "Yes, you have," I answered, "but if you haven't got any better sense than to do as I say, you haven't got sense enough to be on the Institute staff. Didn't you see as you went along that the leads I had given you were going to bring about a foolish result?" "Yes," he said. "Didn't it occur to you that I might have had sense enough to outgrow my own guidelines? And that you should have outgrown them, too, when you saw they would lead you to a dead end?" He got the point and learned the responsibilities of freedom, and we had no futher misunderstanding after that.

I never gave a man a deadline. When I was a five-year-old boy, walking with my grandfather around the farm he said to me: "Son, if you ever haul rock to build a chimney, and haul twice as much as you think you will need, you are likely to have half enough." I found this to be true in assigning problems to my colleagues. When the problem was more difficult than I thought, it would take much longer to handle it, and insistence on a deadline would be an invitation to do a superficial job. When it was less difficult than I thought, the deadline would be an invitation to rest on the oars. Either way, we lost. I discovered that deadlines, like the Kingdom of God, are within you.

I did not want men with conflicting loyalties. I found that one colleague was working eight hours in the daytime for the Institute of Government, and three or four hours in the evening, and full days on Saturdays and Sundays, on unrelated ventures. The Institute was getting his routine efforts while the outside activity was getting the heart and soul and enthusiasm which kept him going to the early hours of the morning. He would frequently come jaded to his work at the Institute, capable only of routine performance. I told him that Samuel Pepys and Walt Whitman had routine clerical jobs to earn their bread and butter, while they put their creative efforts into diaries and poems which were living long after their routine work had been forgotten. I wanted men on the Institute staff who found the fulfillment of their creative efforts in the day's work undistracted by competing sideline activities.

After a year or two of observing me in action, a colleague came to me with the suggestion that we needed to work out a set of personnel policies in the Institute of Government. I referred him to the 22nd chapter and the 35th to 39th verses of the Gospel according to St. Matthew, saying: "Then one of them, which was a lawyer, asked him a question, tempting him, and saying, Master, which is the great commandment in the law? Jesus said unto him, Thou shalt love the Lord thy God with all thy heart, and with all thy soul, and with all thy mind. This is the first and great commandment, and the second is like unto it, Thou shalt love thy neighbor as thyself."

I told him that if he would take the words "the Lord thy God" out of the biblical verses and put in their places the "Institute of Government," he would have the only personnel policy I knew anything about and that I didn't want to know about any other. I told him he could keep on drawing up "personnel" policies for counties, cities, and state departments committed to the forty-hour week, but that I wanted none of them in the Institute of Government. The Institute of Government, I told him, was full of personalities, and had no use for "personnel."

The Staff at Work

Henry Lewis picked up, carried on, and expanded the work with tax officials which had been started by Henry Brandis and continued by Peyton Abbott, Don McCoy, and Robert Byrd.

George Esser and Alex McMahon, the work with city and county governing boards and the structure of local governmental units.

Donald Hayman, the work with state and local officials involved in shaping personnel policies and the Law-enforcing Officers Benefit and Retirement Fund.

Philip Green, Bob Stipe, and Ruth Mace, the work with city and county planning and zoning boards.

Lee Bounds, the work with state and local prison officials and the agencies of probation, pardon and parole.

Ernest Machen, Basil Sherrill, Durwood Jones, Charles Knox, and Ed Hinsdale, the work with the administration of justice in the courts.

Jack Elam, Richard Myren, Zeb Alley, Neil Forney, the work with city, county, and state police officials; and David Sharpe and Roy Hall with teaching criminal law.

Betta McCarthy did the distinctive and thoroughgoing spadework in criminal law which was the foundation for Institute guidebooks for law-enforcing officers on the elements of crime.

Shepard Bryan, William Poe, Edward Lane-Reticker, Joe Hennessee, Bruce Thomas, Robert Montgomery, Walter Lee Horton and Bob Campbell, the work with the State Highway Patrol and other officials involved in the administration of motor vehicle laws.

Clifton Bumgarner, the work with registers of deeds. Dexter Watts, the work with officials involved in the administration and enforcement of wild-life laws and regulations and related law-enforcing officials. David Scott, the work with the legislative service and related activities. Roddey Ligon, the work with the health, welfare, and family law officials, supplemented by Tom Faxon and Tom Devine.

Jim Paul, the work with teaching newspaper law to students in the Journalism School, and with the analysis of problems involved in the 1954 segregation decision by the United States Supreme Court.

154

Paul Johnston, the work of coordinating the research and studies carried on for the General Assembly and the State Commission on the Reorganization of State Government, the operating procedures of the State Highway Patrol, and the jurisdiction of law-enforcing officials.

Robert Giles, the work with state government in general and with the operating procedures of the State Advisory Budget Commission and the State Highway and Public Works Commission in particular.

Jake Wicker, the work with city, county, and state purchasing agents, local public works officials, and problems involved in consolidating the activities of local governmental units.

John Sanders, the work with the General Assembly, history of the Governor's office, and reorganization of state government.

Milton Heath, the work with the legislative service, with water resources, land use, utilities, and environmental problems.

Bill Allen, the work with problems involved in financing *Popular Government* and related and expanding publications of the Institute.

Elmer Oettinger, the work with the editing of *Popular Government,* which he prepared for by examining its issues in detail from its beginning, its relation to the work of individual members of the Institute and the interpretation of Institute activities to officials in particular and the press and public in general. He expanded these activities to include seminars on the problems of free press and fair trial and programs for newspaper reporters covering city halls, county courthouses, and state departments.

There were others, by the end of my directorship in 1962, who came and stayed varying periods of time and were involved in carrying on the day-to-day work of the Institute in a multiplicity of fields, every one of them indispensable in the work of building the Institute of Government. This list includes: Olivia Burwell, Mary Norwood, Katherine Freeman, Norris Snow, Justus Cathey, Kathleen Daniel, Bea Earp, Rosanne Guess, Francis Gust, Ruth Halvorsen, Myrtle Jenzano, Lois Lundquist, Louise Buckner, Nell Markham, Esther Minturn, Priscilla Moore, Julie Morissey, Rose Morrow, Rachelle Marshal, Olga Palatai. The work of all these men and women will be described in detail in the documentary history of the Institute of Government now being prepared.

Range of Activities

The following illustrations will afford a glimpse into the range and depth of the activities which were carried on by members of the Institute staff in the seventeen-year period from 1945 to 1962.

Guidebooks. During those years Institute staff members produced eighty guidebooks detailing the powers and duties of particular officials in over 6,000 pages of text and illustrations. They conducted more than one thousand schools and conferences attended by 5,000 officials in 1957, 6,000 in 1958, 7,000 in 1959, and 7,500 in 1962. The demands for added schools, research and miscellaneous services were growing faster than the staff.

Schools. Institute schools and conferences took many forms: from a twelve-week basic training course for highway patrol recruits, to a three-week course for wildlife protectors, to a two-week course in basic city-planning techniques, to one-week basic courses for many groups of officials, to one-, two-, and three-day meetings for smaller groups.

They included every-other-weekend seminars in municipal administration, extending throughout the school year, and a one-afternoon-a-week five-week seminar series in central-business-district problems for businessmen and local officials.

They included statewide schools in Chapel Hill, district meetings held at key points throughout the state, and national and regional conferences for professional groups such as traffic court officials, urban renewal officials, city planners, prison and jail officials.

They included training courses for local law-enforcement officers conducted by lawyers and judges using Institute materials. In short, they included every conceivable type of pre-service and in-service training which particular officials felt would benefit them.

Clearinghouse. Throughout this period, members of the Institute staff continued putting their knowledge and skills to use in a clearing house of governmental information, transmitted through special studies, bulletins, answers to inquiries, the legislative service,

156

the library, calendars of duties and directories of public officials. They served local officials and governmental units, state departments and agencies, and legislative commissions in research and consultative roles; and, as an outgrowth of continuing spadework studies on city, county, state, and federal government functions, they answered thousands of written and oral inquiries from officials, and wrote more than 300 special studies running to 15,000 pages, numerous bulletins, and 1400 articles and features running to 4200 pages in 172 issues of *Popular Government*.

The Legislative Service. The legislative service, beginning in 1933 and continuing through every legislative session, was expanded in the 1950's.

In 1950-51, a manual of legislative organization and procedure was prepared for the use of new legislators; in 1950-52, a study of legislative committees was made at the request of the Lieutenant Governor for guidance in organizing the Senate of 1951 and succeeding sessions; in 1957-59, the rules of the House of Representatives were revised at the request of the chairman of the rules committee; in 1959-61, the same service was rendered with respect to the rules of the Senate. From time to time during other years the advice of Institute staff members was sought on revision of particular rules and on other procedural questions. Since 1955 the Institute of Government has been regarded as so much a part of the machinery of the General Assembly that an appropriation for its services has been included in the amount budgeted for the legislators.

As individual legislators came to rely on Institute bill digests, they got into the habit of calling upon the legislative service staff for a variety of information. In 1953, for example, our staff was requested to furnish information concerning (1) the experience of other states with annual sessions of the legislature; (2) laws to cut down on the volume of private, local, and special legislation; (3) experience with staggered terms of office in counties, cities, and towns; (4) reapportionment of the membership of the General Assembly; (5) retirement systems in cities, counties, and the state; (6) city and county finance bills; (7) planning and zoning legislation; (8) the feasibility of separating the state prison system from the state highway and public works commission; and many other subjects.

The volume of this work rose so rapidly through the years that it could not be handled by the legislative service staff alone, and many inquiries had to be referred to the Institute's staff in Chapel Hill. By 1960, the value of such assistance had become so apparent that the commission on the reorganization of state government recommended that the Institute of Government furnish a separate legislative research staff to work full-time on such duties in future sessions of the General Assembly.

Teaching in the University. Staff members went beyond officials working on the job and taught courses in colleges, universities, and state agencies, including: the full course on Planning Law and Administration, significant portions of the courses in Urban Design and Introduction to Planning in the University of North Carolina Department of City and Regional Planning; the UNC Art Department's course on Contemporary American Architecture; the Transportation course in the Department of Civil Engineering at N.C. State University; the City Planning course in East Carolina University's Department of Geography; UNC Law School courses in Criminal Law, Municipal Corporations, Family Law; a course in Family Law in the UNC School of Social Work; a course in Law and Government in the School of Journalism; and courses in the School of Public Health, Dental School, School of Nursing, and School of Medicine.

Programs for Citizens. Staff members went beyond colleges and universities, and recognized that local planning programs cannot function effectively without support from citizens at large. They developed and held conferences for citizens interested in community improvement (in conjunction with the National Council of Churches), for business leaders and city officials concerned with the central business district (a five-session series held in two different regions of the state), garden clubs and others interested in improving the appearance of their communities, realtors, and for other groups. They participated regularly in programs of the Institute for media representatives, particularly editorial writers and reporters assigned to cover local governments.

Coming into the University.

Willliam D. Carmichael, Jr.

Frank Graham

John Kerr, Jr.

Robert House

Spencer Love

Governor J. M. Broughton

James H. Clark, Chairman,
Advisory Budget
Commission

159

The Institute of Government is Born Again
Institute Staff: Late 1940's–1962

Henry Lewis—1946

Donald Hayman—1948

George Esser—1948

Alex McMahon—1948

Philip Green—1949

Lee Bounds—1950

The Institute of Government was born again in the lives and work of these men who came to the staff in the years from 1946 to 1950, stayed for periods ranging from twelve to sixteen years by the end of my directorship of Institute affairs in 1962, and became the backbone of the Institute during those years.

The following pages call the roll of men and women who came to the Institute staff and stayed from one to seven years during the years from 1946 to 1962. Pictures of some of them were not available. The records of all of them will be spelled out in a documentary history of the Institute now being written.

Samuel Leager—1946

David Scott—1946

William Allen—1947

David Monroe—1947

Donald McCoy—1948

Dickson Phillips—1948

Ernest Machen—1949

James McMillan—1949

William Poe—1950

161

Basil Sherrill—1950

Shep Bryan—1950

Clifton Bumgarner—1951

Roddey Ligon—1951

Fannie Memory
Mitchell — 1951

Bruce Thomas—1951

Mason Thomas—1951

Max Cogburn—1951

Donald Scarlett—1952

162

Jack Elam—1952

Edward Lane-
Reticher—1952

Richard Myren—1952

Paul Johnston—1953

James C.N. Paul—1953

Robert Giles—1953

John Webb—1954

Zeb Alley—1955

Warren (Jake) Wicker—1955

163

Neil Forney—1956   Roy Hall—1956   John Sanders—1956

Robert
Montgomery—1957

Clyde Ball—1956   Walter Lee Horton—1956

Dexter Watts—1957   Milton Heath—1957   B.J. Campbell—1957

164

Robert Midgette—1957

Robert Stipe—1957

Marion Benfield—1959

Catherine Maybury
Seelye—1959

Robert Byrd—1960

Elmer Oettinger—1960

Edward Hinsdale—1961

Pictures not available for: Mary Oliver, Charles Knox, Tom Devine, Tom Faxon, Mary Gaither Whitener, William Curran, Hurshell Keener, John Alexander, Joe Hennessee, David Sharp, Durward Jones, Alex Biggs, Fred Crumpler, Ruth Mace, Bill Frue, Allan Markham, David Smith, Albert House, David Evans, Perry Powell, Royal Shannonhouse, Betsy Patterson Pace, Marjorie Bounds.

165

Illustrative Schools

Clyde Ball with Registers of Deeds

Henry Lewis, extreme left, with Tax Supervisors

166

Municipal Schools

County Commissioners

Basil Sherrill, center, with Sheriffs

167

Don Hayman with Municipal Officers

Jake Wicker with Municipal Administration School

168

George Esser with Municipal Administration

Alex McMahon and Don Hayman with Municipal Administration School

169

State Highway Patrol School

Highway Safety Conference. Front row, extreme left, McMahon; center, Blair; right, Esser

Traffic Court Conference. Extreme right, Walter Lee Horton

Driver Improvement Representatives

170

State Highway Patrol School

Joe Hennessee points to award

Judges and Court Officials

Recorders Court Judges

Deputy Clerks of Superior Court

172

Superior Court Judges

Recorders Court Solicitors

173

Illustrative Schools

Roy Hall and Law-enforcing Officers

Lee Bounds and Probation Officers

Royal Shannonhouse with class

Donald Hayman with class

Committee of Officials. Extreme right, Alex McMahon

175

Jail School with Bill Cochrane, front and center

Wildlife Patrol

176

ABC Inspectors School, March, 1960

177

Coming out of the capitol. From left to right: Green, Jones, Sanders, Ball, Hennessee

Governor Sanford addresses a joint session of the 1961 General Assembly

Institute legislative staff. Left to right: Esser, Poe, Lewis, Bryan

Institute legislative staff at work. On the right, Clyde Ball, who headed the Institute team. The others, left to right, are Marion Benfield, Milton Heath, Dexter Watts, and Dudley Humphrey

Left to right: Poe, Machen, Lewis, Bryan, Esser

Alex McMahon

Roddey Ligon

Bill Poe

Henry Lewis and Shep Bryan

George Esser

Institute staff taking legislative reports to post office

Clyde Ball and Joe Hennessee

Institute legislative service staff. Front row: Lewis, Pace, Esser; back row: McMahon, Philips, McCoy

182

Illustrative Schools

Henry Lewis, left, with Tax Officials

County Commissioners

County Tax Supervisors School

183

Tax Collectors School

George Esser with class

Basil Sherrill with Sheriffs

184

egisters of Deeds. Front row, **extreme right**: Bumgarner

aw-enforcing Officers

il Management and Prison Supervisors

185

Jailers School. Front row, extreme right, Bill Cochrane

Driver's Licsense Examiners. Extreme right, Ed Lane-Reticher

186

Walter Lee Horton of Institute staff and Colonel Smith of State Highway Patrol greeting cadets attending Safety School

State Agencies in Session at Institute

Governor Umstead with State School Commission

Commissioners revising the State Constitution

Advisory Budget Commission

188

Governor Hodges Addresses State Revenue Officials at the Institute of Government

Court Study Commission at work on improving and expediting the administration of justice. Left to right: Rodman, Brandis, Taylor, Bell

Commission revising the State Constitution

190

Court Study Commission with Chairman Spencer Bell, in front of mantel

Court Study Commission in session, with Clyde Ball at extreme front right

191

Chapter VII Working Patterns

I have asked several long-term colleagues to describe their personal working patterns in the Institute of Government, and to make these patterns more realistic, I have asked them to write informally and in the first person. They represent Institute working patterns at their best: Henry Lewis, Donald Hayman, Philip Green, Lee Bounds, Bob Campbell, Jack Atwater, and Catherine Maybury Seelye.

Henry Lewis (a talk to tax supervisors in 1978)

Following the 1947 General Assembly I was thrust unexpectedly into the Property Tax world, and I did not find the prospect hopeful.

The office of county tax supervisor was commonly combined with some other position; very few supervisors boasted substantial staffs; even fewer had experienced appraisers on whom to rely; most were limited to the puny assistance supplied by township list takers. Neither the tax supervisors nor the county commissioners took strong interest in making discoveries; and administration of the exemption laws was distressingly lax.

At the state level there was an ex officio agency known as the

State Board of Assessment charged with hearing appeals from the counties and with assessing the property of public utilities; but it had no staff and no budget. Utility appraisals were thrown together by an employee of the Revenue Department's Intangibles Tax Division in accordance with statutes that had not been revised since before the First World War. The fact that only rarely was the Board called on to hear appeals from the counties was clear evidence that local decisions seldom offended property owners.

I assumed the Institute's work with the Property Tax because we lost our man in that field, and someone had to keep the program going. But my grade as a student of taxation had almost eliminated me from law school, so I began the task with something very close to fear. But perhaps that fear, that honest sense of ignorance, stood me in good stead, for, from the first, you became my teachers, not the other way around. Together, I think we have had a wonderful time, and I candidly assert that we can take some pride in what has happened to North Carolina's Property Tax since 1947.

I found you a friendly and helpful set of people, associated in a weak organization headed by a few men and women who, with their successors, were the real pioneers in our state's Property Tax advancement. This is not the time to name them all, but I assure you that I could do so.

In our first years together, we spent our time learning the fundamentals of the Machinery Act of 1939, a pretty complex instrument, and as we hammered it out in annual conferences at the Institute, we learned the strengths and weaknesses of both our law and the way it was being administered. We came to understand that the office of county tax supervisor would always be weak if county commissioners, county finance officers, and county attorneys wanted to keep it that way. (Later we added county managers to that list.) We realized that we needed to bring those officials into our pattern for learning, and we did—at commissioners' conventions, in schools for finance officers, in conferences for attorneys, and through your constant efforts to educate them back home.

From the first I was troubled by your lack of training and lack of staff for real property revaluations. A few counties had spent substantial sums for professional assistance, but most counties had no love for outside help, especially if it cost a lot of money. I studied the work being done in other states; I even attended a school for assessors at the University of Connecticut. There, to my surprise, I found that the teaching was being done by the assessors themselves, some of them not doing a very good job of it. This convinced me that North Carolinians were potentially capable of doing the job as well or better. Thus, for a number of years, we devoted substantial portions of your annual conferences to appraisal discussions led by North Carolina tax people who had experience to share. Not until the late 1960's were we convinced that the courses offered by the International Association of Assessing Officers would be worthwhile for North Carolina. Now you use them regularly.

Perhaps the most daring step I took was to develop, publish, and offer you a manual for assessing real property for taxation in this state. Perhaps the most daring thing some North Carolina counties did was to adopt and use that manual. It was a crude beginning, but it was a start. We published the book in 1948; three years later, by accident, I learned that it had been translated into Japanese (without my permission) and used by the United States Military Government for tax appraisals in the City of Osaka. Such treatment for the property owners of Osaka demonstrated that the United States government still believed in strict Reconstruction.

As we learned more together, you moved to strengthen your office staffs. In 1953 the Institute offered its first course for new tax supervisors, and you and your Association worked with me to encourage experienced as well as new supervisors to attend. Those who came taught me a great deal, and we must have taught you something or else you would not have continued to support the school through the years. Just last month Joe Ferrell conducted the twenty-third of these fundamental courses. Similarly, your annual conferences here have become increasingly useful, even sophisticated.

The more we studied, the more we saw the need for changes in the law as well as in its administration. This knowledge, this gleam in your eyes, furnished the spark of initiative that has been the single most important force for Property Tax improvement in our history. Your determination led you to persuade commissioners, attorneys, and legislators to get moving and, together, you won the support of the North Carolina Association of County Commissioners before the legislature.

Now I will take a couple of minutes to point to some of the milestones in our progress:

In 1955 the General Assembly established the first of what became a series of commissions to study the revenue structure of the state, but when that commission made its report it contained no suggestions whatsoever about the locally administered Property Tax. Nevertheless, the General Assembly of 1957 set up a second Tax Study Commission that devoted a great deal of attention to the Property Tax, and its recommendations became the foundation for many of the changes that have taken place since. Together with Hudson Stansbury of the Department of Tax Research, I had the opportunity of working with that commission. Out of its study—fueled by your Association's ideas and initiative—counties obtained authority to establish uniform assessment ratios of less than 100%, thereby, for the first time, giving property owners a solid basis for questioning valuations by forcing county commissioners to record officially the basis on which property was being taxed. A giant step. From the same commission and the 1959 legislature came the 8-year mandatory revaluation schedule in place of the long ignored quadrennial mandate; and, finally, from these sources came authority for counties to levy a special tax that might be accumulated from year to year to pay for expensive revaluation programs—a major blow to the argument that financing good appraisals could not be accomplished under then-existing legal restrictions.

In 1961 you again stormed the General Assembly—through the recommendations of yet another study commission—to attack the shocking legislative habit of allowing individual counties to grant special local exemptions and preferential classifications. You had failed in this effort two years earlier, but this year you succeeded; and in the General Election of 1962 you had the satisfaction of seeing the voters adopt a constitutional amendment requiring that all exemptions and classifications be statewide in application.

As early as 1964 you trained your guns on our antiquated system for appraising the property of public utility companies. Here you took on more than one giant; not only did you shake the utilities in their comfortable tax bed but also you brought into question the effectiveness of an unfinanced and sparsely manned State Board of Assessment. I can testify to the dogged determination of your Association as its officers and legislative committees worked with successive Commissioners of Revenue to develop solutions that they could join you in proposing to the General Assembly. Those efforts began long before 1964, and at times the struggle was disheartening. I know because I was there. In 1966, however, a Tax Study Commission recommended some major changes; and with the strong backing of the County Commissioners Association and the League of Municipalities, the 1967 General Assembly was persuaded to give the State Board of Assessment its first full-time secretary and staff, to be financed—miracle of miracles—from the Intangibles Tax. But the 1967 legislature refused to adopt that commission's proposals for rewriting the statutes governing public utility property appraisal.

By 1969 your colleagues in tax collection had joined you in the movement for complete revision and modernization of the Machinery Act, and the General Assembly responded by establishing a special commission to deal with the Property Tax. Again, I had the opportunity of working with them, and this time Bill Campbell was with me.

There is no time in which to tell the story of the efforts that went into bringing that commission to the point where its members saw the issues and were willing to deal with them. Eventually, they produced the Machinery Act of 1971 which, except for the portions that treated exemptions and classifications, provided a completely new framework for the Property Tax. Five features of the 1971 act merit special mention: (1) For the first time, it required state certification of the qualifications of county tax supervisors. (2) It made the township list taker system optional. (3) It rewrote the discovered property statute to make clear that understatement of value was equivalent to failure to list. (4) It completely rewrote the public utility appraisal and allocation statutes. (5) And, finally, it effected a

196

sweeping repeal of the great bulk of local acts dealing with the Property Tax.

After enacting the revised statute, the 1971 legislature set up still another commission to tackle the thorny subject of exemptions and classifications. Once more we set to work.

Anyone who might have been naive about vested interests in exemptions and preferential classifications surely lost his innocence during that study. But from it, by action of the 1973 legislature, you gained a better organized and less ambiguous set of exemption and classification statutes. What you did not obtain was reduction in the volume of exemptions and preferential classifications. In fact, they were expanded, notably in favor of farm land, forest land, and property of the elderly.

In addition, the General Assembly of 1973 transformed the State Board of Assessment into the Property Tax Commission and established a Property Tax Division in the Department of Revenue; it also restored the 100% assessment mandate that had been dropped in 1959.

Other changes have been effected since 1973, but I will not mention them.

Not everyone is pleased with all the changes that took place or were set in motion between 1947 and 1973 when I was working with you. Some are unhappy with the substantially strengthened state role in supervision and influence; some are unhappy with the revised system of appraising and allocating public utility and similar property values; some fear that the multiplication of exemptions and preferential classifications is laying too heavy a burden on a decreasing set of taxable properties; and some are troubled by the side-effects of 100% assessment.

I share some of these fears; others I do not. I take heart, however, in two fundamental changes that took place during my Property Tax experience: First, the tax statutes were made much easier to understand; most of the hidden favors and pitfalls were removed. Second, the men and women who administer North Carolina's Property Tax law received better training and became far more knowledgeable than ever before. I warn you, however, that the maintenance of clear-cut tax laws demands constant effort by minds trained not merely in law but in North Carolina Property Tax law. If that warning is heeded, you will be able to locate trouble spots; and, with that knowledge, you will be far better equipped to eliminate them than were your predecessors in 1947.

Five years ago, when I was asked to become Director of the Institute of Government, I realized that if I accepted the post I would have to drop out of the Property Tax scene. This was my most difficult choice. I knew that taking the new job would mean that no more could I prod and push you, no more could I grapple with the questions you brought to me, and no more would I have the chance to work with those who studied, proposed, and drafted changes in the tax law. But when I realized that Joe Ferrell and Bill Campbell would be here to take on this work, I was happy and took the decision without regret. They are as good as the Institute's best, and you deserve them.

Now, the time has come for me to step aside completely—like an outdated copy of the Machinery Act, something of a curiosity but not something to rely on.

I add here something of my Institute experiences outside the property tax field.

When I joined the Institute of Government's small post-war staff in 1946 I had formed no firm ideas of what I hoped to do there, and when asked by Albert Coates where I would like to start could only tell him what I preferred not to do: I asked that he not assign me to criminal law (I had disliked the course in law school) or governmental personnel work (I had struggled with manpower classification and assignment for almost five years of military service). He suggested that I examine the efforts George Hampton had made in the thirties to prepare simplified versions of the North Carolina election laws for use by county and precinct officials. This study of both primary and general election laws and practice led me to look also at the subject of municipal elections and, eventually, every provision for special elections and referenda to be found in North Carolina law.

In 1948 I published my first set of instructions for use in party primaries and general elections, a manual that, under varying titles, I took through ten biennial editions until Rod Turnbull came to share the elections work in 1970.

Early in my experience with local election officials I had to face the dilemma posed when an Institute staff member found himself directly involved in partisan political affairs. And, by definition, nothing is more politically sensitive than the statutory and administrative framework in which primaries and general elections are conducted. From the first I made it my business to work as closely as possible with the person who happened to be serving as chairman of the State Board of Elections—often a significant figure in Democratic Party politics—and Raymond C. Maxwell, long the full-time executive secretary of that board. Without their counsel and criticism my work would have been academic and full of holes for the local officials faced with practical problems. I have always placed a high value on the fact that I gained Mr. Maxwell's confidence to the point that he was willing to join me in something theretofore unknown in North Carolina, instructional sessions for county boards of elections members and secretaries, sessions in which he and I shared the teaching assignments. Borrowing from my law school experience, I developed a system for teaching the election law through concrete examples—cases—that appealed to men and women more accustomed to dealing with factual situations than abstract principles.

My studies of the election laws of North Carolina and other states, coupled with the familiarity with the practical workings of those laws I had gained through twenty years of association with election officials were of inestimable help when I was called on to serve as counsel and draftsman for the commission established by the General Assembly of 1965 to revise and rewrite the election laws of the state. Although the commission's work was not intended to be revolutionary, it is clear that when the legislature of 1967 enacted the commission's draft, the North Carolina election laws were laid bare with a clarity that had not been exhibited since 1900, and the stage was set for whatever changes have taken place since 1967.

Late in 1947 I succeeded Peyton Abbott in the field of taxation, while continuing my work with election laws and election officials; and, in my eyes at least, I had a full load of work. But in those days, when the Institute staff was composed of fewer than a dozen faculty members, none could enjoy the luxury of uninterrupted specialization. I was just settling into the tax job when the Institute accepted the invitation of the City of Charlotte and Mecklenburg County to make the first broad study of the possibility of merging the two units of government or, if not the units, at least some of their functions. Naturally I became responsible for examining and analyzing the tax agencies of the county and city—an important and time-consuming step in my professional experience. Others from our staff had equally demanding responsibilities in other areas of study. For some reason that I have now forgotten, we found ourselves without staff to deal with the delicate issue of the public schools. Should the separate city and county school units be merged and, if so, on what basis? In the emergency, and with more loyalty than knowledge, I assumed the responsibility. Although I was competent to develop a legal analysis of the existing situation and propose alternative plans, I had no practical knowledge of school personnel and school politics. Nevertheless, I did my best to listen to the people charged with running the two systems, trying through questions to get a clear understanding of their fears of each other as well as the fundamental issues at stake. But when I came to write my report and offer reasonable possibilities for the future, I almost lost my nerve. I was overwhelmed with ignorance of the technicalities, and I was fearful that whatever I wrote could be decimated by both sets of school officials. In desperation, I decided to try to analyze the problem posed by the two school systems from the point of view of the private citizen and wrote:

> In an essentially adolescent community, it is imperative that plans for future educational development be made in terms of the geographical area, in terms of all the children and in terms of total resources.

In brief, I did what I would never recommend; I attempted to rely on common sense, a very weak weapon without the support power of broad knowledge of a field.

200

Six years later, no action having been taken, *The Charlotte News* began an editorial designed to spur merger by quoting what I have set out above and closed by saying:

> And Mr. Lewis shrewdly noted that "common business experience will make the citizens see chances for economy in one planning program, one building program, one maintenance program, as against two of each."

Not until 1960 did the Charlotte and Mecklenburg school systems become one. (The wheels of local government do not always race toward solutions proposed from outside.) I have quoted from the editorial not wholly in self-praise; I use it as evidence that the Institute faculty member does now and then have the satisfaction of appreciation, although it is rare and often delayed.

Earlier I mentioned my experience with the commission charged with election laws revision; that prompts me to mention the work I did with the series of commissions established to consider the reorganization of the administrative agencies of North Carolina state government. Although I had some responsibilities with several of these commissions, I will restrict my comments to my experience with the first of them. When the Institute was called upon to staff this commission, we felt both honored and (certainly in my case) timid. It was one thing to examine and analyze a unit of county or city government, but examination, analysis, and suggestions for change in an agency of state government—often with an important and well-known administrator—was a horse of distinctly different hue.

And to my lot fell the Department of Revenue, the Tax Review Board, the Department of Tax Research, and the State Board of Assessment. Although I was courteously received by the heads of these agencies, it was soon apparent that the Commissioner of Revenue, who played a dominant role in each, was resentful of what he considered an intrusion—and, worst of all, intrusion by a young fellow with little or no experience in state tax administration. (I could not dispute this analysis, but I had no choice but to proceed to the best of my ability.) Fortunately, the highly respected commission members lent their authority to my efforts, and the numerous division chiefs gave me generous help. At length, I produced a draft report in which I proposed that the reorganization commission recommend the repeal or revisal of a welter of statutory provisions and consider dropping, merging, or reorganizing some of the existing agencies I had examined.

It was unwavering Institute policy to submit reports and proposals for change (we always called them "alternatives") to the agency head directly affected *before* submitting them to the body to which we were to report. This served two purposes—errors of fact were likely to be discovered with less embarrassment, and, more significant psychologically, the person whose agency was being examined could not later assert that he had been surprised by the report. I followed the procedure and made copies of my draft available to the affected agency heads. Time passed, and I received no response from the Commissioner of Revenue, no request that I come to his office for discussion, no written criticisms or suggestions. The day arrived on which I was scheduled to give an oral summary of my work to the full commission. As I entered the Pines Restaurant, where the members had assembled, a Revenue Department representative handed me a thick envelope, saying that the Commissioner had asked him to deliver it to me in person. When the others sat down to enjoy dinner, I lost my appetite; I discovered that the Commissioner had treated my draft as if it were a complaint in a civil action and, paragraph-by-paragraph, he had answered. It was a chilling experience, but I was convinced that he had misinterpreted both the purpose and the purport of what I had written. At that moment, called on to make my oral presentation, I took the only course open to me: I summarized each element of my report, summarized the Commissioner's response to it, then did my best to clarify the issues for the study commission members without taking undue advantage of the Commissioner's absence. Governor Hodges was presiding that evening, a circumstance not calculated to ease my burden, but I do not think I disgraced the Institute. Most of my proposals were adopted, and from the experience I developed friendships with Frank Taylor, William B. Rodman, and others in state government that stood me in good stead throughout my Institute career.

I hope what I have written will be of some help. Since I know that you want something of the flavor of the Institute experience, I have dropped modesty and have written of some of the things that happened to me that produced a bit of praise as well as some of the less rewarding experiences.

Donald Hayman

I started to work for the Institute on April 1, 1948 as a temporary research assistant. The Institute had received several requests for "personnel studies" after World War II, but the Institute's lawyers politely resisted such assignments. Henry Lewis who had done military personnel work for five years was deep in taxes and elections. Terry Sanford had been given the assignments but preferred working with Boys' State, the Highway Patrol, etc. And so the day after Terry entered the private practice of law in his home town, I was given several of the postponed personnel projects.

Evidently I was hired because I had three years experience doing personnel work for the U.S. Department of Labor in Washington. I had completed course work for a Ph.D. in political science from the University of North Carolina and was looking for a dissertation topic and work which would permit my wife and year-old daughter to eat while I completed degree requirements. Mr. Coates asked that I complete the postponed projects and then write a book on public personnel administration in North Carolina which might serve as my dissertation. I developed an outline for such a twelve-chapter study. Professor Charles B. Robson, chairman of the Department of Political Science, urged me to take the position. He wished to bridge the gap between the Department and the Institute. Although bridging the gap was to prove far more difficult than I naively anticipated, I was the first political scientist employed by the Institute of Government.

Thirty-two plus years later I am still challenged by the need for research in public personnel and local administration, by the daily requests for information, and by the opportunity to learn of current personnel and administrative problems from public officials, and by the rewards of planning and directing training for public officials and teaching courses in the Department of Political Science. The postponed projects awaiting me were quickly followed by new assignments. I wished to learn more about North Carolina state and local administration before writing my dissertation. The twelve-chapter book on public personnel administration is still not written. Fortunately, the Department of Political Science accepted one of the twelve chapters, a 173-page book, as my dissertation. Mr. Coates had offered me an opportunity to work "morning, noon, and night, weekdays and on Sunday," and I have enjoyed nearly every minute of the privilege.

My first year was devoted to four projects. The first was a guidebook for law enforcement officers explaining the provisions of the Law Enforcement Officers' Benefit and Retirement Fund. Henry Bridges had just assumed the duties of State Auditor. As chairman of the board of LEOBRF, he and the law enforcement officers of the state were concerned that officers were poorly informed as to their retirement benefits. Lack of information tends to increase suspicion, distrust and dissatisfaction. Suspicion is a common reaction of most of us to people who handle our money. It is an occupational necessity among investigative enforcement personnel. The resulting guidebook explained the provisions of the retirement system and contained worksheets which permitted officers for the first time to calculate their future retirement benefits. The guidebook may have increased understanding and contributed to more officers joining the fund and later to amendments which increased benefits while making the fund more actuarially sound.

The second project involved revising the process for selecting highway patrol recruits. Students in the first recruit school in 1946 were selected by interview panels composed of senior highway patrol officers. When only 53 of the 110 entering the course graduated, the need for a more systematic selection procedure was recognized. Terry Sanford secured the first standardized tests which the highway patrol used in making selections for the second school. By adopting more appropriate standardized tests and physical exams, and more standardized oral examinations, the failure rate was reduced to an average of five to ten per cent. In the absence of a formal state merit system for state funded programs this work led to my assisting the Highway Patrol, Department of Motor Vehicles, and Wildlife Commission in the competitive selection and promotion of employees for fifteen years or until 1963 when the State Personnel Department began offering such a service.

The third project, an in-depth study of the problems and practices of city and county personnel administration, was a part of the Charlotte-Mecklenburg County consolidation study. This project permitted me to examine in detail the statutory, organizational and administrative personnel problems of North Carolina's largest city and county government. I am still appreciative of the time and assistance the public officials of Charlotte and Mecklenburg County gave me in serving as my teachers. The immediate result was more rewarding for me than for the governmental units. I increased my understanding of a wide range of personnel problems and felt better prepared to assist other jurisdictions. Although both governmental units adopted some of the suggestions immediately, others were adopted ten and twenty years later.

Fourth, in 1949 the Institute was asked to provide assistance in drafting legislation to establish a modern personnel system for North Carolina state government. My analysis was first used by Mayne Albright, Clifton Beckwith, and Otis Banks in drafting the 1949 State Personnel bill and later by Senator Joe Eagles in securing numerous amendments to the bill. The result was a compromise which served the state until 1965.

These studies at both the local and state levels were the beginning of the Institute's research, consulting, and training programs in personnel administration. The first four projects opened areas of work which consumed a majority of my time for ten years.

Since the early 1950's, I have been privileged to (1) advise state and local governments on organizational problems, (2) plan and participate in training programs for city and county managers, personnel officers and many groups of state, county and municipal employees, (3) teach, advise and place students desiring public service careers, and (4) supervise the preparation of job evaluation, compensation and a variety of other studies.

Organizations. In 1950 thirty cities and five counties had managers. In 1980, one hundred twenty-four cities and eighty-four counties had managers. I have tried to be factual in pointing out the advantages and disadvantages of every form of government and practice. If I have strayed from objectivity in any presentation, it has been in describing the disadvantages of the city and county manager plan. North Carolina has been fortunate in having a growing number of honest, conscientious, hardworking, professional managers. They have anticipated problems, planned ahead, and initiated improved administrative practice. On some occasions I have been incapable of thinking of as many reasons for not adopting the manager plan as reasons for adopting it. It has been a pleasure to work with the N. C. League of Municipalities and more recently with the County Commissioners Association in visiting governmental units and providing information to governing boards or councils at the time they were considering the adoption of the manager plan.

Research for the State Reorganization Commission led me in 1953 to edit the first Handbook of N.C. Administrative Agencies. Research studies in personnel and natural resource administration over four bienniums resulted in minor changes in state organization. That research led the State Treasurer to request that the Institute study the financial soundness of every retirement system in North Carolina and the feasibility of bringing state and local employees under Social Security. The study was followed by referenda for both state and local retirement systems. Employees of the state and all of the counties have been brought under Social Security. Most municipal employees except a few firemen and policemen have also been given social security coverage.

My 1953 study was followed by Fayetteville and Union County abolishing their unsound retirement systems. Although attention was focused upon the four other unsound retirement systems, they were not immediately abolished. Efforts have since been largely successful in reducing their membership and increasing their actuarial soundness. Most of the recommendations of the 1953 study were adopted within ten years. Although the study has not been criticized since the 1957 heated debate preceding the elections to bring state and most local employees under Social Security, I should have thought bigger and set longer range goals which would have required twenty years to achieve.

I have also worked for a number of other legislative committees and study commissions on such topics as rewriting the state personnel act in 1965 and amending it in 1976 and 1977, state and local employee relations (collective bargaining) in 1970-71, and school board-school employee relations in 1975.

Training. The rapid growth of the city and county manager plan led to a demand for more professional managers and for requests for trained staff to assist the new managers. As early as 1950, I proposed that the Institute cooperate with the Department of Political Science in supporting a Master of Public Administration program. Failing to secure the necessary agreement, five of us on the Institute staff started the municipal administration course to train persons already in local government for positions of increasing responsibility. George Esser led in developing the course. George, Alex McMahon, Philip Green, Henry Lewis and I taught in the course. In the first years I taught over a fourth of this course. After George Esser resigned, Warren Wicker assumed administrative responsibility for coordinating this course. A total of 1,420 public officials graduated from the municipal and county administration course in 25 years. This unique course has familiarized many new public administrators with North Carolina local government law and practice. It has also introduced public officials to the Institute's staff and vice versa. Later we would call on these public officials for help and they would call upon us when legal and administrative problems arose.

In 1953 I planned and directed an institute for personnel officers. The annual institute was formalized in 1958 by the chartering of the North Carolina Chapter of the Public Personnel Association. Now functioning independently of the Institute of Government except as to secretarial services, the chapter sponsors regional meetings in addition to the annual spring conference. Warren Wicker assumed my responsibilities as secretary in 1964 and has continued to serve in that capacity.

In 1953 the Institute of Government was asked to join with the North Carolina Chapter of the International Association of Personnel in Employment Security and the Employment Security Commission to conduct an annual two-day training institute for ESC employees. Mr. Coates asked me to plan and coordinate these institutes. Soon the program committees gained increasing confidence and my role became that of a consultant and eventually a facilitator. After 25 years this annual institute became too large for the Joseph Palmer Knapp Building, and I withdrew as coordinator. The institutes have continued to flourish.

As city and county managers became more numerous in the state, they expressed a need for refresher courses which would be more substantive than their annual conventions. Beginning in 1961, George Esser led in planning two two-day institutes. Later responsibility for two sessions only a month apart became burdensome and a single two and a half day institute was substituted. After the formation of the N.C. City and County Managers' Association in 1964, the session became a joint seminar with the association actively participating in planning the sessions. Since 1966, I have coordinated these manager seminars with the assistance of Warren Wicker and other members of the staff.

In 1959 the Employment Security Commission asked the Institute to conduct management development workshops and training programs for counselors. In 1962-63 and in 1964 the management development workshops were expanded to include additional topics and were offered to state constitutional officers, department and division heads. Between 1968 and 1973 the Institute cooperated with the Office of State Personnel in conducting 40 five-day management development workshops for supervisors. During the 1970's similar one-week workshops were offered employees of local governments by the Institute in Chapel Hill and on a regional basis. During the 1960's and 1970's I planned and directed workshops on employee-employer relations, performance appraisal, and on preparing for retirement. Workshops on the former topics continue to be a part of the Institute's program in 1980.

Teaching and Placement of College Students. In order to attract more college students into professional positions in local government, the Institute began teaching a course in municipal administration in the Department of Political Science in 1955. George Esser was responsible for this course, but Philip Green and I taught portions of it. After George Esser's resignation in 1963, I was responsible for the course and for the personnel administration course offered by the Department of Political Science. Until 1966 I coordinated the joint venture of the political science, industrial relations, education and psychology faculties in offering the master's degree in personnel administration. I represented the Institute in planning and establishing the Masters of Public Administration program in 1966. I have taught in that program, served as a member of the admission committee from 1966-1979, placed graduate students in internships since 1967, and supervised the major papers of numerous students who are today successful administrators.

In order to give college students opportunities to learn about government in action, in 1966 I began helping college students secure summer internships in local government. Between 1966 and 1971 as many as forty-nine students a year served internships and attended Institute sponsored seminars. This program was reduced in size as UNC at Greensboro and UNC at Charlotte established similar programs.

In August 1962 immediately after the close of the first state government summer intern program, Ray Ferris and Joel Fleishman asked the Institute to provide assistance in recruiting, selecting and providing orientation training for summer interns in state government. The interns were placed in state departments for eleven weeks during the summer and given an opportunity to learn about the problems and opportunities of North Carolina government while working in a state department forty hours a week. I have worked with this program since 1962 and have directed the program for all but two years since 1965 when it was officially transferred from the office of the Governor to the Institute. Working with the 448 interns in this program from 1962-80 has been an extremely rewarding experience. It is thrilling to see them learn and achieve what they might have considered impossible at the beginning of the summer. Many have raised their level of aspiration and assumed positions of political, administrative or civic leadership in North Carolina and the nation. Perhaps the greatest reward of this program is the number of interns who have resolved following their internship to remain in the state or return to North Carolina after completing their education. I have been privileged to serve as a member of the North Carolina Internship Council since it was established in 1978.

In order to help both students and public officials learn more of the theory and practice of public administration, I have worked with the American Society for Public Administration. I organized the chapter as a graduate student and served as the first president of the North Carolina Chapter (now Research Triangle Chapter). I have served continuously as a chapter officer since 1951 except when on leave. The quarterly meetings of the chapter permit students, professors, and federal, state and local administrators to meet, discuss current problems, and exchange views concerning public administration.

In order to attract and retain promising employees and trained professionals, public employment in the 1950's had to be made more competitive. In 1950 I published a study of minimum qualifications and compensation of municipal law enforcement officers and a study of the salaries of county employees. A subsequent county salary study in 1952 outlined the problems when employees were compensated by fees and/or by local acts. When the late representative John B. Regan of Robeson County read the study, he introduced and secured the passage of legislation eliminating both practices, and made county commissioners responsible for determining the number, salaries, and conditions of employment of county employees. The county salary study has been continued for thirty years and now Mrs. Elizabeth Pace supervises its annual preparation and publication.

With the increase in the size and complexity of local government, employees and governing boards complained that employees did not receive equal pay for equal work. The Institute was asked to prepare classification and pay plans and personnel resolutions. As the Employment Security Commission agreed to work in this area as a service to local government, I publicized their willingness and prepared pay plans to accompany their classification plans. Since 1956 Elizabeth Pace, Warren J. Wicker, Jim Kweder, and I and fourteen MPA students have prepared classification and pay plans for 28 counties and 53 cities; at least once for each of these counties and cities and three times for several of them.

In 1956 I saw the need for a model personnel ordinance. Although I recognized my own inadequacy, I prepared such a model which has served as a starting place for many of the governmental units of the state which have subsequently adopted a personnel ordinance. In 1976 and 1977 Lynn Burleson and I prepared four model personnel ordinances: for a manager city and county, a mayor city, and a commissioner county. These models have been published by the Local Government Section of the N. C. Office of State Personnel. Many of the personnel ordinances presently in use in medium and smaller cities and counties in North Carolina are variations of one of these models.

When the federal Intergovernmental Personnel Act was passed in 1971, the Institute was asked to increase its training activity and to investigate the training opportunities for first-line supervisors. Richard P. Calhoon and Tom Jerdee, professors in the School of Business Administration, prepared such a study for the Institute. They surveyed the training opportunities for first-line supervisors, by contacting 1,521 first- and second-level governmental supervisors as to their perception of their training needs, and developed a 20-hour Coaching in Supervision course. The employee's booklet and Instructor's Manual have been used widely in training supervisors by federal, state, local governments and community colleges. Both were reissued in 1981 with the help of a second Intergovernmental Personnel Act grant. I coordinated this research and arranged numerous workshops to train supervisors and instructors in using the materials. I served on the North Carolina IPA Advisory Committee from 1972 to 1978.

My greatest satisfaction comes from seeing the accomplishments of the students and officials I have been privileged to meet and work with. Their desire to learn, their energy, analytical ability, creativeness, dedication and success in their endeavors is a continuing inspiration. I was the beneficiary of their achievements in 1978 when I was the first North Carolinian to be named an honorary member of the International City Management Association.

Philip Green

My entry into the field of land-use planning and regulation in June, 1949, was marked by most of the advantages and disadvantages of an almost-clean slate.

I myself knew almost nothing about the field—my only contact having been class discussion of two Supreme Court zoning decisions in a Constitutional Law course in Law School.

The Institute of Government had had greater experience than I but hardly a "program" in the field. During World War II it had co-sponsored a series of conferences on Post-War Planning. And it had assisted in the creation and financing of a graduate-level Department of City and Regional Planning in the University in 1947, for which William M. Cochrane had twice taught a course on Planning Law and Administration.

Fortunately, our state and local governmental clients had had relatively little exposure to planning, so they didn't know what they were missing. Although over 80 of North Carolina's colonial and early post-Revolution towns (plus many of the "company towns" of the late 19th century) were pre-planned, the concept of planning as a continuing process of government had barely taken root by 1949. There were only three full-time planning departments in the state (two city and one city-county) and about 30 active local planning boards, while the legislature had allowed the State Planning Board of 1935-47 to die. (In contrast, by 1980 there were 59 city planning departments, 49 county planning departments, and 18 regional planning staffs; 314 city planning and zoning boards, 85 county planning boards, and 18 regional planning commissions;

several state planning agencies as well as a broad-scale local planning assistance program at the state level; and a myriad of special-purpose boards such as appearance commissions, historic district commissions, environmental protection commissions, etc.)

Truly it was a case of the blind being called upon to lead the blind!

My first assignment was to prepare a guidebook on zoning. In lawyer-like fashion, I began this effort by reading and digesting the North Carolina municipal zoning enabling act, the opinions in the 20 zoning cases decided by the state Supreme Court, and the four U.S. Supreme Court zoning cases. Then I was ready to read the three or four standard texts in the field. Next came a detailed analysis of the provisions of some 25 zoning ordinances found in the Institute library or made available to us by the N.C. League of Municipalities. This gave me my initial "feel" for what zoning was all about.

At this point, as Mr. Coates would say, the ripples began to widen. To provide a legal background against which zoning might be better understood, I analyzed, recorded, and described all North Carolina statutes, court opinions, and (where available) local ordinances dealing with property-related nuisances, restrictive covenants, fire limits, building regulations, filling station regulations, planning boards, housing authorities, subdivision regulation, sanitary districts, hospital districts, drainage districts, agricultural development districts, soil conservation districts, and the state rural rehabilitation law.

Having initially completed the "law library" portion of my study, I finally began to contact real live zoning officials: city planners, building inspectors, board of adjustment members, planning board members, and the like. I interviewed officials in Charlotte, Durham, and Winston-Salem at length, seeking to identify their problems, understand their procedures, and learn their functions in detail. I reviewed their records, secured copies of their forms, read their minutes, and talked with them both in their offices and at their homes. All of this was faithfully logged, and I began to see ways in which I might be of help to them.

One problem sent me back to the law library. It became apparent that boards of adjustment were generally confused as to the rules they should follow in dispensing justice, and there appeared to be no handy guide for them. There were relatively few North Carolina cases concerning their functions. So I explored at length the case law from other states, and on the basis of this put together what I believed to be the first set of rules in print for such boards.

All of this was ultimately written up, edited, revised, re-edited, and turned over to the printer. Finally, after six months of proofreading and corrections, it was published as a 430-page book called *Zoning in North Carolina* in the spring of 1952—almost three years after I began.

This doesn't mean that I was sitting idly on my hands. Mr. Coates never felt contented when he had less then three or four projects under way at one time, nor did he allow us the luxury of focusing on one thing at a time.

By the time the zoning book was published, I had thrice taught the semester-long course on Planning Law and Administration for the Department of City and Regional Planning (striving mightily to keep a class or two ahead of my students as I explored more broadly the full range of activities involved in local planning programs); had taught about a third of the Law School's course on Municipal Corporations in collaboration with George Esser and Alex McMahon for three successive years; had started holding monthly meetings of the few professional planners in the state beginning in January, 1950, had become their permanent secretary when they formally organized as the North Carolina Section of the American Institute of Planners in December, 1951; had written and published a 375-page, 3-volume *Guidebook for City Planning Boards*; had made and published a study of rural fire protection programs in the state; had made and published studies of fire protection, building regulation and inspection, and water and sewerage services in Charlotte and Mecklenburg County, as parts of a city-county consolidation study; in collaboration with Ernest Machen and Donald Hayman had made and published a study of stream pollution in North Carolina and developed the state's first comprehensive stream sanitation legislation; had studied and published a report on roadside

214

control and development measures for a Highway Safety Study Commission; had analyzed administrative procedures of six state departments and agencies for a State Administrative Procedure Study; had written nine articles on miscellaneous subjects for publication in *Popular Government* and another for the *North Carolina Law Review*; had audited two courses offered by the Department of City and Regional Planning; had served a stint on the Institute's legislative reporting service in Raleigh; had reviewed proposed zoning ordinances and answered inquiries from city and county officials concerning planning and land-use regulation; and had prepared a new perimeter zoning ordinance for the town of Chapel Hill. One might say there was never a dull moment.

Zoning in North Carolina and *A Guidebook for City Planning Boards* were distributed to planning board members, zoning administrators, board of adjustment members, and other interested officials at a series of two-day district meetings in the Fall of 1952. At the conclusion of these meetings I felt I had enough grasp of the field to take stock of where we stood in our overall program for planners and related officials.

First, I listed the many types of people involved in local planning:

1. Professional planners, either working in local planning departments or serving as consultants

2. Students preparing for careers as professional planners or attorneys

3. Sub-professional planners—lower level personnel in planning departments

4. Local board members
   a. Governing boards
   b. Planning boards
   c. Zoning boards of adjustment
   d. Housing authorities
   e. (Later: redevelopment commissions, economic development commissions, appearance commissions, historic district commissions, historic properties commissions, environmental advisory boards)

5. Other local officials more or less directly involved with planning programs
   a. Managers
   b. Attorneys
   c. Building inspectors, housing inspectors, zoning administrators, etc.
   d. Engineers
   e. Housing authority directors and urban redevelopment directors (and later: community development directors)
   f. Health officers
   g. Registers of deeds

6. Citizen groups and individuals

7. The Governor and the various state departments and agencies

8. The General Assembly and legislative study commissions

Next, I considered what I had offered or was offering to each of these groups, so that I could identify gaps and set priorities. There was an on-going program for *professional planners*, for whom I was holding monthly meetings with programs on topics of interest to them, assisting in the development of legislative proposals (including bill drafting), reporting on legislation enacted by the General Assembly, and answering their inquiries. For *students* I was teaching courses on planning law both in the Department of City and Regional Planning and in the Law School. For *board members* and *related officials* I had written the two major books and a series of *Popular Government* articles, held one series of meetings, and answered inquiries. For the other potential clients I had done precious little.

On the basis of this analysis I planned a comprehensive program of stepped-up activities which would touch all of the clients in varied ways. Unfortunately, the next five years brought so many diversions that I was hard put to maintain the programs already in being. But the analysis became the basis for the enormous flowering of our planning program which began in 1958.

The diversions took the form of other assignments: to participate in a study of Guilford County's organization in 1953; to participate in studies for the Commission on Reorganization of State Government from 1953 through 1959, with responsibility for overall coordination of that work in the 1955-57 biennium; to serve as editor of *Popular Government* for 1954, 1955, and 1956; to work on our legislative reporting service and serve as editor of our Legislative Summary in 1955 and to serve as director of the service during a special short session of the General Assembly in 1956 and its regular session in 1957; and to assume many administrative responsibilities as an assistant to Mr. Coates.

There were a few advances in the planning field in this period. In 1953 I published *Cases and Materials on the Law of City Planning in North Carolina* for my Law School teaching, as well as serving on the organizing committee of a Roanoke Congress on City Planning sponsored by the Southern Regional Education Board and undertaking preparation of new planning legislation. In 1954 I held a week-long course on basic city planning techniques for sub-professional planners and related officials. I attempted (with partial success) to produce at least one *Popular Government* article on a planning-related topic for each issue. Periodically I mailed out materials on special subjects to board members. The volume of inquiries increased. And most important of all, in 1955 the Institute began holding its annual 160-hour course in Municipal Administration for managers, department heads, and persons aspiring to such posts, which enabled me to bring a substantial amount of background material on the nature and conduct of local planning programs to an important audience.

The most frustrating activity of this period was a major study of industrial development programs which extended through several years. The first eight chapters of this publication were complete and in stencil form, with the first draft of the remaining chapters almost finished, when I was forced by other assignments to put it on the back burner and ultimately abandon it.

The winter of 1957-58 was the major turning point in the development of the Institute's activities in the planning field. Ruth L. Mace and Robert E. Stipe joined our faculty, bringing new talents, insights, and manpower, and their impact was immediately noticeable. Both had master's degrees in City and Regional Planning, and Bob Stipe also had a law degree. His knowledge filled in vast areas of ignorance in my background, and his extraordinary diligence led to undreamed-of expansion of our program. For almost 17 years, until he left to become head of the state's Division of Archives and History, we worked as a team in the closest and happiest association I have ever experienced.

Rather than describing our activities year-by-year, it will be easier to comprehend our total program in terms of the clients outlined earlier.

For *students*, I published *Cases and Materials on Planning Law and Administration* for the Planning Department course and, in collaboration with George Esser and Alex McMahon, *Cases and Materials in Local Government Law* for the Law School course. Bob started teaching a segment of an undergraduate course in Municipal Administration in the Political Science Department, a segment of traffic engineering course at North Carolina State University, a planning course at Shaw University, a course on urban design in the Planning Department, and segments of an introductory course in that department. In the 1960's we began to rotate responsibility for the course on Planning Law and Administration in alternate years.

For *professional planners*, while continuing our earlier program, we began to offer a series of one- to three-day seminars on specialized subjects, such as "Perception and Environment," "Underground Wiring," "British New Towns," "Rural Zoning," and "Development Timing." I compiled and published *Planning Legislation in North Carolina* in 1957 and continued biennial revisions. Bob offered detailed review and consultation concerning subdivision regulations, urban aesthetics, mapping for planning, and historic preservation. In the later '60's he achieved national recognition with a series of one-week courses on historic preservation. And for a time we reviewed and commented on almost every zoning ordinance or subdivision regulation adopted anywhere in the state.

For *sub-professional planners* and *related officials* Bob initiated and taught with distinction a series of two-week short courses in basic city planning techniques, after which he helped the state's new local planning assistance agency to take over continuing responsibility for this program.

For *local board members* we began in 1958 an annual North Carolina Planning Conference which has continued to the present. Bob and I traveled all over the state holding one-day schools for mayors and governing boards, for planning boards, and for boards of adjustment; some of these were "orientation" schools for new board members and some were schools on special topics of interest at the time. (Fortunately the emergence of a well-staffed state-level local planning assistance agency with regional offices reduced this work load before it became overwhelming.) In addition we taught segments of the Institute's newly-established biennial courses for new mayors and councilmen and for new county commissioners. We decided that *Zoning in North Carolina* and *A Guidebook for City Planning Boards* were too big a dose for the average board member, so we published a series of 50-100 page publications: *City Planning in North Carolina, An Introduction to Municipal Zoning, An Introduction to County Planning, An Introduction to Subdivision Regulations, Organization for Local Governmental Planning, Regulating the Subdivision of Land*, and *Enforcement of the Zoning Ordinance*. These were distributed in numbers sufficient for every board member to have an individual copy. Even this appeared to be too much for the average board member to read, so after Bob's departure Michael Brough and others prepared audio-visual materials for training board members plus a series of four to eight-page *Planning Memoranda* on smaller topics which were designed ultimately to make up a working manual for planning board members. Finally, there was an increased flow of *Popular Government* articles aimed at board members, which has continued more recently under the pen of Richard Ducker.

Our activities aimed at *other officials involved with planning* also expanded greatly. We began regular participation in seminars for city and county managers. Ruth Mace began a newsletter for local redevelopment officials; we also participated in their programs, and I worked with their attorneys in developing biennial legislative programs. We began publishing, with periodic supplements, a compilation of *North Carolina Supreme Court Cases on Zoning, Subdivision Regulation, and Urban Renewal* as an aid to city and county attorneys, and we regularly participated in their conferences when they formally organized associations in the 1960's. We taught major portions of Institutes on local government law sponsored by the N.C. Bar Association.

We began in the 1960's an extensive program for building inspectors, beginning with a basic course on building code enforcement, adding an advanced course, and then adding one-week courses on zoning administration and housing code enforcement. This program led eventually to our playing a major role in the creation of a state-level certification program for all local code officials, with training programs decentralized throughout the state through its community colleges and technical institutes. As part of these programs I have issued multiple editions of *Legal Responsibilities of Local Building Inspectors in North Carolina, Legal Responsibilities of the Local Plumbing Inspector in North Carolina, Legal Responsibilities of the Local Housing Inspector in North Carolina,* and *Legal Responsibilities of the Local Zoning Administrator in North Carolina.*

We reached out to other officials. One of the North Carolina Planning Conferences was focused on problems of environmental health, and half our attendance was from health officers and others in that field. We hosted a national workshop of the National Association of Housing and Redevelopment officials. We hosted a regional conference of the American Association of State Highway Officials, devoted to highway planning. We hosted several conferences for state and local industrial development officials in the state. We participated in annual conferences of registers of deeds, tax supervisors, and city and county recreation officials, as well as occasional conferences of city engineers and public works directors.

For the first time we made significant efforts to reach *citizen groups* interested in planning. We co-sponsored with Sears Roebuck and Company a major conference on civic improvement, to which the company bused hundreds of garden club members, members of civic clubs, etc. On Ruth Mace's initiative, we set up a seminar series on central business district problems with attendance from local business men, chambers of commerce, and local government officials from seven North Carolina cities, followed up by publication of *Guidelines for Business Leaders and City Officials to a New Central Business District*. She also made an extensive study of public and private industrial development programs in the state and published *Industry and City Government*. In cooperation with the National Council of Churches, we held a well-attended conference for planners and churchmen. Bob Stipe taught in annual Realtors' Institutes held by the School of Business Administration and in conferences of the North Carolina Merchants' Association. All of us talked to a variety of local preservation societies, garden clubs, 4-H clubs, women's clubs, civic clubs, and similar organizations. And Bob played a central role in planning for and conducting the Governor's Conference on Beautification in 1966.

At the *state government* level, we served on a variety of agencies advising the Governor, including the Advisory Committee on Low Income Housing, the Technical Advisory Committee on Area Development, and the Advisory Committee on Beautification. At various times we gave significant assistance to the Department of Conservation and Development, especially in its industrial development programs, its mapping programs, and its regulation of surface mining; the Department of Local Affairs, particularly in training programs for local planners; the Department of Natural Resources and Community Development and the Coastal Resources Commission in developing and implementing the Coastal Area Management Act; the Recreation Commission, especially in a compilation of recreation laws; the Division of Archives and History, in a number of historic preservation projects and courses; and the Division of Engineering and Building Codes of the Department of Insurance, the State Building Code Council, and the North Carolina Code Officials Qualification Board, with reference to improvement of the state's building laws and training programs for code officials.

We assisted the General Assembly and various legislative study commissions in the development of a great deal of planning-related legislation. The Commission on Reorganization of State Government in the latter half of the 1950's, the Municipal Government Study Commission of 1957-59, and the Local Government Study Commission of 1967-74 (for all of whom the Institute furnished staff services) produced a tremendous amount of legislation of interest to planners. In addition, the North Carolina Section (later Chapter) of the American Institute of Planners and the directors and attorneys of the state's urban redevelopment commissions used our services on a biennial basis for the preparation of legislative programs, drafting of bills, and monitoring of legislative activity—and much of this legislation was enacted.

And finally, our program provided another type of assistance to local governments. Over the years we actively participated in two major city-county consolidation studies for Charlotte and Mecklenburg County, two similar studies for Durham and Durham County, and one for Sanford and Lee County. In all of these our role was to describe existing planning-related elements in the government and suggest alternative ways in which the proposed units could organize their planning programs in the event of consolidation. While none of these efforts resulted in successful consolidations, they offered us convenient forums in which we could present additional suggestions, many of which were adopted.

All of these activities were illuminated and informed by professional contacts and experiences beyond the borders of the state. Both Bob Stipe (in 1968-69) and I (in 1963-64) were awarded Senior Fulbright Research Fellowships in London, on the basis of which we were able to make useful comparisons between the English system of land use regulation and our own. For many years he served on the executive committee of the Board of Trustees of the National Trust for Historic Preservation. I had a comparable experience as a member for ten years of the Advisory Committee for the American Law Institute's Model Land Development Code project.

Both of us served in a variety of positions in the American Institute of Planners, its Southeast Chapter, and its North Carolina Section; made multiple appearances at conventions of the above groups and the American Society of Planning Officials; and taught at classes and conferences offered by many universities both here and abroad. And we got down into the trenches of local government to serve three terms each on the Chapel Hill Board of Adjustment and the Chapel Hill Community Appearance Commission.

Lee Bounds

Lee Bounds started working with the Governor, the Chairman of the State Highway and Public Works Commission, and the operating staff of the state prison system, at the beginning of the 1950's. He was both apprentice and assistant in succession to practically every successive division head, and the overall directors of the state prison system. He analyzed their powers and duties, outlined their operating practices and procedures, wrote them into guidebooks, taught them in training schools which he organized in every division of the prison system.

All of the administrative heads of the state prison system with whom he worked would agree that Lee Bounds did most if not all of the backbone research which was the underpinning of their innovative programs, helped to formulate most if not all of the policies behind them, drafted most if not all of the legislation which brought these programs to life, wrote most if not all of the departmental rules and regulations to carry them into action, and provided a resulting continuity and a growing comprehensiveness of vision that no one of them was in a position to supply.

The Director of the Department of Prisons under whom Lee Bounds served had this to say about Lee's work:

> Since assuming my responsibilities as Director of Prisons, I have found that one of the major deficiencies in the North Carolina Prison Department is due to the lack of written policies and until these policies can be formulated, it is my opinion that North Carolina will never have a sound penal system.
>
> Therefore, in light of the above fact we sought advice and guidance of the Institute of Government with the result that Lee Bounds was assigned to the Prison Department to assist us in our mission. The result is that not only have we formulated twenty-four prison policies, but we have completely revised the basic organization. Without the help of the Institute of Government and Mr. Bounds, all

of this would have been impossible. It is my sincere hope that the Institute of Government can continue to render this fine service to the Prison Department as we have only made a beginning. Many more policies must be formulated; after this, a training program in order to familiarize our personnel with the contents of each policy.

The Governor of North Carolina said this:

Soon after I became Governor I learned the State was paying the Institute of Government a substantial amount for consulting services in connection with the State prison system and that Lee Bounds was the individual who was providing these services. I further learned Lee was an expert in the field and had been primarily responsible for designing the successful work-release program and other forward-looking innovations in the system. I decided it would be sensible to acquire his full-time services as Director of our prison system rather than to continue this consulting relationship, and in October, 1965, he finally agreed to accept the challenge to help provide North Carolina with a modern penal system.

He went before the General Assembly and the public generally and informed them not only about the good things in the system but especially some of the intolerable conditions existing which required correction. The prison employees were undertrained and underpaid. Many of the buildings were out of date and thoroughly inadequate. Living conditions of the inmates in many instances were degrading and dangerous.

He was constantly seeking more funds for training and paying personnel, devising new programs and advocating better living conditions and more humane treatment for the inmates.

His campaign for funds to correct some of the existing conditions gradually began to bear fruit. The pay for personnel was increased. Better training was initiated. College graduates were recruited, and funds for capital improvements were increased. Hospital facilities at Central Prison were improved, and in 1967 the General Assembly appropriated $4.2 million for a new medium security prison to be constructed near Morganton. This building was designed by Lee and his associates to alleviate the conditions created by the design and the crowded conditions in some of the older buildings. New work programs and new training courses for the prisoners were devised. The prison administration was reorganized. Many of his forward-looking goals were being reached. My original faith in his ability was completely confirmed.

Lee is now Kenan Professor in the Political Science Department where he is bringing to his students the results of his studies and researches in the Institute of Government and his experience in working on the job with the Department of Prisons which became the Department of Correction during his administration.

Bob Campbell

One day I, B. J. Campbell, doctoral student in Psychology, was called to the chairman's office. It was the spring of 1955, and the chairman said there was a job possibility for a psychologist at the Institute of Government. The job was to involve construction of driver license examination and teaching of Department of Motor Vehicle employees.

She asked me if I was interested in this part-time job to support my graduate training. I said yes and set off to see Mr. Coates. Before I left, Dorothy Adkins, in her gruff but motherly way, told me I must wear a suit to suitably impress the lawyers at the Institute. I later found out that Coates had said that he wanted a psychologist that didn't look too much like a psychologist—a sensible requirement in view of the looks of some of my classmates. However, I didn't know about his request, so I wasn't too comforted when during that first interview with Coates he said I didn't look much like a psychologist.

In my first months at the Institute of Government I thought it was a mighty strange organization, lacking in understanding of the scholarly ways of Psychology, populated by nothing but attorneys, etc. After a year at the Institute of Government, we got a grant from the American Administration of Motor Vehicle Administrators for a study of the point system and I was actually put in charge of the study.

I was dazzled and frightened—*dazzled* at the prospect of directing a major project while still only a graduate student, and *frightened* that I probably couldn't cut the mustard. Coates handled me just right. He gave me all the leeway I wanted to carry out the study but was there to back me up when I needed help. The study worked out nicely, and was one of the most valuable parts of my education. I learned the true meaning of working "day and night"—Monday through Friday and then coming back and working day and night Saturday and Sunday.

I had the experience of learning that you might have a conference with Albert Coates at 6:30 a.m. on his sun porch, or walking through Battle Park on the way to the Institute of Government, or in the cool of the evening after a full day, or any other time of the week.

The study gained recognition and received the *first* annual prize called the Metropolitan Award for Research in Accident Prevention, judged to be the best accident prevention research that year. The report was a book published by the Institute of Government and called *Driver Improvement: The Point System.*

All during 1955, '56, '57, '58 and through most of '59 while I pursued my graduate education I was also a member of the Institute of Government staff.

In the fall of 1959 I left the Institute of Government to become Assistant Director of the Automotive Crash Injury Research Project at Cornell University in New York City. I remained in this capacity even after the project was moved to Buffalo.

In 1965 and 1966 discussions began about the creation of a Highway Safety Research Center at the University of North Carolina. I was interested, and I talked to UNC officials over a period of months.

In conducting the business of HSRC, lessons I learned at the Institute of Government came back. There was no course, no project, no internship, no ingredient in my education that matched the learning value of my time at the Institute of Government. This shows up in several aspects of HSRC's work. For example, I insist that HSRC reports serve two masters—they must have the rigor to gain the respect of our most critical scientific colleagues in the field, but they must also be understandable to the untrained motor vehicle administrators who must use the report. I insist on plain, simple writing.

My lesson in plain, simple writing came at the hands of Basil

Sherrill. The first report I wrote for the Institute of Government was something rather special to me, so I made sure it was filled with scholarly language, written with full expression of the scientific knowledge I had. Mr. Coates asked Basil Sherrill to go over the report with me and Basil did. He went through it word by word. When he was through, my report was like the prophetic status of the city of Jerusalem—not one stone laid on top of the other. Every time he took a word out of my text, he took a square inch of the skin off my body. When he got through Campbell was a quivering bloody mass, his scholarly language in shambles. But you know what?—the report was *readable*. That was Campbell's lesson in report writing.

I had a lesson in staff-hiring while at the Institute of Government. I heard Albert Coates tell his personnel selection philosophy. He said he didn't want a man serving at the Institute of Government unless that man had the potential to outstrip Albert Coates. Coates said his ambition was to have a staff *full* of men, with the potential to outstrip Mr. Coates. At first I thought that he couldn't be serious. (Later I had contact with organizations where obviously the top man sought out pygmies rather than giants and saw how the organization could falter and die.)

Coates was right, and I have adopted the same philosophy. I hope to be the least capable statistician among my statisticians, the least capable psychologist among my psychologists (of course, it may be easier for *me* to be "last among equals" than it was for Albert Coates, but at least the philosophy is the same.) That's what I learned about personnel selection at the Institute of Government. I learned about being a teacher and working with administrators from Albert Coates. Albert Coates said that when we worked with administrators and wanted to put forth an idea, we ought to broach the idea in such a way that the administrator would think it was his own idea. I watched Coates do it, and I've tried to follow that practice. That's how I learned about relationships.

I learned about the notion of an organization within the setting of a great university from Albert Coates. Albert Coates had much to say about the University of North Carolina. He spoke of it with an awe and a respect that I couldn't grasp when I was a graduate student. He spoke to me about the University in its role for the century past and the centuries in the future, and I didn't grasp it. I saw the University in terms of "right now"—a place to go to school. Oh I loved the dogwoods, and the sand walkways, and the sports teams and the Bell Tower, but I loved it in pieces and didn't grasp the whole.

Maybe I still don't, but in these later years I think I have a better feeling for the institution of the University of North Carolina. And now on University Day when I walk in the Faculty Parade and go into the Hall, and hear the songs and the words and renew my sense of community with the University, I realize the greatness and importance of this institution, and am thankful once again that the Institute of Government is a part of it, and that Albert Coates is a part of it, and that he opened the doors for so many others of us to be a part of it.

Catherine Maybury Seelye

When the National Association of County Commissioners met in Asheville, the officers and directors wanted to come by Chapel Hill to visit the Institute of Government. We decided to put up an exhibit to illustrate the Institute's activities from its beginnings in the late 1920's and early 1930's to the present. I called on Catherine Maybury Seelye, the Institute librarian, to assemble it on short notice. She knew, better than I, what was involved, and moved her home into the Institute building for the duration of the project; asked me to rent a television set to take the place of a baby-sitter for her small daughter, and went to work.

I have asked her to write her memories of those days, and here they are:

> I remember we had less than 2 weeks to prepare the exhibit (12 days?) and I told you (and all others who would listen) that what you were asking could not be done. As usual, it was shouting into the wind and I was sent back upstairs with feet of lead and a sinking heart. I was so tired of impossible tasks.

We were to display the entire history of the Institute (about 30 years?—at any rate, the number of years doesn't matter since you accomplished in a relatively short period what it takes others twice, three times, or four times and time to accomplish—and thus our task was gargantuan). We had no notion of where to begin. How to show what Brandis, Gardner and Grice and all those who followed had meant to the development of the Institute? How to exhibit strength, frustration, fury, brilliance, devotion and loyalty? How does one present these qualities which in essence were the Institute?

My only thought was to center the exhibit around staff publications (hardly the kind of creativity that had played so large a part in the growth and development of the Institute, but it would at least give us a focal point and I did believe that much of the work and inspired performance of the Institute would be reflected by these publications). So we had now a vague concept of the exhibit but that was all we had. We had no materials—no poster board, no paint, no tape, no crayons or ink, no saws, no lumber, no hammers or nails, no letters or letter-making equipment—NOTHING—nor anyone who could work with these materials if we had them. We didn't even know at this time what was needed or how much. We did have your history of the Institute but no documentation—files had to be scrutinized and raided, pictures found and reproduced, persons, places and things identified, copies of out-of-print publications located.

By now two days had passed—there·were about 10 left. A tightening around the heart. At what point any clear notion formed of what we were to do (or of what we were actually doing) I have no recollection at all. Somehow (evidently) things began to move and we with them. We recruited law students to make our display boards and cases and we recruited as many of the staff who would allow us to do so to help out with specific jobs. We began the exhibit in the governmental lab from which it oozed out into the north (?) corridor and flowed down to the foyer, surged around the corner and gushed down the south(?) corridor, finally filling the large basement room below. Most of this activity was largely due to Bob Stipe and Bill Frue, the former acting as art director and chief contractor, the latter as photographer and general handyman.

The pace increases. Orders went out thick and fast, both for supplies and to workers. Our normal 8-hour day turned into 10-, 12-, and 14-hour days and finally for some into 24-hour days. I topped out at 20. Panic turned into nightmare, nightmare into hysteria and hysteria into delirium. On one occasion Bill Frue and I and another (since forgotten) person were spread-eagled on the floor (terrazzo, but oh! what bliss to be horizontal) of the main exhibit corridor. Someone had given way and the rest of us wordlessly followed. I don't know how we ate or when or what. Our legs hurt terribly and I remember crawling on my hands and knees one night up to my dormitory bedroom at the Institute. We loathed each other and hated you much of the time. But we never lost our affection for each other or our respect and admiration for you—which was ultimately the enabling force which saw us and the exhibit through.

One sharp image which will never leave me: after HOURS of work in the darkroom, Bill Frue emerging (often we feared he was never to emerge again), soaked to the skin, motionless at first from the shock of the light, then shaking himself like a great shaggy dog after its bath.

One very troublesome aspect of the project for me was my 10-year-old daughter, who, during the early days of this period, was ill, and although she was looked after by a neighbor, she was forced to spend much time alone. I thought perhaps a television set would relieve some of her loneliness and you (someone) agreed that the Institute should fund the renting of a set since my finances would not allow me to do so. I believe she had the set for a week, after which time we both took up residence in the Institute dormitory until the project was completed. This episode, as I recall, was looked upon later with some disfavor by the State Auditor and singled out as a misuse of State funds.

Institute colleagues Robert Stipe and William Frue were the chief assistants and co-workers who shared her labors. They agree with me that Catherine Maybury Seelye was the organizing genius and undisputed heroine of this story.

Jack Atwater

Jack Atwater came into the University's service as janitor for the Institute of Government on July 1, 1940, shortly after it got into its building on Franklin Street. He retired after thirty-five years of service, on July 1, 1975, because of health problems which have since been happily resolved. He is now living on Old Lystra Road, in a house of his own building, located on five acres of land bought from his own savings.

230

Jack Atwater

He began working with the Institute as janitor in charge of building and grounds. He kept them clean—as a working place for himself and all other members of the staff. But that was only his starting point—he magnified his office.

He brought in the mail, including: letters of inquiry and information from city halls, county courthouses, and state agencies throughout North Carolina and communications from other states—all of which he sorted out and put on the desks of staff members; daily and weekly newspapers, around two hundred and fifty of them, from all over North Carolina; magazines and books and other materials coming from all sections of the country—all of which he distributed to the appropriate places in the library.

He brought in Institute supplies from the University storehouse, ran the mimeograph machine, assembled and bound the reports, brochures, and guidebooks prepared by the Institute staff, put them in envelopes, figured out the mailing rates, and took them to the post office.

He was an ever present help to all members of the Institute staff in a multiplicity of ways and on a multiplicity of fronts—making himself a general favorite among his fellow workers.

231

He continued these services as the Institute moved from its home on Franklin Street into the Joseph Palmer Knapp Building. They expanded as the staff grew to thirty or more members with attendant secretaries and research assistants. They expanded further as the mimeograph machine was replaced with Xerox machines, off-set machines, machines making plates to be used in off-set machines, addressograph machines, keeping the mailing list of 10,000 constantly changing officials up-to-date.

His own abilities grew with these increasing responsibilities and at the time of his retirement in 1975 he had become supervisor of the activities of five full-time assistants who were kept as busy as anybody in the building. There was not a person on the Institute staff who did a better job in his field of work than Jack Atwater did in his.

He had barely finished high school studies, but his native abilities and mastery of all the activities in his charge to the last detail, together with a marvelous personality, won him the respect and affection of his five full-time assistants and fully as many part-time helpers who were college-trained students in the adjoining Law School. All accepted his briefings, directions and supervision without question because they knew he knew his business, loved it, and tended to it.

Jack's friend and colleague, Dexter Watts, writes this of him:

> Two of my most vivid memories of Jack Atwater over the eighteen years he and I were both at the Institute of Government center on his readiness to sacrifice personal convenience to assist others in performing their tasks for the Institute.
>
> Every evening Jack would have the responsibility for taking first class mail to the Post Office after locking up the building. Invariably staff members would straggle down with letters and other materials needing urgently to be mailed. Jack's patience in again unlocking the postage meter and accepting further mail was remarkable. It was rare for Jack to be gone from the building before 6:00 p.m.—at least a half hour past his nominal departure time.
>
> Another persistent memory is of Jack's amazing ability to accept and squeeze in rush duplicating jobs that staff members would bring down for impending schools, important mailings as to recent court

decisions, or other matters submitted at or past the deadline. Though we appreciated then his capacity to cut short his personal breaks and lunch hours, to stay past normal quitting time, and to come back on Saturdays, it is only after his departure and the loss of much of this extraordinary flexibility that we can fully appreciate how much he did.

Everyone on the staff, from the Institute Director to the lowest paid employee, felt the same way about him and for the same reasons.

Gladys Hall Coates

These observations on my colleagues are no less true of my wife, Gladys Hall Coates, who has given five years of full-time work, and a large part of the fifty-two years of our married life, to the Institute of Government—all without pay.

I saw her for the first time in the summer of 1923, after her junior year at Randolph-Macon Woman's College (she graduated there in 1924), was engaged to her in 1925, and brought her to Chapel Hill as a bride in 1928, while the Institute of Government was taking form. As we passed in review before students standing on the Law School building steps, one student observed: "There goes tidewater Virginia and rainwater North Carolina."

Shortly after coming to North Carolina, she got acquainted with the location of cities and towns of the state and with many officials by filing thousands of early Institute of Government letters. She stuffed, sealed, and stamped envelopes; worked up mailing lists and addressed early issues of *Popular Government;* entertained prospective staff members and found them places to live in Chapel Hill; cooked meals for officials and visitors who came to give advice and counsel; discussed programs and policies with me throughout the years, and chauffeured me on countless trips crisscrossing the state while I prepared for the next day's law classes. She helped plan both Institute buildings and superintended the furnishing and decoration of them when they were built.

She has edited nearly everything I have ever written—cutting out

Gladys Hall Coates standing at the entrance of the first
Institute building.

purple passages, frying off fat, and adding insult to injury by improving the final product in ways which could not be denied.

There was the time I spelled out the story of the Institute of Government. I wrote it in the glow of creation, carried forward by the
momentum of my feeling about it, with commas, colons, semico-
lons, dashes, and periods incidental to the movement—as indeed
they were. I thought I was turning a perfect thing over to her. When
the manuscript came back to me, every page was blemished by un-
seemly marks. Whole sentences were marked out and here and there
a paragraph entire. Deflation did not describe my feeling. Nor did
dehydration. That night I went to bed in worried sleep. Some hours
later she woke me up—entranced by Thomas Hardy's description
of Eustacia Vye as Queen of the Night in *The Return of the Native*. It

was a glorious description full of the same sort of hyperboles and figures of speech she had just cut out of my pages. Half awake and in dead earnest, I replied: "It's a god's blessing that Thomas Hardy got his manuscript to the printer before you got hold of it."

She has done independent research on her own. Her largest venture was a study of the structure and workings of student government in the University of North Carolina at Chapel Hill. I stated the scope and character of her work in accepting the Di-Phi award for public service in 1951: "A five-year quest led her through a hundred and fifty years of Trustee minutes, Faculty minutes, Dialectic and Philanthropic Society minutes; through the pages of the *University Magazine* from its beginning in the 1840's, the *Tar Heel* from its beginning in the 1890's, the college humor publications from their beginning in the early 1900's; state newspapers of the various periods of University history; the *Yackety-Yacks* and the *Hellenians*; the University catalogues and other formal records; diaries of students and writings of faculty members, and the priceless recordings of Cornelia Phillips Spencer. In this five-year vigil and epic of research she uncovered and tracked out a story of governmental evolution on this campus which I believe to be without parallel in this country or any other. I could not say more without violating her own canons of propriety and good taste. I could not say less without losing my own self-respect."

Most of this work was done in the North Carolina Room of the University library where the records were kept. I got into the habit of dropping in for a few minutes conference with her around the middle of the morning. The young lady at the library desk observed these tete-a-tetes and feared an "affair" was in the making—as indeed it was. Later she came up to my wife and said with a smile: "Now I know who you are. For a long time I thought you were his secretary and I felt so sorry for his wife."

Another cooperative venture was the history of the University Law School. I stated the scope and character of her work in a special issue of the *North Carolina Law Review:* "This story could not have been told without the underpinning of three months of meticulous and painstaking research by my wife, Gladys Hall Coates."

She has not been above the protective use of astringents. I do not believe she ever forgot a thing I ever said that she could use to advantage later on. I once told her that as a five-year-old boy I won fifty-two brightly-colored celluloid butterflies for walking two miles to Sunday school and not missing a single Sunday for a year. A long while later, when I was about to win an argument on some religious point, she blurred my argument with the observation that it was a pity I had not gotten something out of Sunday school besides celluloid butterflies. In fifty years of married life, I do not believe I have ever won an argument she did not want to lose.

There was the time when she went to the library to read Macaulay's essay on Samuel Johnson in the *Encyclopedia Britannica* and was so entranced by the editor's note that she copied it down, brought it home to me, and said with great glee that it was a perfect description of her husband. The note stated that Macaulay's essay had been retained " . . . with a few trifling modifications in those places in which his invincible love of the picturesque has drawn him demonstrably aside from the dull line of veracity."

Every year she would plan and carry through a Christmas party for staff members and their wives and as many more secretaries and research assistants. She garlanded the house for these parties, made eggnog which spoke with authority, hot spiced punch, ham biscuits, sandwiches, fruitcake, and added raisins, nuts, mints, and other good things. Moving pictures of some of these parties were made for the record. Fun, frolic, and fellowship ran riot on these occasions.

She has lit up the path we have travelled with music and art and many a heartening observation. Once, when we were driving over a river and the wind had stirred the water into ripples which caught and reflected the morning sun, she said: "It looks like a place where bright angels' feet have trod." In the middle of ups and downs and numberless frustrations I heard her say: "All these woes shall serve for sweet discourses in our time to come." And then again: "These are they which came out of great tribulation."

And there is a line from Virgil that I often heard her repeat: "These things I saw and of some of them I was a part."

Chapter VIII   The Joseph Palmer Knapp Building: 1956

Outgrowing Living Quarters

During the 1940's the Institute building on Franklin Street was outgrown, cramping Institute activities to the stifling point with staff offices taking over the basement and attic bedroom space originally designed for visiting officials; with secretarial workers taking over the one and only classroom; with the library overflowing its single room into the hall and spilling out to shelves in private offices; with mimeograph, assembly, and mailing facilities operating in the corridors of the basement, and storage space non-existent. University dormitories and classrooms were filled with students, with the result that no space was available for officials coming to school. Hotel rates prohibited attendance by officials from the smaller towns and counties, and cut it in half for the larger ones.

We desperately needed more room to house the growing Institute activities, and I started laying plans to acquire the houses adjoining the Institute building. This would give Institute activities freedom to overflow into those houses without delay, and later we could replace them with expansions of the existing building. I got options on some of these houses, though not all of them; but without getting them all we were still hemmed in and I had to drop this plan. Prospects of raising building money at that time appeared non-existent, and I contemplated using the $50,000 gift of Spencer Love either to build an extension to the rear of our Franklin Street building, giving it a T shape, or to buy the Barbee property across the street (now a part of the Morehead Planetarium site). I got an option on this property and was ready to buy it to house overflowing work, when an unexpected visit interrupted and terminated this process.

An Unexpected Visit and its Consequences

Frank Aycock, who had gone into schoolteaching and had become superintendent of schools in Currituck County, came back to Chapel Hill to finish his Law School training. He asked me if I had ever received a letter from Joseph Palmer Knapp, a New York publisher and philanthropist who had built a home in Currituck County and taken a deep-rooted interest in its people. "Not that I remember", I replied. "Why do you ask?"

"A year or two ago," he said, "I was sitting with Mr. Knapp in a duckblind in Currituck County, and while we were waiting for the ducks to come over he got to talking about the need for training public officials. He had run into the need for it in Currituck County. If men needed training to be lawyers, doctors, ministers, and school teachers, they needed training to become public officials. I told him my old Law School teacher had been working for years on that problem on a statewide scale. He took down your name and address and said he was going to write to you."

My heart nearly missed a beat for fear that a letter of inquiry had come and I had not responded adequately, promptly, or at all. I went from my Law building office to the Institute in a hurry, agonizing all along the way. I found Mr. Knapp's letter:

My dear Professor: Senator Dudley Bagley was discussing with me the question of training for public service, and he said that in the book on "The Institute of Government" I would find much of interest. I would be glad to have the opportunity of reading it, and if not too much trouble, will you kindly ask the proper people to forward it to me, with bill.

I found also a letter from Frank Aycock describing in detail the duckblind conversation, written to me about the same time:

One of Mr. Knapp's pet peeves was the ignorant, untrained public servant. He was a cussing man and he reserved his most choice expressions for this gentry. One reason that he felt so strongly about this was that he was acquainted with Mr. Robert Moses, how well I cannot say, and he considered Mr. Moses to be an ideal public servant. He described in detail Mr. Moses' early life, how he went to school and when he came before his father to decide as to his college education, he informed his father that he didn't see any reason why he should go to college to learn how to make a living since his father was already wealthy and had enough for him to live on comfortably for the rest of his life. The elder Moses, according to Mr. Knapp, was scandalized until he found that his son wanted to take advantage of his father's wealth to be trained for public service. This pleased the elder Moses, and Mr. Knapp told me that this was exactly what was done. Mr. Knapp realized that not every one had the wealth of the Moses family but he could not see why every one in public life should not have training before he put himself up as a candidate for public office. He pointed out that lawyers have licenses, doctors, dentists, nurses and others have licenses. Why should a sheriff hold office without license? Why should any public official be elected or appointed without a license to show that he was competent to hold the office?

After quite a long conversation along this line, I ventured to say one day that his idea, while a good one and possessing considerable merit, was not practical but that I knew a man who had the same idea but in a practical form. He was extremely interested and had me describe in great detail, in so far as I knew, the work of the Institute. He wanted to know all about you and why and how you had started the Institute. Naturally I did not know as much as he wanted to know. He finally asked me if I knew you personally and when I replied in the affirmative he asked that I write to you and ask you to write to him about your work. Your letter greatly pleased him and we had one or two conversations after that. I felt sure that he wanted to help you with your work. Why he did not do more I do not understand since I think your work held greater appeal for him than any other single project he had in mind with the single exception of universal education.

In my subsequent conversations with him, few in number since I left shortly after, he told me that he had checked up on my story with Mr. Dudley Bagley. He informed me that Mr. Bagley had backed my story to the limit and said that you had done and were doing a wonderful work for the state. This encouraged me to believe that he would some day do something handsome for the Institute.

I had answered Mr. Knapp's letter, thank God, and, miraculously, on the day that I received it! Here is my letter:

Dear Mr. Knapp,

In the 1920's I was teaching courses in the University Law School dealing with legal problems involved in state and local government; found that my knowledge of law in books did not go far enough to meet my students' needs; and went out to study government in action as an apprentice to officials working on the job in city halls, county courthouses and state departments.

I found these officials needed to know what I had learned from the books as badly as I needed to know what they had learned on the job and started swapping my theory for their practice, my reseach for their experience, my government in books for their government in action.

This swapping continued as they followed me to Chapel Hill— singly at first, then in groups for consultation and assistance on particular problems, and finally for systematic courses of study and instruction, which I would like to feel were worth as much to them as to me.

In this swapping process I began to see my classroom as a statewide center—with lines of communicaton to every city hall, county courthouse, state department and federal agency in North Carolina; with all I was learning about government in books flowing out to the officials in these local centers, and all they were learning about government in action flowing back to me, coming to a focus in the classroom at the classroom hour.

As these lines of communication opened and expanded through the years—by letter, telephone, radio, publication, conference, school, and grapevine—my Law School classroom has grown into the Institute of Government for the continuous study of the structure and workings of government in the cities, the counties and the state of North Carolina, going far enough into the federal system to round out the state and local picture.

In all of these activities I am looking for ways and means of: (1) bridging the gap between outgoing and incoming officials and cutting down the lost time, lost motion, and lost money involved in a

240

rotating governmental personnel, (2) coordinating the interlocking, overlapping, and sometimes conflicting units and officials, (3) raising the standards of governmental performance in city halls, county courthouses and state departments by lifting the poorest practices to the level of the best, and (4) putting the people in touch with their government and keeping them in touch with it.

Mr. Knapp had replied:

My dear Professor: It would be difficult to express sufficiently my appreciation of your letter of January 1st and of the merits of the publications and *Popular Government* which you so kindly sent to me at Mackey's Island. They will be preserved carefully—read and re-read. After I have had an opportunity to study them, I will write you again.

But he had not written again, and I wondered why. I remembered a telephone call I had received from Dudley Bagley about that time, saying he was going to see a man in New York who had expressed an interest in helping the Institute of Government, and that he would let me know how he came out. But no word had come, and I knew no news was bad news.

Shortly afterward, I saw in the paper that Joseph Palmer Knapp's ashes had been brought from New York to be buried in Currituck County. My wife and I stopped over at the Bagley home in Moyock on our way to her home in Portsmouth, Virginia, for the Christmas holidays and found out why Mr. Knapp had not followed up his letter. The coming of World War II had carried him to New York for closer supervision of his business interests; but he continued his interest in the work of the Institute of Government and invited Mr. Bagley to New York to talk about it. However, on the very week of Mr. Bagley's visit to New York, the *Saturday Evening Post* had carried the extended feature on the Institute of Government. Mr. Knapp had no love for this rival of his magazine, *Collier's,* and this was not the time for Mr. Bagley to ask for help. So the moment had passed, and shortly after Mr. Knapp had died.

The Bagleys told us of the Knapp Foundation and its continued interest in North Carolina; and Mrs. Bagley told us that while Mrs. Knapp had been discussing gifts for fisheries and curriculum studies, she had said she would like to see her husband's name on a building symbolizing his interests in Currituck County and North Carolina.

Then and there, in the Bagley's dining room on Highland Farm while we were eating lunch, I described the building that would be the center, the symbol, and the workshop of one hundred county courthouses, three hundred town and city halls, and the score or more of government buildings in the state capital.

The Bagleys had been long-standing friends and supporters of the University and were favorably inclined toward me and the Institute of Government. They knew that Mrs. Knapp was the starting point of any efforts we might make for a building bearing her husband's name, and they arranged for my wife and me to meet her on one of her visits to Nags Head, a North Carolina beach resort in Currituck County.

Mrs. Knapp listened to what I had to say about the work of the Institute of Government, saw that it could fulfill Mr. Knapp's interest in the training of public officials, and invited us to present plans to the Joseph Palmer Knapp Foundation for a building to house the work of the Institute.

Gordon Gray, then President of the University, accompanied by University Comptroller Billy Carmichael, went to New York to appear before the Knapp Foundation Board with the request for a half-million dollars to be matched by the state for a million-dollar building for the Institute of Government. It was suggested in the meeting that the Knapp Foundation put up one-fourth of the money and the state three-fourths. At that point, Mrs. Knapp rose to her feet and said: "Joe Knapp pulled his weight in everything he did as long as he lived, and now that he is dead he is going to keep on pulling it in everything done in his name as long as his name is in my keeping." That one sentence meant a quarter of a million dollars to me, for in a matter of seconds the half-million-dollar gift was approved on condition that the State of North Carolina would match it.

At this point President Gray was faced with a problem: Other departments in the University needed buildings and were pressing

242

the University to go to the legislature for them. It was a problem of priorities. The problem came to a head on a memorable morning in the President's office. Powerful advocates were urging other claims, worthy claims. The President was the ultimate judge. I will never forget his decision and the words with which he announced it: "All of these claims are good claims. I do not have to decide that one is worth more to the state than another. Let me assume that they are all of equal value. I am making my decision on the ground that I don't know of anyone in competing departments of the University who has gone as far as Albert Coates and his wife have gone in making personal sacrifices to carry out a program they believe in, and I want to recognize that fact."

Under the leadership of Governor William B. Umstead and his legislative counsel Frank Taylor, the General Assembly of North Carolina matched the Knapp Foundation gift at the legislative session in 1953 and the building was assured.

The Joseph Palmer Knapp Building

The building was put on the high ground at the eastern gateway to the University near the point where in colonial days the road leading from the eastern shore to the western mountains was crossed by the road running from the north through Petersburg, Virginia, southwards through Pittsboro, North Carolina, and beyond. We moved into the building in the spring of 1956.

There was a research and teaching wing, including twenty-four staff offices; seminar rooms for smaller groups, classrooms for groups ranging in size from fifty to one hundred; an auditorium equipped with visual aids for teaching purposes and laboratory space for demonstrating differing methods, practices, and techniques in government.

There was an administrative wing, including offices for administrative personnel; secretarial space; reception center and conference rooms; library and publication center; mimeograph, assembling, mailing, and storage rooms; staff lounge, roof deck, and a service kitchen.

243

There was a bedroom wing, including sixty-five double rooms with twin beds and connecting baths; with bookshelves, chairs, desks, and lamps for study and writing; and with living rooms on all floors for the use of students and their visitors.

There was an auditorium seating three hundred fifty people. An added gift of $100,000 from the Joseph Palmer Knapp Foundation decorated its walls with fourteen murals, seven by fourteen feet in size. Painted by Francis Vandeveer Kughler, the murals portrayed significant moments and turning points in the history of North Carolina.

The photographic murals in the building on Franklin Street, representing the geography of North Carolina from its shoreline and coastal plain through the piedmont section to the mountains and beyond, were moved to the basement walls and corridors of the Knapp building.

Hugh Morton, a prominent citizen and expert photographer, gave dozens of pictures of a variety of North Carolina scenes for the walls of bedrooms and offices and classrooms.

The state had not begun to provide air-conditioning for public buildings at that time, but we persuaded the authorities to allow us to include ducts in the building plans, and within a year or two funds were raised to air-condition the building from basement to attic.

There was a full-time staff of twenty-four professors, associate professors, and assistant professors of public law and government. There was a librarian and there were two full-time assistants, a housing officer, fourteen secretaries, two mimeograph operators, three janitors, and from ten to twenty part-time research assistants who worked on schedules ranging from a few hours a week to full-time for the summer months. And there was a salary scale as good as the best in the academic division of the University of North Carolina in Chapel Hill, and working facilities in the University surpassed by none.

244

Presenting the Building to the University

In presenting the building to the University, I had this to say:

I knew of Joseph Palmer Knapp but never saw him while he was living in the flesh. I have seen his face in photographs and himself in action in moving pictures taken as he worked and played. I have followed his tracks in Currituck County and looked at him through the eyes of friends and neighbors who knew and loved him.

In the lives of people who walked on crutches and now walk on legs.

In the lives of children—like the little boy who learned what seeing was when the school health clinic discovered and corrected his defective vision and who walked from shadows into light; and the little girl who did not know she could not hear as others heard until the clinic's hearing aid opened to her ears the wonders of the world of sound.

In the lives of men and women caught in the bind of failing crops and falling prices, whose homes he saved from mortgage sale and tax foreclosure.

In the lives of three hundred farm families who brought him Christmas gifts of home-grown fruits and vegetables preserved according to their choicest recipes—in their appreciation of better cooking, better diet, better health, and better living from knowledge spread by home economics courses and home demonstration agents.

In the sound of music carried into homes throughout the county by children who learned from music courses in the schools and played in bands and sang in music festivals.

In wreaths of flowers brought by children from the schools to put upon his grave at Christmas time—childen who never saw or knew him any more than I did, but felt through parents, friends, and neighbors a magic force working in their lives.

In the vacant place he left against the skies of Currituck, there is coming into focus the form and figure of a man who went local when he saw the ducks in Currituck; went native when he saw that hunting guides respected him for the shots he could make rather

245

then the checks he could sign; went North Carolinian when he built his home at Mackey's Island and turned from a periodic visitor into a resident citizen; went Southern while reading Claude Bowers' *The Tragic Era,* and started doing what he could to right the wrongs of Reconstruction at his doorstep; went American in wanting a child on Knott's Island in Currituck County to go to teachers and buildings as good as any child would have in Brooklyn where he was born and raised.

In this form and figure of Joseph Palmer Knapp coming to us through the noise and fog and static of the years, with a face rugged with the wind and weather of Currituck winters, we see the spirit and image of a man—

Who loved to try a marksman's skill against the curve and speed of a duck in flight;

Who loved to test his mettle in a battle of wits with trout, salmon, friend, or foe;

Who loved excelling to the point of quitting violin lessons after hearing Kreisler play;

Who hated cruelty to the point of firing a keeper from his job for leaving a dog to suffer with a cankered ear;

Whose poker face in a business deal became an open book in the fellowship of friends;

Who lived and died with the look of eagles in his eyes, the sweep of wings in his spirit, the love of human beings in his heart, and left this building signed with his name, and "the vivid air signed with his honor."

Accepting the Building

Chancellor Aycock accepted the building for the University, saying:

> The growth of the Institute of Government always has been dynamic and sometimes has been turbulent. Its history reveals that it has always been long on hope, vision, energy and effort but short on tangible assets. Today we recognize an important tangible achievement by the dedication of the Joseph Palmer Knapp building. This splendid laboratory in which many vital problems in human rela-

tions may be discovered, tested and disseminated, is made possible by the joint effort of the Knapp Foundation and the people of North Carolina. A million-dollar laboratory for science is not unusual because the need for the advancement of scientific knowledge is widely understood. An investment of this proportion in a laboratory to the science of improvement in human relations is in the realm of the exceptional. Thus it is appropriate for us to ponder for a moment and to inquire into the purposes underlying this magnificent gift . . . .

The vital characteristics of the Institute of Government which appealed to the Knapp Foundation and caught the imagination of the people of this state is that it was not merely discovered but rather it was created. In this particular, discovery was merely a prelude to creation.

A program of education for public officials in the Institute of Government has emerged as the means to perpetuate and extend our democratic heritage. So today we dedicate this building which stands as a dynamic symbol of one of the finest creations of mankind. It illustrates effective cooperation between private contribution and public support. It provides a suitable home in which those who seek to serve their fellow man may study and learn. It will become more and more the center of creative thought to improve human relations through the establishment of a higher sense of justice.

Threats of Encroachment

No sooner was the Institute of Government settled in the Joseph Palmer Knapp Building than I had to protect it from encroachment. The University Comptroller felt that we would never be able to fill the new building, that it was far too big for our uses, that we would rattle around in it, that other departments in the University needing greater space should move in and occupy parts of it for the time being. I pointed to the fact that the Institute, too, had been bursting at the seams and overflowing its quarters, and that was why we had been fighting for a new and larger building. I further pointed to the fact that the University had already commandeered for other purposes the building we had just moved out of without saying a word to us, despite the fact that I had raised the money for it from private sources; that for seventeen years we had been operating as a private enterprise and had bought and paid for with private funds the land on which that building stood.

This threat of encroachment ended as the steadily-growing programs of the Institute of Government brought over five hundred local, state, and federal officials to the building in the closing months of 1956, five thousand in 1957, six thousand in 1958, and seventy-five hundred in 1960, for schools and conferences running from two days to twelve weeks, and future needs for still more space were appearing as Institute horizons were expanding.

No sooner was the Institute saved from this encroachment than it faced another. One morning, a year later, I noticed three men surveying the land within a hundred yards of the Institute's new building and driving stakes into the ground. I casually wandered over in their direction and off-handedly asked what they were doing. "Locating sites for new dormitories," they said. "This is my land," I answered. "It is needed for expansion of the Institute of Government." They said they were under the impression it belonged to the University, since the University building committee had sent them to stake out the sites for new buildings, and that I had better go to see the Chancellor. There was no time to lose. I went to see Chancellor Aycock before going back to my office and told him of this invasion, and asked him to get me a hearing before the building committee. He did.

The hearing came six weeks later while I was in bed with a combination of cold and flu, with eyes and nose running, along with a fever. My wife came into the bedroom with the word that the committee was in session and would hear what I had to say at eleven o'clock. My mind cleared in an instant; so did my eyes and nose, while my fever soared. I went to the meeting, where the committee heard me for an hour with patient courtesy.

"Have you got the money for your future building?" they asked. I had to say no. "What reasons do you have for thinking you will get it?" I pointed out the fact that we had raised the money for the old building on Franklin Street and had outgrown it; that we raised the money for the new building and were outgrowing it; and that I believed we could raise the money for more room, as we needed it. The committee in good will and good humor told me that it would take my case "under advisement." I had heard that tune before and I knew its meaning. I had at that point lost the argument.

In that precise moment, a scene in the home of Harvard University's President on a Christmas afternoon flashed across an interval of thirty-seven years into my mind. President Lowell was giving the boys around him a new twist on the old story of the difference between an optimist and a pessimist. "An optimist," he had said, "is one who sees a light that isn't there. A pessimist is one who blows out that light." I told the committee that story, and reached my climax with this plea: "On that land, right now, I see buildings that are not there. I am asking this committee not to tear those buildings down."

When I went out of that room, I felt in my heart that I had won my case. This feeling was confirmed a few days later when the Chancellor said to the committee: "Boys, get out your pencils and figure out another site for the dormitories." Taking time, place, and circumstances into account, I never heard a sentence packed with more pure, simple, and heart-warming eloquence than this statement of Bill Aycock. It ended the second encroachment threat. It meant freedom and room to grow and expand. And that is what we kept on doing.

Appraisals of Institute Work: 1945-1962

From the Chairman of the Guilford County Commissioners:

The Institute's guidebooks relating to the collection of taxes and supplement thereto have been loaned by me temporarily to our tax collector, who is now studying them. After he has completed the study, it is his purpose to loan them to various employees in his office in order that all of them may be acquainted with these books.

On next Monday after serving sixteen years, I will retire from the board of commissioners, and feel my work would not be complete until I wrote and thanked you and the staff of the Institute of Government for the many courtesies shown me, personally as well as officially. I want to compliment the work the Institute is doing for the cities and counties of our state.

A certified public accountant has just completed his audit of our books and has advised our governing board that in all his experience of more than 20 years he has never seen a better report. Naturally this makes all of us feel good. The Institute of Government has been of such great assistance in handling our affairs that we are sending you a copy of this audit report.

Our Board knows of nothing you or your staff have left undone that you should have done in our county. We know of nothing you or your staff have done that you should not have done. We would like to see you and your staff in the years ahead continue and expand your services to local and state government. This gives us the opportunity to say that in the opinion of this board the Institute of Government has been the chief factor in developing in North Carolina the best and most effective and economical local government to be found in any state.

From the Chairman of the State Board of Elections:

In my opinion, the three greatest educational achievements of North Carolina in the present century are (1) the rediscovery by Governor Aycock and his contemporaries of the duty of democratic government to provide for the education of its youth through a publicly supported school system; (2) the decision of the Legislature of 1933, under the courageous leadership of Governor J.C.B. Ehringhaus, to equalize the minimum educational opportunity of all the State's children by providing a uniform eight-months public school system in every county in the State, and (3) the creation ... of the Institute of Government.

The first two of these achievements illustrate what the State can do for education, and the third illustrates what education can do for the State.

I use the word "creation" advisedly because that is exactly what the Institute of Government has done—it has made something where there was nothing before.

From the Dean of the Harvard Law School, Erwin Griswold:

I think it is one of the glories of this Law School that a number of its graduates have done distinguished jobs in fields which were not confined to the narrow realm of the practice of law. Among those, your work in North Carolina stands very high and I would like to join with Dean Pound in the statement which he gave you a number of years ago.

I have read your Story of the Institute of Government with a great deal of interest. I had heard in a general way about your work, but I had not before had a chance to know about it in any detail. The whole field of local government is one in which much needs to be done, and

250

I do not know of any more effective means which has been developed to do something about it than what you have done with the Institute of Government.

Frankly, I do not have any suggestions to offer. My own work is so closely confined to the handling of problems arising here at the Law School that I have not had any opportunity to do any constructive thinking in related fields. Nor do I know of any persons in this area who are doing anything even closely approximating what you have undertaken. It is good of you to look to others for information and suggestions, but I think that the actual flow of ideas is almost entirely the other way. It is you who have had the ideas and the experience, and we should hope that others will profit from what you have done.

From the President of the American Bar Association:

It has been my good fortune to visit the Institute of Government in the University of North Carolina at Chapel Hill and meet with its staff and research assistants and observe the effective training and excellent results of the Institute's operation. The research specialists have studied state and local government in the library and in the field; made studies of current problems for government departments and official commissions; assisted in the drafting of legislation; published guidebooks for officials; and conducted numerous schools for officials and employees of the state and local governments. The Institute is worthy of investigation by any local, state or national group that is interested in establishing a similar institute or training center.

The Joseph Palmer Knapp Building

253

The Joseph Palmer Knapp Building

254

Institute of Government
versity of North Carolina —

255

Joseph Palmer Knapp

Margaret Rutledge Knapp

256

Frank B. Aycock, Jr. in his law office in Elizabeth City. In a duckblind in Currituck County, Frank Aycock kindled Mr. Knapp's interest in the work of the Institute of Government.

Joseph Palmer Knapp
We train people to be lawyers, doctors, preachers, and school teachers. Why not train people to be public officials?—Joseph Palmer Knapp

Dudley Bagley
Dudley Bagley and his wife, Ida, with Albert and Gladys Coates made the plans which led to the Joseph Palmer Knapp Building.

William B. Umstead,
Governor of
North Carolina

Frank Taylor,
Legislative Council

Under their leadership the General Assembly of North Carolina
appropriated a half million dollars to match a half million dollar grant
from the Knapp Foundation.

Senator Sam J. Ervin, Jr., and Senator Everett Jordan at the dedication of the Knapp Building

Chancellor William B. Aycock

Mrs. Coates and Mrs. Knapp conferring on furnishings for the Knapp Building

The Building in Use

A meeting in the government laboratory

The auditorium of the Knapp Building

A staff office

261

The crime laboratory used in law-enforcement instruction

The staff lounge

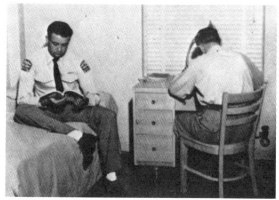

262

Men studying in one of the bedrooms
of the Knapp Building

A view of part of the library

Superior Court Judges at a luncheon in the Institute Building.
Left to right: Froneburger, Seawell, Moore, Fountain

Chapter IX   Changing of the Guard

Albert Coates to John Sanders: 1962

Chancellor William B. Aycock appointed John Sanders to succeed me as Director of the Institute of Government. At the end of the working day on the 31st of August, 1962, I took down my name from the door of the Director's office, put up the name of my successor, John Sanders, took the keys of the Institute building to his home, and gave them to him in the common law tradition of "livery of seisin."

John Sanders was one of the ablest students in my Law School classes during my nearly forty years of teaching. In his senior year, he undertook for me research on the history and powers of the Governor's office that resulted in a study so comprehensive and useful that Governor Luther Hodges publicly referred to it as an invaluable service when he took office. After a clerkship with Judge John J. Parker and law practice in Raleigh, John joined the Institute of Government in 1956 and proceeded to perform work of such uniformly high quality that it caused me to advance his salary faster than that of others who came to the staff at the same time. He had first-rate native ability, developed and sharpened by professional training and experience.

John Sanders directed the affairs of the Institute of Government for eleven years, from 1962 to 1973, when he left to become Vice President of the over-all University of North Carolina in charge of planning. One of his colleagues, Jake Wicker, wrote this assessment of his directorship at that time:

> If it is true that an administrator's chief role is to expedite the work of his colleagues and bring out the best in them, then John Sanders was an unqualified success at the Institute. First of all, he had a strong concept of the Institute's mission in serving the people of North Carolina, and all of his leadership was directed toward that end. He was utterly fair with all who work at the Institute, and his colleagues knew that his comments and criticisms came from perceptive insights and were aimed at improving the Institute's service to the state. Members of the staff and faculty during his directorship did not work for John Sanders; they worked for the people of the state and their governments through the Institute and with Sanders.
>
> In his vision for the Institute, he saw its work expanding steadily, but had constant concern for its quality. He was not interested in empire-building—he sought the growth and well-being of the Institute solely in order that its mission might be better accomplished. He believed strongly in the Institute's operating principles of competence, objectivity, and non-advocacy, and he saw the Institute as being in the service of all the people of the state, of all political factions and parties, and of all levels and units of government.

John Sanders to Henry Lewis: 1973

Chancellor Ferebee Taylor appointed Henry Lewis to succeed John Sanders as the Institute Director. He was the first of the new group I had started bringing on the staff of the Institute after World War II. He came in 1946, worked in its service without a break for twenty-seven years, except for the year he served as a Vice President of the University of North Carolina, and was second to none in ability and experience.

One of Henry's colleagues, Elmer Oettinger, wrote this about him as he came to the directorship:

> Over the years Henry Lewis has come to have strong convictions about the relationship of the Institute of Government to the Univer-

sity at Chapel Hill. He states them succinctly: "The Institute of Government is fortunate to be University-based. I am confident that a major reason for the Institute's success is the kind of people we have been able to attract to our faculty. The reason we have been able to attract and hold them is that they are able to identify with the University as faculty members." Even so, he adds emphatically. "The objective for every Institute of Government faculty member is that he or she maintain close contact with people on the job in governmental service."

His major fields of research, teaching, and writing have been property taxation, organization of state tax agencies, legislative organization remains a continuing thread in his career. Even in November of this year, his first month as director of the Institute of Government, he presided over one of his regular schools for tax officials.

Through the years Lewis has served with three tax study commissions. He was consultant and draftsman for the Commission for the Study of the Revenue Structure of the State (1957-58), the Commission for the Study of the Local and Ad Valorem Tax Structure of the State (1969-70) (and drafted its Machinery Act of 1971), and the Commission for the Study of Property Tax Exemptions and Classifications (1971-72). For this last commission, he drafted its revisions of the statutes dealing with exemption, classification, and preferential tax treatment of property.

When working with the organization of state tax agencies, Lewis served as consultant and draftsman for the Commission on the Reorganization of State Government (1953-54), with emphasis on the Department of Revenue, the State Board of Assessment, the Tax Review Board, and the Department of Tax Research. In the study and reworking of legislative reorganization and procedure, he did research and analyzed the standing committee system of the North Carolina Senate for H.P. Taylor, Sr., who was then Lieutenant Governor; initiated proposals to decrease the size and number of Senate committees; and made comparable studies of committees in the State House of Representatives. His background in election law and procedure includes serving (1966-67) as consultant and draftsman for the Election Laws Revision Commission, recodifying the primary and general election laws of North Carolina.

Lewis has been called upon to serve in administrative capacities before being appointed as director of the IOG. He was in charge of the Institute's Legislative Service in 1949, 1951, and 1953 and shared that responsibility with George Esser in the 1955 session. During

Gordon Gray's administration as president of the Consolidated University of North Carolina, he served on a committee to investigate hazing at the University and wrote a report that became rather celebrated. He also served as chairman of the committee to inaugurate William B. Aycock as Chancellor of the University.

More administrative challenge came when he consented to take leave from the Institute faculty to serve one year as Vice President of the Consolidated University. His principal responsibilities for the University's general administration included acting as liaison official between the Board of Trustees and the University administration and as legal counsel to the President of the University, the Chancellor, and the Board of Trustees on matters affecting labor relations and student disruption and discipline. He also had supervision of the University's television system during that year.

Henry Lewis to John Sanders: 1979

Chancellor Ferebee Taylor appointed John Sanders to succeed Henry Lewis as Director of the Institute of Government in 1978. He took up his duties January 1, 1979.

John's colleagues welcomed his return with this statement from Philip Green:

> Institute of Government faculty members and clients greeted the announcement this fall of John Sanders' appointment as the Institute's new Director with the enthusiasm of a Homecoming . . . .
>
> John Sanders grew up in the town of Four Oaks, and thus is one of the remarkable group of Johnston County men who have served on the Institute's faculty: Albert Coates himself, . . . Paul Johnston (later the state's first Director of Administration) and Dean Robert Byrd of the UNC Law School.
>
> Sanders' education reinforced this heritage, first at North Carolina State University and then, following a stint in the U.S. Navy, at the University of North Carolina at Chapel Hill. At N.C. State he started to become an architect. At UNC he majored in history with a minor in political science; did a year's graduate study in American history; and finally graduated from the School of Law.
>
> Throughout the years he was marked as a leader. At UNC he capped an active career in student government by winning election as president of the student body, and he was tapped for both the

Order of the Golden Fleece and the Order of the Grail. He ranked near the top of his law class, was elected to the Order of the Coif, and served as editor of the UNC *Law Review*. As a result of his law school record he received the singular honor of being chosen to serve as law clerk to Chief Judge John J. Parker, U.S. Court of Appeals for the Fourth Circuit.

In view of this background, it was natural that Albert Coates offered Sanders a position on the Institute faculty in 1956 and that he accepted this offer. He had worked as a research assistant for the Institute while a law student, and he had been impressed with its opportunities for public service while he was impressing the Institute faculty with his ability. Neither set of expectations was disappointed.

During the six years that preceded his directorship and on a part-time basis thereafter, Sanders' principal fields of interest were state government organization and administration; state constitutional revision; legislative representation; and higher education organization and administration.

In the area of state government, he served as principal staff member for a series of Commissions on Reorganization of State Government. Among his major accomplishments was drafting the legislation under which the state's first Department of Administration was created.

He assisted two commissions concerned with revision of the State Constitution: The North Carolina Constitutional Commission in 1958-59 and the North Carolina State Constitution Study Commission in 1968-69. The latter produced the extensive constitutional revisions that were adopted in 1970.

Sanders was recognized as the state's foremost authority in the field of legislative representation. As a disinterested expert he was consulted by the attorneys on both sides and the presiding federal judge in the landmark case which led to reapportionment of the General Assembly, and he assisted the legislative committee that drafted the new plan of representation in response to the court's decision.

As a staff member for the Governor's Commission on Education beyond High School and adviser to subsequent commissions and the Governor, he played a key role in developing the plans by which the state's system of higher education was reorganized in the 1960's. This experience was supplemented by extensive assignments within the University at Chapel Hill, including terms as chairman of the Chancellor's Advisory Committee; chairman of the special committee that produced the University's first affirmative-action plan;

chairman of the University Faculty Advisory Council; and first chairman of the All-University Faculty Assembly.

Obviously this background and experience fitted Sanders perfectly for the assignment as Vice-President for Planning of the University System to which he was called in the fall of 1973. And it explains why he has been at the center of most of the major struggles involving the University since that date.

To such a man the Institute faculty bade a reluctant farewell in 1973. With great pleasure, they now say, "Welcome home!"

John Sanders

The three directors of the Institute of Government; Henry Lewis, 1973—1979; Albert Coates, 1927—1962; John Sanders, 1962—1973; and 1979—

Chapter X My Personal Appraisal of Institute Activities: 1930-1962

I believe it may be fairly said that the Institute of Government has made measurable progress toward the goals it set for itself in the early 1930's:

Toward bridging the gap between outgoing and incoming public officials and cutting down the lost time, lost motion, and lost money involved in a rotating governmental personnel;

Toward coordinating the activities of officials in interlocking, overlapping, and conflicting governmental units, and reducing duplication, friction, and strife;

Toward keeping up the continuity between the government of yesterday and the government of tomorrow by improving methods, practices, and techniques from year to year, and avoiding the necessity of wholesale reorganizations from generation to generation;

Toward bringing to every official on the job the improving methods, practices, and techniques of every other official, and thus raising the standards of governmental performance by lifting the poorest practices toward the level of the best.

If I had to put the story of government in North Carolina from the 1660's to the early 1900's into one sentence, that sentence would be this: It is the story of multiplying governmental units and expanding governmental services. To illustrate:

271

For some years after 1663, under the charter from the crown, the state was the one governmental unit in North Carolina. It was the only one that was needed for fifteen hundred people living on a piece of land "fortie mile square." As people spread two hundred miles down the coastal plain and five hundred miles across the piedmont plateau to the mountains and beyond, the state was divided into one hundred counties. These counties were subdivided into thousands of townships and special districts. Across this subdividing structure of counties, townships, and special districts was thrown the overlapping framework of cities and towns.

By the latter 1920's this dividing, subdividing, and crisscrossing process reached its peak and the consolidating process began. School districts which had run into the thousands began merging into one hundred county-wide school systems. Road districts which had run into the thousands began merging into one hundred county-wide road systems. Within the county limits the process began of merging separate city and county offices, such as city and county tax collecting offices, city and county libraries, city and county election boards, and so on. Study commissions began to explore the possibilities of consolidating city and county governments in counties with one predominating city, such as Wilmington and New Hanover, Charlotte and Mecklenburg, Durham City and Durham County. By the early 1930's the state was beginning the process of absorbing separate city and county school systems into one statewide school system and city and county road systems into one statewide road system.

Throughout these same years the state had begun to take on more and more services to the people on a statewide basis and the process of multiplying state departments, agencies and commissions had begun. There were around seventy-five of them by 1925 and three hundred by the 1960's. The process of grouping and consolidation began in the 1930's, went forward in the 1940's and 1950's, and reached its peak in the early 1970's with the consolidation of the three hundred or more into around nineteen cabinet departments.

During the last fifty years there have been more basic changes in the structure and the workings of government in the cities, the counties, and the state of North Carolina and their interlocking rela-

tionships with each other and the federal government than had occurred in the two hundred seventy years from the 1660's to the
1930's.

I think it may be fairly said that the men and women of the Institute of Government have been at the working center of most if not
all of these changing patterns in state and local government. This is
illustrated by successive undertakings beginning in the 1930's:

By their work for the state commission authorized by the General
Assembly to rewrite the state constitution in the middle 1930's.

By their work for the city council of Charlotte and county commissioners of Mecklenburg in exploring the possibility of consolidating city and county governments in the 1940's, and their
work with the General Assembly on the problems of private, local,
and special legislation.

By their work for the state commission on the reorganization of
state government in the 1950's.

By their work on the problems growing out of the U.S. Supreme
Court decision in the case of Brown vs. Board of Education in 1954.

By their work for the state commission on improving and expediting the administration of justice in the courts in the 1950's.

By their work with city, county, and state officials on the continuing governmental problems confronting them from day to day
and from year to year.

By their work in creating a new university of public officials in
the framework of the old University of North Carolina.

A New University of Public Officials

In the latter 1920's local schools for law-enforcing officers were
growing into statewide schools. By the early 1930's the statewide
school of law-enforcing officers was growing into a statewide
school of governmental officers—including all groups of public
officials at city, county, and state levels—coming together in the
Institute of Government. By the latter 1930's the Institute of Government was growing into a new university of public officials in the
framework of the old University of North Carolina at Chapel Hill.

Our first courses were short courses running two and three days, usually on weekends—including Friday, Saturday, and Sunday—to avoid more than one day's loss of time from the job for an experiment of doubtful promise. As these short courses proved their worth to those attending, they were expanded to one week, then two weeks, and then, with the State Highway Patrol to twelve weeks.

At first we gave certificates of attendance—the fact that they had been there meant enough to the attending officials to be framed and hung on their office walls. Later, examinations were given at the end of each course, certificates of attendance only were given to those who did not pass the examination, and certificates of proficiency were given to those who did. The difference soon became known, and soon eliminated those who attended out of curiosity or for the sake of a few days off.

Our first examination was given in the middle 1930's at the end of a ten-day school for law-enforcing officers with fifty or more officers attending. We followed this with ten one-day district schools where the officers could leave home early in the morning, arrive at the district center by nine o'clock, have four hours of instruction in the morning, an hour for lunch, and four hours in the afternoon—the only cost being the midday meal and the travel. We found that as many officers would come to each of the one-day district schools as would come to the ten-day statewide school. And we also found that district schools were feeders for statewide schools.

In the early 1940's, I wrote this report on the progress of this new university of public officials:

> In a two-weeks school for federal, state and local law-enforcing officers conducted by the Institute of Government not long ago, there were men whose ages ranged from nineteen to sixty; whose schooling ranged from the third grade in public school to one year in college; whose experience in law-enforcement ranged from one month to thirty-two years; and who had previously worked as salesmen, bookkeepers, textile mill employees, plumbers, saw mill operators, soldiers, sailors, painters, merchants, newspapermen, construction engineers, steel mill employees, electricians and radio workers, baseball players, bankers, carpenters, machinists, truck drivers, and stenographers.

274

Expand this class to the ten thousand or more officials and citizens who have attended Institute training schools within the past ten years and you have a cross-section of the men and women of the cities, the counties, and the state of North Carolina. Most of them do not have the sixteen units of book study listed as college entrance requirements, and college doors refuse to open at their knock. But while others have been laying books end to end in schools, these men and women have been laying moments of insight and experience end to end in working at their jobs. The Institute of Government accepts these credits for admission to its training schools; and the University of North Carolina thus finds its rootage extended beyond the public schools to include the city halls, county courthouses, state departments, and federal agencies of North Carolina and the civic organizations of the men and women on whose shoulders these governmental units rest.

These men and women come into our classrooms in statewide, district, and local schools charged with interest in the subjects to be taught and with first-hand impressions of the problems to be discussed. Where the students with book-learning backgrounds draw on their imaginations for hypothetical questions, these men and women draw on their experience for questions filled with the realities of the life in which they live. Their interchanges in these classrooms lift the classroom hour above the level of supposititious considerations and infuse it with the "hum and shock" of life. The clashes of their minds in free and open discussion now and then strike off sparks already beginning to light up the face of the state like matches struck in darkness. The schoolrooms of the people are becoming the crossroads of the commonwealth.

The results of these activities are already appearing. I have seen official leaders come into departments with a vision lifting their co-workers out of ruts and routines, releasing their frustrated energies, and bending their cross-purposes to a willing focus on the common task, in the spirit of all for one and one for all. This new spirit among departmental employees has turned the irritating trivialities of daily contacts into opportunities for collaboration giving dignity to their employment. It has translated the moral values of their own good fellowship into economic assets of their respective governmental units.

I went to the Deans of the College of Arts and Sciences and the Graduate School to discuss the possibility of credits toward A.B. and Master's degrees for those public officials who could qualify—

to be achieved through a combination of correspondence courses and courses in residence on periodic weekends. After some discussion the Dean of the Graduate School came up with another idea: "Albert," he said, "the School of Public Health is continually bringing in students who do not qualify for A.B. or Master's degrees, but who have a rough equivalent in experience from working in the public health field. The School gives them a certificate with built-in values which is accepted by public health authorities as the full equivalent of a professional degree."

This suggestion took root in my mind: It could start with an overall certificate for county and city managers and administrators whose work on the job covered the whole range of local government, and state department heads whose work on the job was directly related to local government. It could go forward with certificates in more limited fields of knowledge for clerks of court, registers of deeds, accountants, and so on—the guidebooks already being prepared in those fields could be the beginning textbooks with Institute staff members working in those fields as teachers.

Just as the schools for law-enforcing officers had led to the schools for all governmental officers, the schools for all governmental officers would grow into and find their fulfillment in a new university of public officials within the framework of old University of North Carolina.

The Course in County Administration. Here is a description of the course in County Administration as it was given in the winter and spring of 1977-78:

> The course will be held over ten weekends between October 6, 1977, and May 6, 1978. Weekend sessions are scheduled from two to four weeks apart for the convenience of officials who must keep up with their jobs.

> Within time limitations, an attempt is made to cover all phases of county government and administration. Emphasis is placed on the job of the county manager and county department heads. The course will cover the following subjects of importance to county administrative officials:

> The County as a Governmental Unit. The legal position of the

276

county and its relationship to the state. County powers, functions, and organization. Forms of county government.

Techniques of Administration. Administrative-governing board relationships. Role of the county manager. Relationships between the county commissioners and other special governing boards. Techniques of administrative organizations; motivation; delegation of authority; supervision, leadership; communications; human relations and public relations; ethics.

Local Government Finance. Statutory and constitutional requirements with respect to county revenues and expenditures; budgeting; budget control; property tax administration; debt limitations and policies; purchasing and contracting.

City and County Planning. The purpose and methods of planning; devices for carrying plans into effect; joint city-county programs and relationships between city and county planning programs; zoning and sub-division control administration; developmental policies.

Personnel Administration. Classification and pay plans; recruitment; conditions of employment; training; retirement systems; organization for personnel administration; employee relations; merit system requirements.

Functions and Activities. Special problems in the organization and operation of schools, health programs, welfare programs, the court system, libraries, recreation programs, and other county activities.

Final Problem Session. Solution by students of typical problems in county administration.

The Course in Municipal Administration. Here is a description of the course in Municipal Administration as it was given in the winter and spring of 1977-78:

The course will be offered in two sections for 1977-78. Section I will follow a weekend schedule with ten sessions. Section II will follow a weekly schedule with six sessions.

Within time limitations, an attempt is made to cover all phases of municipal government and administration. Emphasis is placed on the job of the city manager and of department heads. Extensive use is made of problems drawn from the experience of cities and towns in the State, large and small alike. The following subjects are covered:

277

Introduction to Municipal Government — (18 hours) — Background, types, functions, and legal status of local governmental units; state-local and city-county relations; forms of city government.

Public Personnel Administration—(10 hours)—Classification and pay plans; recruitment; conditions of employment; employee training; retirement and disability benefits; employee relations.

City Planning—(14 hours)—Types and contents of various city plans such as population studies, economic base studies, and street plans; devices for carrying plans into effect such as zoning and subdivision control.

Municipal Line Functions and Policies—(30 hours)—Special problems in the organization and operation of police, fire, public works, public utility departments, etc.; development of policies governing operation of each department.

Municipal Management Seminar—Solution by students of typical problems in city government, individually and in groups.

Techniques of Municipal Administration — (30 hours) — Basic administrative principles; administrator-governing body relations; problems of organization; techniques of direction; supervision; leadership; communications; human relations.

Municipal Finance — (48 hours) — Organization; thorough study of revenue sources; budget preparation and accounting systems, debt administration; purchasing.

A Student's Comment. The North Carolina Association of County Commissioners and the North Carolina League of Municipalities each year give an award to the most outstanding member of each graduating class and recognize him at their annual conventions. Here are the appraising remarks of Ray McClees, Tyrrell County Coordinator, to the North Carolina Association of County Commissioners at Pinehurst, August 21, 1976:

I am grateful for the Outstanding Graduate Award, and I just want to take a minute of your time to say something about the Institute of Government at Chapel Hill. There is no other place that I know of where you'll find so much talent and energy and enthusiasm for telling the story of local government. The faculty there has that special

278

quality of being able to draw from the students many of their experiences "on the firing line." Our class of 55 people came from every part of the state, too, and from the towns, counties, the State government, the Federal, and even two of the employees of your Association staff who are sitting here tonight, and of whom you can be proud.

It is fair to say that the Institute's Municipal Administration Course has become the top-ranked course for North Carolina's top municipal administrators.

Its importance lies not in the large number of graduates, but in the breadth and depth of the course and in the central management posts held by those who have completed it. About 75% of the state's city managers have been graduated from the course, and new managers coming into the state are uniformly advised by their fellow managers to enroll in it as soon as possible.

Competition to enroll in the course on the part of the department heads and other key administrative officials is keen. Despite the expansion of capacity, it has been impossible to meet all enrollment requests. City managers who have themselves taken the course are especially anxious for their department heads to have the advantage of enrollment.

While the course is not designed to "produce" city managers, many of those who have taken the course while in some other administrative post have since become managers, and completion of the course is viewed with favor by governing boards in selecting a manager.

The interaction of students from such varied backgrounds, bringing with them experiences we lived each day during the months the course ran, and the faculty which specialized in the problems those students faced, created a classroom atmosphere, to my mind, far more productive in concrete answers to everyday problems than any other type of schooling you could imagine.

You commissioners here tonight: I urge you to go back home and encourage your young and aspiring administrators in the court house to attend the Administration Course at the Institute of Government in Chapel Hill. County government touches every citizen in this great State, and they deserve the best possible government we can provide. That means having available to you and the people in your county the services of trained, professional administrators to handle the ever-growing complexity of government problems. And one of the best ways to ensure that is to send your administrators to the Institute of Government. I am grateful that my county commissioners, from the smallest county in North Carolina, thought it wise to send me.

In the Context of History. From the Lords Proprietors of Carolina in the 1660's to the General Assembly of North Carolina in the 1980's. In the 1660's, the Lords Proprietors of Carolina called on John Locke, in his middle twenties, to draw up the *Fundamental Constitutions of Carolina*—for a land three thousand miles away, which he had never seen, for people living under conditions he knew nothing about and facing problems he was not aware of. Except for two or three provisions, it was ignored in its verbiage and its content by colonial governors and legislators who saw that it could not be fitted to the ground of Carolina.

There were five men on the staff of the Institute of Government in the middle 1930's, twenty-five by the latter 1950's, and thirty-three by 1980. Like John Locke these men were in their middle twenties; unlike John Locke they were born, brought up, schooled, and experienced in the structure and the workings of local, state, and federal governmental institutions in this country, and familiar with the problems faced by the people in the cities, the counties, and the state of North Carolina. They have been working hand in glove with local governmental units and officials throughout the fifty years of the existence of the Institute of Government.

I think it is not going too far to say that the Institute of Government, culminating in a new University of Public Officials, is becoming as significant in the lives of the public officials of the cities, the counties, and the state of North Carolina in the middle 1900's as the University of North Carolina was significant in the lives of the people of North Carolina when it opened its doors in 1795.

Chapter XI   My Personal Appraisal of Institute Colleagues: 1930–1962

If I had to put my finger on the finest thing I did in the forty years from September 1923 to September 1962, it would be on the quality of the men and women I have been privileged to bring into the public service by way of the Institute of Government of the University of North Carolina at Chapel Hill. In 1979, at the dedication of the Local Government Center in Raleigh, I spoke this appraisal of these men and women:

Recognitions of the work of the Institute of Government have come to me through the years with my name on them in big letters, but if you read the fine print as I have read it, you will find that every one of them, without exception, goes on to say that my name is there because of the work of men and women of the Institute of Government. And so of this building wearing the legend of the Albert Coates Local Government Center.

I may have been the spearhead of the Institute of Government, but these men and women have been the force behind the spearhead, giving it the forward thrust and cutting edge. I may have drawn the outlines of the Institute of Government, but these men and women have filled in its features and breathed into them the breath of life. I may have dreamed of a new University of Public Officials within the framework of the old University of North Carolina, but these men and women have built it.

For thirty years the highest compliment I could pay to any man on earth was to invite him to join the staff of the Institute of Government. I am talking out of my knowledge when I say that I never brought on the staff anyone who I did not think was actually or potentially a better man than I was, or who I did not think could push me for first place.

I owe the Institute of Government to these men and women who came to the Institute staff during the years from 1946 to the end of my directorship in 1962, to those who came during the years from 1933 to 1939 and laid its foundations, and to those who came during the years between bases and kept its life lines open. When I say that the men and women coming from 1946 to 1962 carried the Institute of Government farther forward than it had gone before and rebuilt the Institute in their own image and likeness, I am not stepping on the toes of their predecessors, I am standing on their shoulders.

If I owe the Institute of Government to these men and women, let me tell you what I think they owe to me—no more and no less. Years ago I stood on the shore of New York harbor and saw a steam tug pull an ocean liner out to sea. I noticed that after the steam tug had got the ocean liner into deep water, it turned around and came back to shore and left the ocean liner going on its own. That is what I did for my colleagues: I brought them on the staff of the Institute of Government, got them going, got out of their way, and left each at the mercy of his own genius. I gave them the opportunity "to bourgeon out of themselves all that there is within them." The Institute of Government is the product of their assorted abilities.

The Pioneers in the 1930's. Throughout my years as Director of the Institute of Government, I told all the people I talked to about coming on the staff that I did not want them to come until they had studied and thought about the work we were doing to the point that they would not come unless they were satisfied they were coming for a life work and not for a temporary job. I believe that the people coming to the staff in the 1930's—Henry Brandis, Dillard Gardner, Buck Grice, Marion Alexander, and Harry McGalliard—came with that in mind, and I have no doubt they would have continued in the work they had begun if Institute funds had not run out in the latter

1930's and they had to leave for bread and butter reasons after staying from three to six years.

Henry Brandis went on to become Director of Research in the State Department of Revenue, Professor of Law and for fifteen years Dean of the Law School of the University of North Carolina at Chapel Hill. Dillard Gardner to become Marshall and Librarian in the Supreme Court of North Carolina, Buck Grice to become Deputy State Auditor, Harry McGalliard to become Deputy Attorney General, Marion Alexander to become the Executive Officer of the newly incorporated bar of North Carolina—all in the public service.

Holding the Line in the 1940's. I could not offer a life-time job to the men who came to the Institute in the early 1940's while the Institute was living from hand to mouth and from year to year, between bases and in the uncertainties of wartime. After keeping the life lines of the Institute open most of these interim staff members went on to other public service jobs. Peyton Abbott became Assistant Attorney General and legal advisor to the Commissioner of the State Revenue Department. Clifford Pace became City Manager of Asheboro, and later of New Bern. Malcolm Seawell became Superior Court Solicitor, Superior Court Judge, and Attorney General of North Carolina. Bill Cochrane became Administrative Assistant to Senator Kerr Scott, later to Senator Everett Jordan, and later Executive Director of the United States Senate Committee on Rules. Terry Sanford became a member of the State Senate, then Governor of North Carolina, and later President of Duke University.

Careers in the Institute. I could, and did, offer a life work rather than a temporary job to the succession of people coming to the Institute staff in the latter 1940's and throughout the 1950's. Henry Lewis coming on the staff in 1946, just out of Law School and World War II, stayed the course for thirty-one years, became Director of the Institute in 1973, and retired at the end of 1978 with the distinction of becoming the first to devote all of the years of his professional life to the Institute of Government. Elmer Oettinger retired in 1979 after serving the Institute for twenty-one years.

As of 1980, Don Hayman has already worked for thirty-two

years with the Institute, and has nine years to go before he reaches the mandatory retirement age at seventy. Philip Green, thirty-one years with thirteen years to go. Jake Wicker, twenty-five years with thirteen years to go. John Sanders, twenty-four years with seventeen years to go. Milton Heath, twenty-three years with eighteen years to go. Dexter Watts, twenty-three years with eighteen years to go. Ed Hinsdale, nineteen years with eight to go.* Betsy Pace has worked full-time for nine years and part-time for thirteen years with fourteen years to go. Marjorie Bounds, twenty years, with eleven years to go.

All of them have been, and still are, a seasoning influence in breaking in the newer faculty coming to the Institute during the administrations of John Sanders and Henry Lewis. They are continuing as backbone joints in the new administration of John Sanders starting in 1979, and have from eleven to eighteen years to go in the Institute's services if they serve out their allotted time.

Careers beyond the Institute. Others have given substantial parts of their lives to the Institute of Government and gone on to public service employment in this and other states.

After twelve years as Assistant Director of the Institute of Government,· Alex McMahon became General Counsel of the North Carolina Association of County Commissioners and served on many State Legislative Commissions, Executive Director and President of the American Hospital Association, and Chairman of the Board of Trustees of Duke University.

After fifteen years with the Institute of Government, George Esser became Executive Director of the North Carolina Fund; Program Advisor, National Affairs Division, Ford Foundation; Executive Director, Southern Regional Council; Executive Director, then President, National Academy Public Administration, Washington, D.C.

Henry Brandis, Dickson Phillips and Robert Byrd became Professors of Law and Deans of the Law School of the University of North Carolina at Chapel Hill. Ernest Machen became Professor of Law at Wake Forest University. Durwood Jones, Professor of Law at the University of Tennessee. John Scarlett, Professor of Law and

*Retired, 1981

Dean of the Law Schools in the University of South Dakota, Drake University, and Wake Forest University. Richard Myren became Professor of Law at the University of Indiana, then went with the International Police Chiefs Association, later became Dean of the School of Criminal Justice in the University of the State of New York, and then Dean of School of Justice, American University in Washington, D.C. James C.N. Paul, Professor of Law at the University of Pennsylvania, then at the University of California at Los Angeles, later Professor and Dean of the Rutgers University Law School in New Jersey. Royall Shannonhouse, Professor of Law in the University of Georgia and later in the University of Baltimore. David Sharpe, Professor of Law in George Washington University. Marion Benfield, Professor of Law in the University of Georgia, later in the University of Illinois. Mary Oliver became Librarian of the UNC Law School. William J. Curran became Professor of Public Health Law at Harvard University. David Smith became Secretary of International Legal Studies and Professor of Law at the Harvard Law School.

Bob Campbell became Director of Research for the Cornell University Automotive Crash Inquiry Program, then Director of that Program, later Director of the Highway Safety Research Center for North Carolina in the University of North Carolina at Chapel Hill. Louis Cherry became Librarian for the Armed Forces Staff College at Norfolk, Virginia, and later went to the staff of the Library of Congress in Washington, D.C. Catherine Maybury Seelye became head of the Public Documents Department of the University of North Carolina Library, and later held a similar position at the University of Connecticut. Robert Stipe, Director of the State Department of Archives and History, and now Professor of 'Design, N.C. State University. Hugh Cannon, Director of the North Carolina Department of Administration. Clyde Ball, Professor of Law in Memphis University and later Legislative Service Officer for the General Assembly of North Carolina. John Webb, North Carolina Superior Court Judge. Fannie Memory Farmer became a Juvenile Court Judge, then Attorney for the State Department of Public Welfare and Social Services, and later head of the

Public Records Division in the State Department of Archives and History. Zeb Alley became State Senator. Mason Thomas, Juvenile Court Judge for Wake County. Max Cogburn, District Judge for Buncombe County. Paul Johnston, Administrative Assistant to the Governor of North Carolina, then Director of the State Department of Administration, later Administrative Assistant to the United States Secretary of Commerce. Robert Giles became Assistant Attorney General of North Carolina, then Administrative Assistant to the Governor of North Carolina, later General Counsel, United States Department of Commerce, and is now Director, Research and Planning Division, North Carolina Administrative Office of the Courts. Basil Sherrill became Assistant Attorney General of North Carolina, and later Director of the State Department of Probation. Alex Biggs, member of the State Utilities Commission. Roddey Ligon, County Attorney and County Manager of Forsyth County. Dickson Phillips, Judge of the Circuit Court of Appeals for the Fourth Judicial District.

In the Context of History

In the year 1830, when the University of North Carolina was thirty-five years old Chief Justice Thomas Ruffin of the North Carolina Supreme Court wrote a memorial to members of the General Assembly, saying: "In North Carolina every person who is old enough to remember when the University was not, must have observed, and cannot but testify to the effects most salutary, of its establishment." He went on to say that four hundred sixty men had graduated from the University and almost as many more had studied here since the opening of its doors in 1795. "These Seven or Eight hundred of the Alumni of Chapel Hill," the Chief Justice continued, "now fill with honor to themselves and the College and with usefulness to their country most of her posts of distinction, trust, labor, and responsibility .... Many who have sought employments and homes in distant sections of the Union make us favorably known in Sister States, ..."

I can say the same things about the men and women of the fifty-year-old Institute of Government in 1980.

After the great London fire in the 1660's, Sir Christopher Wren stamped with his genius a great number of churches, libraries, hospitals, and other public buildings, scattered throughout the city to the point that his son wrote these words into his epitaph in St. Paul's Cathedral: "If you would see his monument, look around you." I think it is not going too far to say of the men and women of the Institute of Government: "If you would see their monument, look around you—in the city halls, the county courthouses, and the capital of North Carolina."

Chapter XII   On Looking Back

My working life in the University of North Carolina has been something of an obstacle course—full of rocks in the road, stop signs at intersection points, rapids and countercurrents, swimming upstream in water all too often over my head. But it has not been so bad. I go along with the author of *Pilgrim's Progress* in saying: "Though with great difficulty I am got hither, yet now do I not repent me of all the trouble I have been at to arrive where I am."

In all the ins and outs, and ups and downs, and run arounds throughout the years, my work has been interlaced with stretches of free and open road—go ahead signs, sheltering arms, helping hands, encouraging words, understanding hearts.

As I look back, I am certain that the most priceless gift that an all-knowing God can offer to any man at the beginning of his life is the privilege of choosing his own life work—for his life is the only thing he's got to work with. The tragedy is that so few people have that privilege. And just as tragic is the fact that so many of the people who have it do not know what they want to do with it. Charles B. Aycock, Governor of North Carolina, had put it this way around the turn of the century when he called for "the equal right of every child that is born on earth to have the opportunity to bourgeon out all that there is within him." I have had that opportunity.

Some men are born knowing what they want to do with their lives. I was not. I did not find out until I was in my late twenties, on a train coming from the Mayo Clinic in Rochester, Minnesota, to the University of North Carolina at Chapel Hill. I have described that moment of insight earlier in this story, and I have never doubted its validity. One thing I have learned from my experience: that every point along the way is a starting point, and that you have got to start from where you are, with what you've got, how it works, and ask the question—"Where do I go from here?" There is the old truism, born of frustration: Nobody can get anywhere from here. It is truer to say: Nobody can get anywhere from anywhere else.

I have done my share of those things I ought not to have done, and left undone my share of those things I ought to have done, and wanted to do. I have learned not to worry too much over mistakes I have made—if I did the intelligent thing in the light of all the facts I had, or could have had, at the time. But I still worry too much, as perhaps I ought, when I could have avoided the mistake by a proper judgement under the known or knowable facts.

I have not been unaware of my personal limitations. As a small boy, walking from my home in the country to the public school in Smithfield I crossed the railroad track, and looking down it in the distance saw the rails appear to run together—but this didn't seem to bother the train when it got there. It was the built-in limitation of my own vision that made the difference between the appearance and the reality. On that same walk I passed the county fair grounds, and noticed that the fuss and noise and raucous cries of the crowd all but drowned out the music of the band, but that as I walked toward my home the false notes of the racket died away and in the distance only the clear tones of music lived. These experiences became symbolic in later years—as they are today.

I have lost more battles than I have won, but I have learned to live with my defeats without blaming my losses on those who in one way or another have crossed my path, stepped on my toes, or got into my hair. I have no doubt that most, if not all of them, were going their own way as I was going mine, "doing their own thing" as I was doing mine—for similar reasons and equally praiseworthy or blameworthy motives—and that clashes at intersection points

could, and should, be charged off to the slings and arrows of out-
rageous fortune. I go along with the observation of Mr. Justice
Holmes in Abrams vs United States:

> But when men have realized that time has upset many fighting faiths,
> they may come to believe even more than they believe the very
> foundations of their own conduct that the ultimate good desired is
> better reached by free trade in ideas—that the best test of truth is the
> power of the thought to get itself accepted in the competition of the
> market . . . .

Sometimes I have met that test, and sometimes I have not.

I commented to a colleague once that I thought the truest and
most eloquent line in all literature was a common saying that we
had heard all of our lives: "It's a great life, if you don't weaken." I go
along with his answer: "Yes, and it's not so bad if you do." Now
and then, toward the end of a long hard day, I may begin to weaken;
but up to this time, my critics to the contrary notwithstanding, I
have not weakened to the point that a good night's sleep wouldn't
put me back on my feet.

In the ins and outs and ups and downs and run-arounds of a life
time I have had my share of fulfilling moments—

Times when I had "the wonderful feeling that everything's going
my way"

Times

> *When the morning stars sang together,*
> *and all the sons of God shouted for joy*

Times when I felt with the poet that

> *God's in his heaven—*
> *All's right with the world!*

Times when I sang the song of Solomon

> *For lo! the winter is passed, the rain is*
> *over and gone; the flowers appear on the*
> *earth; the time of the singing of birds is*
> *come, and the voice of the turtle is*
> *heard in our land*

290

I have had my share of frustrating and despairing moments when I got into situations where, no matter which way I got out, I got out the wrong way.

Times which taught me the meaning of the legend of the American eagle—shot down and weltering in its own blood, ruefully observing that the shaft which had brought him to the earth was tipped by a feather from its own wing.

Times when I learned the meaning of the words of the Greek dramatist written twenty-five hundred years ago, proclaiming

> the God whose law it is that all who learn must suffer—and in the night sorrow falls drop by drop upon the heart, until, against our will, and even in our own despite, comes wisdom to us by the awful grace of God.

In these moments I find myself going along with the philosophy of an eighty-year-old janitor who met Chancellor House on the street in Chapel Hill: "How are you feeling this morning?" the Chancellor inquired. "Mighty porely, Mr. House, mighty porely. I've got a misery in my back. It kept me awake all night long."

"Don't you let that thing get the better of you, go see a doctor," the Chancellor suggested.

"No, Mr. House, I'm not going to see no doctor," the old janitor said. "I'm going to get on with my work. 'Cause when I gets to working, I gets to singing. And when I gets to singing, I gets to praying. And when I gets to praying, the Spirit comes and moves my misery away."

The trustees retirement policy for UNC division heads in administrative work caught up with me at the age of sixty-five in 1962. At the end of the working day, on August 31, 1962, I took down my name from the door of the Director's office, put up the name of my successor, and went home.

I left behind me a faculty of twenty-four full-time professors, associate professors and assistant professors, with fifteen to twenty part-time research assistants.

A supporting staff of fourteen secretaries, a housing officer, office manager, two mimeograph operators, and three janitors.

The first full-time Director in the Institute's history, with sufficient funds provided by his predecessor to lift the salary scale to the level of the best in the academic division of the University of North Carolina at Chapel Hill.

The Institute of Government as a going concern—keen, pushing, and enthusiastic—a new university of public officials within the framework of the old University of North Carolina.

On leaving the Institute in 1962 I said to my colleagues:

> Years ago I read about a man who left his work unfinished, saying: "My dreams will come true to other men." I do not have that much conceit, for my dreams have already mixed with the dreams of my colleagues to the point that I cannot always tell where my dreams leave off and theirs begin. Let me say that the dreams of all of us in the Institute have mixed with the dreams of those who have gone before us, and will mix with the dreams of those who come after us, in the spirit of all for one and one for all—and let it go at that.
>
> Robert House told me not long ago that leaving the Chancellorship of the University involved no great climactic moment. He said that in his college days at Chapel Hill, he would get on the train to go to his hometown of Thelma for the Christmas holidays, strike up an acquaintance with a stranger, and in the middle of a fascinating conversation hear the conductor coming through the car crying out: "Thelma! Thelma!" He would turn to the companion and say, "I'm sorry but this is where I get off the train—at Thelma."
>
> And that is the way I find it now. I am getting off the train at Thelma, with my desk full of loose ends and unfinished business which will be picked up, carried on, added to, and subtracted from by my successors, who will go along in their own way as I have gone along in mine. Individual Directors of the Institute will come and go. But the Institute of Government, like Ol' Man River, will keep on rolling along; with added sweep and power as every man on the staff builds his division of the Institute to a size as great as the Institute of Government today, and the whole continues to be greater than the sum of all of its parts.

That is the way I felt about the Institute of Government and its staff when I left it in 1962. It is the way I feel about it now—in 1981.

292

Chapter XIII   Addendum

In the Service of the University

No one can read the annual reports of John Sanders who was Director of the Institute of Government from 1962 to 1973, and the reports of Henry Lewis who was Director from 1973 to 1979, as I have read them, without realizing with all the stinging freshness of demonstrated truth that during the first fifty years of its existence the Institute of Government has gradually worked its way into the heart and center of the internal administrative framework of the University of North Carolina at Chapel Hill.

At the end of the year 1978, according to the Director's report for that year, the Institute faculty and staff were serving on a multiplicity of administrative boards and committees, including: University Committee on Staff Grievances, Faculty Council and its Committee on the Status of Women, Chancellor's Affirmative Action Committee, Faculty Committee on University Government, Continuing Education Council of the University of North Carolina, Committee on Instructional Personnel, Advisory Board of Ackland Art Center, North Carolina Law Center Board, Law Foundation, Friends of the Library, Traffic and Parking Committee, Curriculum Committee School of Nursing, Faculty Club House Committee, Advisory Board School of Social Work, Co-ordinator of Master of Public Administration Program, Advisory Committee for Title I Education Act of 1965, UNC-Chapel Hill Representative of University of North Carolina Faculty Assembly, University of North Carolina Urban Affairs Council, Chancellor's Advisory Committee. Two Institute faculty members have been called into service as Vice President of the overall University of North Carolina.

In the Service of the State

No one can read the annual reports of Institute activities, as I have read them, without realizing that members of the Institute faculty have been steadily growing into the confidence and service of the state. At the end of the year 1978, Institute faculty and staff members were serving on a multiplicity of boards, commissions, committees, and other agencies of state and local government, including: State Advisory Committee on Libraries, Human Resources Advisory Council, Orange County Precinct Registrar, Chapel Hill Township Planning Advisory Council, State Task Force on Rural Energy, North Carolina County Commissioners Association Advisory Committee, North Carolina Code Officials Qualification Board, Water Resources Research Institute, Board of Directors Chapel Hill-Carrboro United Fund, Board of Directors Low Income Housing Development Corporation, North Carolina Internship Council, Personnel Advisory Committee of Department of Public Instruction, Secretary-Treasurer of Research Triangle Chapter of American Society for Public Administration, North Carolina Coastal Resources Advisory Council, Board of Directors of Water Resources Institute, Triangle Universities Consortium on Air Pollution, Board of Directors Institute of Environmental Studies, North Carolina Bar Association Committee on Administration of Justice, North Carolina Criminal Justice Education and Training System Council and its Curriculum Committee, Advisory Committee for the Governor's Conference on Economic Development and Balanced Growth, Secretary North Carolina Youth Advisory Council, Legal Consultant North Carolina School Boards Association, Permanent Legislative Commission on Children with Special Needs, Counsel for State Board of Education, Council on the Education of Exceptional Children, Consultant Family Law Committee North Carolina Bar Association, Human Rights Committee-Murdock Center, Camp Butner.

In the Service of the Nation

At the national level, at the end of the year 1978, Institute faculty and staff members were serving on a multiplicity of national agencies, boards, and commissions, including: United States Council on Environmental Quality-Extramural Panel on Incentives, National Air Pollution Manpower Development Advisory Council, Board of Directors Institute of Environmental Studies, American Association of University Professors Committee, American Bar Association Committee on Fair Trial-Free Press, Media Law Committee and Privacy Committee, Chairman Special Committee on Uniform Privacy Act, National Conference of Commissioners on Uniform State Laws, Chairman National Organization on Legal Problems in Education, Phi Delta Kappa Committee on Impact of Court Decisions in Education, Governmental Affairs Committee National Association for Retarded Citizens, Council Member Research Triangle Chapter American Society for Public Administration, Executive Board of Committee on Chemical Tests for Alcohol, North Carolina Representative in National Association of Prosecutors, Research Review Committee of National Rural Water Survey, Advisory Committee for Title I of the Higher Education Act of 1965, Secretary North Carolina Chapter International Personnel Management Association.

State of the Institute in 1978

The Henry Lewis report on the *State of the Institute* in 1978 outlines the growth of the Institute of Government since my retirement as Director in 1962, and gives a picture of the Institute as a going concern on his retirement at the end of his administration of Institute affairs:

Role and Method

For those not familiar with the Institute, we should point out that, as a part of the University, it has a two-fold mission: to help public officials and employees perform effectively the tasks of governing the State of North Carolina and its counties, cities, and towns, and to help increase public understanding of state and local government. The Institute's work is reflected in teaching, research, publishing, and professional advisory services ("consulting"). While necessarily concerned with questions of public policy, we leave to others the initiation and advocacy of changes in policies and programs of government.

Schools, seminars, courses, conferences

Teaching activities of the Institute usually take the form of intensive courses of short duration, primarily designed for the in-service training of elected and appointed governmental officials. While many courses are planned to help experienced officials increase and update their knowledge of both the laws they administer and methods of administration, the Institute continually offers introductory courses for those who find themselves in government posts without training or experience.

During the past year the instructional activities that have consumed the longest periods of time have been:

—16 weeks of basic training for new State Highway patrolmen
—13 weeks of in-service schools for Wildlife Enforcement officers
—A 165-hour course in Municipal Administration (two sections)
—A 165-hour course in County Administration.

In the same period we offered introductory courses for new:

—county commissioners
—tax assessors
—tax collectors
—municipal and county finance officers
—registers of deeds, and
—magistrates

Outreach

In the nine months opening on July 1, 1976, and ending on March 31, 1977, 6,000 people attended Institute schools and conferences held in Chapel Hill; by the end of June 1977 this number should exceed 8,000. For the same nine-month period, hours of contact with students at these Chapel Hill events totaled 108,000. When figures for the final three months of the reporting year are included, the total Chapel Hill contact hours will exceed 145,000.

For the first nine months of the current reporting year, 7,000 people attended schools and conferences outside Chapel Hill sponsored or co-sponsored by the Institute, for a total of 26,000 student contact hours. A reasonable projection suggests that by the end of June, attendance at events outside Chapel Hill will exceed 8,000, for a total of 52,000 student contact hours.

Thus, if our projections are correct, in the current reporting year the Institute of Government's faculty will have reached 16,000 persons in the classroom, for a total of 197,000 student contact hours.

Publications

Enrollment figures at Institute events are impressive, but they must be read with an understanding that our faculty spend only about 20 per cent of their time in formal teaching. Since the Institute's large constituency cannot all be brought into classroom settings with any degree of regularity, the.faculty must reach them through technical publications of a high order. Our publications include treatises, guidebooks, textbooks, monographs, special studies, bulletins, and a variety of other items. Our most recent catalog shows more than 700 Institute publications listed under 61 subject headings and 95 authors. During the last ten years our records show that, on the average, the Institute issues more than 65 new publications each year. We now publish nine periodicals. These are:

Popular Government, published since 1931, and eight series of special bulletins—*Health Law, Local Finance, Local Government Law, Property Tax, School Law, Trial Judges, Administration of Justice and Planning.*

The following selection of 1976-77 faculty publications illustrates the breadth of Institute concern:
—Clarke, Crowell, Drennan, and Gill, *North Carolina Crimes: A Guidebook for Law Enforcement Officers.*
—Dennis, *The North Carolina Local Government Commission; a Descriptive and Interpretative Analysis.*
—Hinsdale (with R. Chaney), *Conditions of Adult Probation—Legal and Illegal.*
—Lawrence, *Local Government Finance in North Carolina*
—Ross, *Boards of Health in North Carolina; a Guidebook for Board Members*
—Solberg (with R. Leonard), *Notary Public Guidebook for North Carolina*

—Thomas, *Protective Services in North Carolina*
—Farb, *Chart of the Administrative Organization of State Government and a set of supplements, Internal Organization of North Carolina State Executive Department.*
—Vogt, *Capital Improvement Programming: A Handbook for Local Government Officials*
—Watts (with L. Hogue), *Abating Obscenity As a Public Nuisance by Local Ordinance.*

Advisory Services

Consulting and other professional services, which require about 30 per cent of our faculty's time, are made available on request to state and local officials and agencies (including study commissions). They constitute both a useful aid to clients and a valuable means of expanding the competence of Institute faculty members. Advisory assignments carried out by Institute faculty members in the current reporting year include:
—Commission on Correctional Programs. Legislation on public drunkenness (Michael Crowell); sentencing and parole (Stevens Clarke); and motor vehicle law (James Drennan)
—Four committees of the Legislative Research Commission. Water resources (environmental laws and utilities law) (Milton Heath); improving the professionalism of local building inspectors (Philip Green); sex discrimination (Michael Crowell); and land records information systems (William Campbell)
—Group Child Care Consultant Services (Mason Thomas)
—Commission to Revise the Public School Laws (Anne Dellinger)
—Criminal Code Commission (Poindexter Watts and Douglas Gill)
—Land Policy Council (Milton Heath and Philip Green)
—Mental Health Study Commission (H.R. Turnbull)
—Administrative Office of the Courts. A study of local court facilities and financing (Joseph Ferrell)
—A consortium composed of representatives of the Criminal Justice Training and Standards Council, the Community College System, the Justice Academy, and the Law Enforcement Training Officers Association as well as the Institute of Government to develop a basic training curriculum in criminal justice (Douglas Gill).

Work with the Legislature

Since the 1930's one of the principal clients of the Institute of Government has been the General Assembly. We have maintained, primarily for the members of that body, a reporting service comprised of daily bulletins summarizing proposals introduced and calendar action taken, weekly local legislation bulletins, computer-prepared status reports on public and local bills, weekly summaries, and special bulletins in the fields of Criminal Justice, Higher Education, Public Education, Liquor Law, and Property Tax. Other beneficiaries of this reporting service are numerous state and local governmental officials, newspapers, and television stations.

A second aspect of the Institute's legislative work is offering counsel for standing committees, some for full-time service, some for limited subject matter. In the recent session, members of the Institute faculty worked regularly with ten Senate and thirteen House standing committees.

New Programs

During the past year we have continued to initiate new instructional programs—some of a one-time nature, some planned for continuation; some in Chapel Hill, some at regional locations; some sponsored by the Institute; some co-sponsored. Here is a selection of these new programs and events:
—Three two-day training programs for experienced magistrates (Joan Brannon)
—A conference for attorneys for and administrators of the community college system and a course in school law for presidents of community colleges and technical institutes (Robert Phay)
—A series of regional schools for jail personnel co-sponsored by the Jail and Detention Services Unit of the State Department of Human Resources (Stevens Clarke and Anne Dellinger)
—A series of eighteen regional six-hour seminars on public health and mental health law co-sponsored by the UNC School of Public Health (H.R. Turnbull and Patrice Solberg)
—A series of child-abuse workshops in each of four regions of the state (Mason Thomas)
—A school for new local finance officers (David Lawrence and John Vogt)
—Three regional training programs for State Department of Correction pre-release and after-care trainers (Richard McMahon)
—Sixteen three-day programs in management by objective for the State Department of Correction (Ronald Lynch and Richard McMahon)
—A five-day basic course for industrial developers co-sponsored by the UNC Department of Geography and the State Division of Economic Development (Donald Liner)

299

—A week-long training program on environmental monitoring and planning for the State Department of Natural and Economic Resources (Milton Heath).

Program Flexibility

Although the Institute of Government's substantive programs are developed, assigned, executed, and evaluated on a long-term basis, the orderly process of program development is subject to the practical effect of the Institute's commitment to be responsive—to the needs of state and local government in North Carolina. This responsive role makes it impossible to plan and staff the entire work program at the beginning of a year, then leave it to realize itself without further administrative concern. Almost daily, requests for assistance (through instruction, research, and consultation) are received that had not been anticipated when the year's work was being laid out. Yet each requires a response—affirmative if possible—and that often requires faculty members to shift emphasis and much effort to be made in determining which staff members are available to attend to the request, in making arrangements for financing, and in dealing with the client.

Faculty and Supporting Staff

Today the faculty of the Institute of Government (including the Librarian) has grown to an authorized complement of 34 positions; the full-time supporting staff has stabilized at 39 positions. In a typical year, we will also employ from eight to ten full-time law clerks and research assistants in summer and five part-time during the academic year. Although the administrative structure of the Institute is simple—we have no divisions or sub-structures within the faculty—we do have effective working teams or groupings based on fields of interest and responsibility—for example, our Criminal Justice Administration, Local Government, and Court groups.

Facts about Faculty

Twenty-four members of the current Institute of Government faculty were trained as lawyers; three were trained in Public Administration; and one each was trained in Psychology, Social Work, Economics, and Library Science. The lawyers come from a wide selection of law schools—six from Harvard, five from the University of North Carolina, four from Duke; two each from Vanderbilt, Yale, and Columbia; and one each from George Washington, Miami, and the University of California at Los Angeles. Half the faculty are native North Carolinians; the other half come from almost every region of the country.

The longest tenure of any member of our present faculty is 31 years; the shortest, one month; the average tenure of the present faculty is eleven years, five months; the median, eleven years, three months.

Financing the Institute

For convenience, the current financial status of the Institute of Government may be presented under three source headings:

State appropriations: There are two state appropriation budgets totaling $1,078,896 for the year—the regular operating budget ($1,043,986) and the State Government Intern budget ($34,910).

Revenue accounts: There are three budgeted revenue accounts that total $596,996—the short-course account ($459,809), the Legislative Reporting Service account ($86,500), and the residence hall account ($50,687). Income for these accounts is derived from many sources, including some fifty contracts, retainer arrangements, grants, and special projects.

Trust funds: The Institute administers two small special-purpose funds that come to a total of $37,607.

Persons Coming to Institute Faculty from 1962 through 1980

Robert L. Gunn—1962
Jesse R. James—1963
Robert T. Daland
   (visiting, 1963-64)—1963
James C. Harper—1963
Dorothy Kiester—1963
Richard R. McMahon—1963
Ben Overstreet, Jr.—1963
George A. Coltrane—1963
Joseph S. Ferrell—1964
Ben F. Loeb—1964
J. Taylor McMillan—1964
David G. Warren—1964
Allan Ashman—1965
William A. Campbell—1965
Douglas R. Gill—1965
S. Kenneth Howard—1965
Robert E. Phay—1965
Norman E. Pomrenke—1965
Rebecca Ballentine—1965
George M. Cleland—1966

Lee Quaintance—1966
David R. Gergen—1967
C. Paul Brubaker, Jr.—1968
William E. Benjamin—1968
Harvey D. Miller—1968
David M. Lawrence—1968
William H. Cape—1969
H. Rutherford Turnbull,
   III—1969
Philip T. Vance—1969
Michael Crowell—1970
Joan G. Brannon—1971
Stevens H. Clarke—1971
Robert A. Adman—1971
William B. Crumpler—1971
Gloria A. Grizzle—1971
C. Donald Liner—1971
Ernest E. Ratliff—1971
Ronald G. Lynch—1971
Robert L. Epting—1972
A. John Vogt—1973

Michael B. Brough—1974
Anne M. Dellinger—1974
Stephen N. Dennis—1974
James C. Drennan—1974
L. Lynn Hogue—1974
John T. Greenwood—1974
George T. Rogister—1975
Thomas A. Ross—1975
Robert L. Farb—1976
M. Patrice Solberg—1976

Bonnie E. Davis—1977
Richard D. Ducker—1977
Grainger R. Barrett—1978
Sue B. Rankin—1978
Ann L. Sawyer—1978
Michael R. Smith—1978
Jacqueline B. Queen—1980
Robert P. Joyce—1980
Kenneth S. Cannaday—1980